Social Media, Crisis Communication, and Emergency Management

Leveraging Web 2.0 Technologies

Connie M. White

CRC Press
Taylor & Francis Group
Boca Raton   London   New York

CRC Press is an imprint of the
Taylor & Francis Group, an **informa** business

CRC Press
Taylor & Francis Group
6000 Broken Sound Parkway NW, Suite 300
Boca Raton, FL 33487-2742

Printed in the United States of America on acid-free paper
Version Date: 20110815

International Standard Book Number: 978-1-4398-5349-8 (Hardback)

Visit the Taylor & Francis Web site at
http://www.taylorandfrancis.com

and the CRC Press Web site at
http://www.crcpress.com

To my mother, JoAnn White

CONTENTS

PREFACE

This book is written for those who want to learn how to leverage social media to support many of the needs required when managing emergencies and public safety. It is intended as both a reference for the self learner and is structured to support academic courses on both the undergraduate and graduate levels. The information in this book has been developed to teach anyone the skills necessary to build social media to help manage emergencies.

Most of the applications and social medias covered throughout the book are available to you for free. As a result, you will be able to use the information acquired from these lessons to build your own solution sets. It will cost you nothing more than a bit of time, some patience, and a little dedication. Much of this book provides a *hands-on* approach to learning. In particular, information is catered to support those on the local level where there is a deliberate effort to integrate usefulness encompassing a comprehensive emergency management approach: preparedness, mitigation, response, and recovery. Although the focus is on emergency management, other crisis communications groups, such as dispatchers, business continuity planners, nongovernmental organizations (NGOs), security, volunteer organizations, and other organization types will benefit from the information provided in this book. Multiple organizations network together and plan for disasters that cross both manmade geographical and organizational boundaries. The same groups who network, plan, and partner together on the ground in face-to-face interactions can be supported and further connected using social media. New groups can be easily formed and members can collaborate in real time to best support the decision-making needs to manage both the expected and the unexpected.

The information in this book comes from a variety of sources. As is the philosophy behind this book, the formation of it is truly a collaborative effort between the academic community and real-world practitioners. Many people contributed to the information provided in this text. Some information comes from prior research conducted exploring how social media can be used for emergency management. I was fortunate enough to conduct research in this area then create a course based on this content. It was through teaching the information to real-world practitioners that the "rubber hit the road."

Over the years, I have conducted numerous formal and informal studies using my emergency management practitioner students, the International Association of Emergency Managers (IAEM), along with an academic community who specializes in Information Systems for Crisis Response and Management (ISCRAM.org). Together, these groups helped develop a framework to match existing technologies to tasks to further support the actualization of using social media for emergency management. The IAEM mailing list served as a wealth of information from experts when conducting questionnaires by both me and those who studied under me over the years. A lot of the material generated for this book is a direct result of me creating and teaching the first university-level course focusing on implementing social media to support the needs of emergency management. Teaching this class on both the undergraduate and graduate levels to experienced practitioners active in the field proved invaluable. I can never thank those students enough, especially those who went the extra mile on this endeavor. Many of these students are listed in the acknowledgment or as contributors to this book.

I have a growing concern that we are creating a digital divide between those who use Web 2.0 technology and those who don't. There are a number of reasons for the lack of adoption and implementation. There is a strong need to level the playing field. It is my hope that through the lessons laid out in this text, the insight provided from practitioners, and from the case studies providing real-world examples, practitioners can add one more "tool" to their toolbox.

Social Media, Crisis Communication, and Emergency Management: Leveraging Web 2.0 Technology is in no way a comprehensive attempt to cover everything one can do with social media and Web 2.0 technologies. Although the needs defined by crisis communication remain the same, the technology to support these needs changes rapidly. For example, so many updates have occurred with sites and technologies and smart phones just while writing this book. It would take another book to cover everything that's changed and, then, by the time it was published, it would be outdated and another would have to be written. However, the good news is that there is a set of basic features that are common to all applications that exist to support the needs of agencies and the public.

Facebook, Twitter, YouTube, and other very popular sites are covered in an effort to teach what functions exist to meet objectives. These lessons are demonstrated by using these and other popular sites. Popular now, Twitter was hardly known a few years ago and now it's the latest rage, but something else is sure to come along and be the latest, greatest thing since, well, the last latest, greatest application or technology.

I was invited to workshops, exercises, and meetings funded and hosted by the Naval Postgraduate School (NPS) Center for Homeland Defense and Security (CHDS), the Department of Homeland Security's Office of Emergency Communications (OEC), the Office for Interoperability and Compatibility (OIC), The Army Research Office, the National Science Foundation (NSF), and by others where we explored the possibilities of government groups formally leveraging social media. As I attended these various workshops, conferences, and round table discussions, I noticed that most people wanted to know more about social media. Many people were interested in using it, but there was no one comprehensive source providing this information in an organized manner. Over time, I realized there was a critical need to put together a book that explains what social media is, provides information on what is out there, describes how to use it, and, further, pushes these concepts by introducing more cutting-edge concepts supported by Web 2.0 technology.

So, in essence, this book describes how social media, along with a variety of tools and technologies, can be leveraged together to create a synergistic effect that can help provide people the right information at the right time in order to make the best decisions possible.

ACKNOWLEDGMENTS

Marianne Hart Arensmeyer
Deputy Site Manager/Mechanical Engineer
Science Applications International Corporation (SAIC)
Milwaukee, Wisconsin

Peter F. Buck
Petty Officer First Class
United States Navy

Jonathan Cook
Emergency Communications Specialist
Bloomington Police Department
Bloomington, Illinois

Skot Covert
Storm Chaser, Search and Rescue Tech III
National Registered Emergency Medical Technician (NREMT)
Special Projects Director
Office of the Lt. Governor of Arkansas
Little Rock, Arkansas

Mark A. Cromer
National Registered Paramedic, Instructor Trainer
Carilion Clinic
Roanoke, Virginia

Dawn Dawson
Kansas City Metro
Kansas City, Missouri and
Kansas City, Kansas

Rosalie A. Huff
Emergency Management Planner
DynMcDermott Petroleum Operations
New Orleans, Louisiana

Jeremy Jacobs
Real Estate Broker
Help-U-Sell
Florence, Alabama

Kristopher Kendrick
Project Manager
Lockheed Martin–Training Solutions, Inc.
Little Rock, Arkansas

Jim Lanier
Emergency Communications Center Division Manager
Manatee County Public Safety
Bradenton, Florida

Jason Milhollin
Director, Emergency Management
Douglas County, Georgia

Kristy Posey
Security
The Children's Place
Fort Payne, Alabama

Michael Posey
Telecommunicator
Dekalb County Sheriff's Office
Fort Payne, Alabama

Robert L. Rosser
Logistics Specialist
Emergency Management Agency
Marshall County, Alabama

James Soukup
Emergency Communications Director City/County of Durham
Durham, North Carolina

Diana Tamayo
Master Sergeant
United States Air Force

Christopher Andrew Walker
VP Disaster Response Group
Garner Environmental Services, Inc.
Deer Park, Texas

Lakeita Windham
Training Support Specialist
Department of Homeland Security
Anniston, Alabama

ACADEMIC COLLEAGUES

Thanks to

Dr. Star Roxanne Hiltz for contributions to the numerous studies that we've conducted over the years.

Dr. Bartel Van de Walle for requesting that the ISCRAM community go on Facebook.

Dr. Frank Friedrich for helping disseminate surveys to larger groups of EM students at various stages of this work.

Dr. Leysia Palen for all of the quality research she and her colleagues conduct and inspire others to do.

I would like to give special thanks to my colleague, Dr. Linda Plotnick, who spent countless hours brainstorming, debating, and contributing to the effort of this work in its foundational stages.

I would like to thank the publisher, Taylor & Francis Group, and the staff. A special thanks for the guidance, help, and patience from my editor, Mark Listewnik.

AUTHOR

Connie M. White earned her PhD in information systems from the College of Computing Sciences at the New Jersey Institute of Technology. She is an assistant professor with the Institute for Emergency Preparedness at Jacksonville State University, Alabama. Dr. White is the director of Information Technology Solutions for Emergency Management (ITSFEM), an education and consultation firm. She has published work in the *Journal of Emergency Management* (JEM), *The International Association of Emergency Manager's Bulletin* (IAEM), and the *International Journal for Information Systems for Crisis Response and Management* (IJISCRAM).

Her current work explores how collaborative applications, social media, Free and Open Source Systems, and Web 2.0 technologies can be leveraged together to support the decision-making needs of crisis managers. Challenges arise in capturing the important information and directing the right information to the right people at the right time. Another research focus is using spatial-temporal geographical information systems and social media to help provide information on the outer rural areas that have the least amount of connectivity through crisis mapping. Other research efforts explore using virtual worlds, such as Second Life, as a teaching tool for practitioners. Her dissertation, *A Dynamic Delphi System to Support Decision Making by Large Groups of Crisis Management Experts*, focused on the creation of a crisis management system that is used by large groups dispersed geographically when decisions must be made under uncertainty and among domain-driven subgroups. The end result of this effort produced an application that contributed to the Sahana Disaster Management System, Eden, a free and open source system created in response to the Asian tsunami (which has been used all over the world), most recently in the Haiti earthquake response, and the floods of Pakistan. Her research interests include social media, decision making, scales, Sahana, Thurstone's law of comparative judgment, artificial intelligence, and emergency management. Her homepage is http://sites.google.com/site/conniemwhite/

CONTRIBUTORS

Michael Amberson (Chapter 5) is an emergency management specialist with the Gadsden/Etowah County Emergency Management Agency in Alabama. Previously, he served as the Public Information Officer. In this position, Amberson helped establish the agency's social media sites and policies. He worked to incorporate the use of social media sites as part of the agency's standard operating procedures during emergencies. In addition to emergency management, Amberson has an extensive background in radio.

Joel Aud (Chapter 8) works as a senior analyst in support of the Texas Department of Public Safety and in direct support of the Texas Rangers. His focus is on the pragmatic and cost-effective use of technology in the service of public safety. He is a student of the military theories of John Boyd as they relate to Web 2.0, a hardware/software tinkerer with too many projects, and a continual advocate for leaner, more efficient government through public engagement and emergent technology.

Fran Boon (Chapter 7), technical director of AidIQ, has spent 15 years since graduating from Oxford University using technology to provide solutions for the developing world. Working with Oxfam, NetHope, Tactical Technology Collective, Sahana, Inveneo, Asterisk, and OpenStreetMap, he has traveled extensively providing relief during major humanitarian disasters, such as in Haiti and Indonesia, and working on longer-term sustainable development projects. Boon is also the chair of the Sahana Eden Project Management Committee. His main interests include Mapping (GIS) and mobile technologies.

Tim Brice (Chapter 4) graduated from the University of Missouri in 1992 with dual bachelor's degrees in journalism and atmospheric science. Brice joined the National Weather Service in 1994 and has served in the El Paso, Texas area office for the past 16 years. He has led the way in helping the National Weather Service develop its Internet presence and incorporating the latest technologies into operational uses. He currently serves as the office GIS (geographic information system) and strategist.

Greg Carttar (Chapter 9) wears two hats. The first, in the private sector, is as a provider of very large, temporary voice communications and data systems for special events and circumstances. Two examples are the 2004, 2005, and 2007 DARPA Grand Challenge series of robotic vehicle trials in the Mojave Desert, and the Sundance Film Festival for 11 years; both of which are difficult and demanding communications environments quite different from each other. The second, in public safety, is 10 years in the Fire Service, currently as a safety and communications officer. Other certifications include HazMat tech, fire service instructor, emergency management for fire service, and LP Gas emergencies. He is a member of Missouri-1 DMAT in the Logistics Branch. His experience with communications systems extends back to the late 1960s in his father's radio business, which serviced and maintained all nontactical radio systems on McConnell AFB and its missile sites. He is actively involved in research regarding the likely effects of the New Madrid earthquake scenario on critical communications systems of all types.

Elizabeth Clark (Chapter 1), business continuity and emergency management planner, began her public safety career in 1993 with Public Safety Communications in Calgary, Alberta, Canada. Currently working for the City of Calgary, Utilities and Environmental Protection Department, Clark is an associate business continuity professional, secretary of the Alberta Chapter of the International Association of Emergency Managers, and a member of ASIS. She earned a B.S. in emergency management from Jacksonville State University, Alabama and plans to further her education by pursuing a Master's.

Sean Conner (Chapter 7) is an innovation expert and technology strategist with Kila Ventures, where his primary roles are future-casting and ideation. He holds a degree in physics and a graduate degree in mechanical engineering from the University of Washington in Seattle. Conner is a passionate entrepreneur who has launched startups in fields ranging from consumer goods to information technology.

Hal Grieb (Chapter 2) is currently a senior emergency management specialist with the City of Plano Department of Emergency Management in Plano, Texas, where he has been since June 2008. Grieb created the "Prepared in Plano" (www.preparedinplano.com) campaign in 2008, allowing the city to leverage web-based technologies in all phases of emergency management. He has helped frame the City of Plano's social media and Web 2.0

policy and is a co-chair on the city's Web 2.0 committee. Grieb is also a community administrator on the Department of Homeland Security's (DHS) Science and Technologies R-Tech Program's First Responders Communities of Practice, the Making America Safer Using Social Media community at https://communities.firstresponder.gov/.

Daniele Malerba (Chapter 7), IT consultant to United Nations World Food Programme, Rome, has studied international relations at the University of Sussex, Brighton (U.K.) where he graduated with a dissertation titled Tweet Me Your Location: The Use of Social Networks in International Emergencies. His main interest is on the use of media during times of great distress as a means by which to better affect people's lives.

Matthew Miller (Chapter 5) works for SRA International and is a contractor at the Centers for Disease Control and Prevention's BioSense program. He is the lead analyst, situational awareness lead, and GIS officer for the program. Prior to his time at the CDC, Miller worked as a firefighter/paramedic in various jurisdictions in Georgia. He also recently completed his master's in emergency management at Jacksonville State University.

Keith Noble (Chapter 2) is currently a paramedic captain with Austin–Travis County Emergency Medical Services, Austin, Texas. His current position is the lead instructor of the local high school EMT-Basic program and an ATCEMS academy instructor. He is a member of the department's disaster medical response team and motorcycle medic team. Captain Noble is a nationally registered paramedic, licensed Texas paramedic, Texas EMS instructor, and has a BS in administration of justice from the Pennsylvania State University. He is currently pursuing a master's degree through Jacksonville State University in emergency management.

Brandi Simpson (Chapter 7) works with the Highway Patrol division of the Alabama Department of Public Safety as a police communications officer. Prior to working for the Department of Public Safety, Simpson worked for the county coroner's office for six years. She also worked for an E-911 agency for a little over a year. She is pursuing a degree in emergency management with a minor in homeland security.

Pat Tressel (Chapter 7) has been writing software since computers lived in refrigerated rooms and ate punched cards, and networks consisted of friends and family. Now that networks have come full circle, she is interested in how machine learning, web services, crowd sourcing and collaboration, and social networking can be applied in arenas where they are underrepresented, such as humanitarian work and organizational intelligence.

Murray Turoff (Chapter 6) is faculty emeritus in information systems at the New Jersey Institute of Technology (NJIT). He earned his PhD in physics from Brandeis University. Dr. Turoff has studied emergency management information systems and other computer-based collaborative systems since the late 1960s. He designed and implemented the first Emergency Management Information System (EMIS) for the Office of Emergency Preparedness in the Executive Office of the President to manage the 1971 wage price freeze. He implemented the first computer-based Delphi Conference Systems in 1969 and, after joining NJIT in 1973, he created the Electronic Information Exchange System (EIES) to study implementing computer-augmented communications and tailored the nature of the application and the group. It contained features such as group chat, internal linking of all communication objects by the users, much as in the early Internet. It integrated computer conferencing, messaging, chatting, personal notebooks, and other forms of synchronous and asynchronous group communications in a seamless, single interface. Turoff is a cofounder of a community of researchers dedicated to improving Information Systems for Crisis Response and Management (ISCRAM) emergency management information systems.

Jack "Robby" Westbrook (Chapter 3), director of EMA and Homeland Security in Cherokee County, Georgia, is a practicing emergency manager and has been the director of the Cherokee County Sheriff's Office Division of Emergency Management since 1994. He is responsible for all aspects of the county emergency management program. Director Westbrook has led the response and recovery to 11 presidentially declared disasters and been assigned to incident management teams that deployed to Hurricane Katrina, the South Alabama–Georgia tornadoes of 2007, and many smaller community-wide incidents. Director Westbrook has participated in developing and exercising a wide range of public health–related plans including the Strategic National Stockpile, Cities Readiness Initiative, and Pandemic Influenza.

1

Why Social Media?

INTRODUCTION

We are all members of some social network, by choice or by default. Some social networks are goal driven and others are not. Volunteer firefighters of a rural community are networked together. They have a common goal and work together as a team toward this effort. This network may extend to other rural areas where firefighters come to one another's aid in the event that the local team is confronted with a situation that is beyond their capacity to control. These networks can be further extended to include other local-, county-, and state-level firefighters. This can be through larger wildfires, training exercises, conferences, particular events, and specialty groups. A family is a social network of members who are linked together by default. We do not select our family members and yet we are connected in a very structured, sometimes peculiar series of nodes where edges forever connect us, linking us together (e.g., a family tree). Neighbors and neighborhoods are networked as communities based on proximity. Although we may choose where we live, we may not be able to choose who our neighbor is and, yet, we are networked as a group this way. Members of a social network can be linked together by ideas where they demonstrate support for one another and can be goal driven, such as the Al Qaida social network of terrorist groups. Social networks are a reflection of society.

The Internet has changed the way we interact and work together. It has revolutionized the way in which relationships are created and maintained as well as how groups of people link up and interact. Online social networks are supported by a variety of applications, which we will refer to as *social media*. For our purposes, we will use the definition adapted from some of our foundational-level research, which originated in 2007. Social networks are defined as "links from people to other people, groups, or information objects. Such objects may be messages, photos, videos, wall postings, notifications, current activities, events, widgets, etc. Such links might be created by intelligent agents or by the users" (White, et al., 2009). Social media, in particular, has captured and supported a rather large population of users who have taken some of their existing traditional social networks and moved them over to an online environment. The transformation of communications being replaced by alternative Internet solutions is an ever-growing trend where new applications are a daily occurrence.

Social media can be used as a primary means of communication or it can be used as an alternative or additional method for communication. Additionally, new social networks linking people who may not have been linked together before are created, supported, and strengthened. Social media provides many ways to disseminate information in a fast, inexpensive, and efficient manner. When combining the ability to disseminate information to a network of people online, and then have this initial group extend the information in a variety of other electronic and non-electronic ways to reach those networks that are online and not online (i.e., going viral), demonstrates the foundation upon which social media can be further leveraged. This helps get the right information to the right people at the right time. This real-time environment helps support the decision-making needs of the public and emergency management during time critical situations.

Social media is being used as an alternative way for emergency managers to communicate with the public and with each other. Many organizations, agencies, and individuals within a variety of areas in the emergency domain are pioneering efforts, exploring strategies, and paving the road to help develop sets of best practices. Social media provides a free and easy way to disseminate large amounts of information to large groups of people very quickly and efficiently. With today's budget deficit affecting all levels of government's ability to meet its goals and objectives, social media and Web technologies are being turned to as alternative solutions to the many problems that exist and are proving to be a better form of crisis communications under some circumstances.

2

The information presented in this book is important because it provides the emergency manager, public information officer, dispatcher, first responder, volunteer organization, or any other group challenged with the task of managing crises, with a tool set that will complement a comprehensive approach to emergency management including preparedness, mitigation, response, and recovery. The information that will be learned over the duration of this text can be used immediately. Most of the software applications and social sites covered in this text are available for free, so they can be used now. This is important because many people don't know about social media or the host of applications that are available for free to help fulfill the numerous objectives of any agency. This information will not only teach you about the many applications that are out there to use, but also will attempt to create a new mindset of collaboration and collective intelligence. The Internet, along with the new technologies created to use it, such as smart phones, is changing the way we work and interact. It is important to learn how to utilize these systems and incorporate this new way of "sharing" information, collaboration, and interaction using online Web-based real time tools.

The power of social media has yet to be unleashed. This book provides state-of-the-art ways to further leverage these technologies. This chapter will answer the questions: What is social media and *who* uses it? We will explore some of the reasons practitioners choose to use social media and will cover some of the common concerns. This is followed by some words of wisdom about the integrity of the information you will instigate as well as some basic introductory security tips. The remainder of this text is organized such that each chapter builds on the prior chapter's information. Although some particular aspects can be covered independent of one another, there is a unified approach that is taken and needs to drive designs. This is to help manage information overload and direct the right information to the right people at the right time. Therefore, the concepts are integrated and build on each other in a dynamic manner. Case studies are provided as real-world case examples to give the user ideas and models upon which to build his/her own sites and social media. This text is a teaching and reference guide. For those using this text as a teaching aid in a course, exercises are provided throughout the text to help synthesize the materials and provide challenges to students. These exercises can be conducted with individuals, but it's suggested to have teams collaborate and share ideas.

ONSITE WITH LIZ CLARK

SOCIAL MEDIA IN CANADA: A TIME FOR CHANGE

Communication and collaboration are critical cornerstones of emergency management. After-action reports of disasters in both Canada and the United States abound with examples of how limited communication and poor information-sharing processes have impacted response and recovery. Social media offers a solution to some of our communication challenges. To be sure, it is not the silver bullet that will solve all; however, its effectiveness, as one tool amongst many, is hard to dispute.

The power of social media was demonstrated in Calgary, Alberta, on Monday, October 18, 2010. On that date, Calgarians

FIGURE 1.1 Liz Clark, Business Continuity and Emergency Management Planner, Calgary, Alberta, Canada.

gained international attention when they elected as mayor a political newcomer by a considerable margin over other more well known and experienced candidates. Further, voter turnout set a record at 51 percent. How did this happen? With the use of Facebook and Twitter, Mayor Nenshi informed, energized, and motivated a significant portion of the population, particularly the young, into political action. Upon winning the election, he said that he was as proud of having mobilized people to vote as he was of his own victory. Nor has the engagement or the tweeting died down. Two days after being elected, Mayor Nenshi was still Tweeting his constituency:

Nenshi: Sitting down with @starwestbureau she wants questions from tweets for me. Send them now! #yycvote.
   And, receiving answers such as:

#yycvote question: What can we (the public) do to sustain the momentum for positive change in Calgary? How can we help you follow thru?

While the use of social media in this election is worthy of further research, two important points emerged immediately. Firstly, traditional polls, conducted right up until polling commenced, suggested that the more experienced politicians would take first and second place, with Nenshi likely to follow in third place. A social network tabulation, however, conducted by blogger Mike Morrison showed the results exactly as they occurred, with Nenshi having a substantial lead followed by the other two main candidates. This suggests that traditional means of collecting information may not be providing the most accurate information. The second point of note for emergency managers relates not only to the accuracy of information that can be obtained through social media, but also to the potential for capturing "onsite" information early. As polling stations were closing, Twitter users reported that some people had not been able to vote because the polling stations had run out of ballots. The returning officer discounted this report initially indicating that although some stations had been running low, extra ballots had been couriered out and no one had been prevented from voting. It was later determined that, in fact, the courier had been unable to deliver extra ballots and indeed some people had been unable to vote.

While Calgary is an international player, it has suffered from an unshakeable image of red-neck conservatism. This week, however, one man's vision and the effective use of social media tools have done much to dispel that image.

During the month of October, an informal survey of members of the International Association of Emergency Managers (IAEM) Canada discussion list was posted to get a sense of the prevalence of social media usage in emergency management in Canada. The original request for information was followed up with the posting of a brief online survey. It is unknown how many people received the request for information; however, 57 respondents completed the survey. One person provided a similar survey that they had conducted within their organization in July 2010, and those responses are included in the following numbers. Respondents were asked whether their agency was using social media, what they were using it for, who the intended audience was, what applications they were using, and if they were not using it, why not? Not all respondents answered every question.

Responses were received from a great variety of agencies representing the diversity in the Canadian emergency management community from coast to coast. Nevertheless, for several reasons, including the fact that this survey was only vetted through one source, some early problems in the survey design, and the relatively small sample size, this survey should be viewed as the basis for further dialogue and not as a scientific research analysis. Comments from respondents suggest that opportunity exists for further dialogue and sharing of potential application uses across the field of emergency management.

Of the 51 responses to the question asking whether your agency uses social media, 49 percent indicated they did and 51 percent indicated they did not. The three agencies with the greatest number of responses were health representing 32 percent of total responses, emergency management agencies at 29 percent, and first responders at 13 percent. The category "other," which provided 9 percent of responses consisted of emergency management practitioners from utilities, ARES, and search and rescue. Figure 1.2 presents the results from the survey tallying which *Agencies* are using versus the *Agencies* that are *not* using social media.

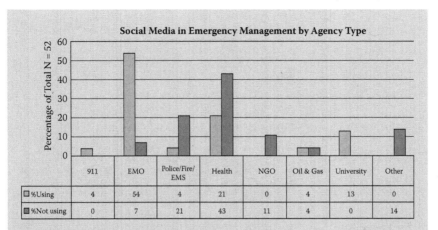

FIGURE 1.2 Social media use by agency type. One agency provides oversight for both 911 and health functions. These functions are separated here to illustrate the different agency types. Percentages represent the agency in relation to total responses received. N = 52 in this table.

Although many are not presently using social media, results indicate that the greater majority is interested in implementing such technologies. Figure 1.3 presents the findings of the agencies that were surveyed.

The survey revealed that 77.78 percent of those not currently using social media are interested in doing so, with 11 percent actively pursuing implementation. A further 11 percent are not interested at this time.

In response to a question asking what applications agencies are using, 49 percent indicated they are using Facebook, 40 percent indicated they are using Twitter, and another 12 percent are using other applications including LinkedIn, RSS Feeds, Blogs, and Websites. Emergency managers in Canada are using social media to post educational information (26 percent), to post information during emergencies (23 percent), to post regular updates on agency activities (16 percent), and to gather intelligence (16 percent). Also, 8 percent of respondents are using applications to engage their intended audience in dialogue. Other uses include weather alerts, emergency notifications, organizational communication following

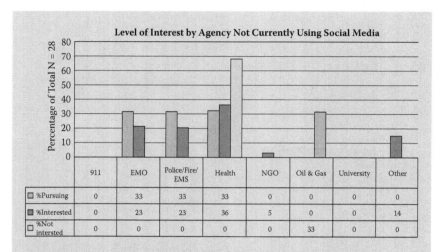

	911	EMO	Police/Fire/ EMS	Health	NGO	Oil & Gas	University	Other
☐ %Pursuing	0	33	33	33	0	0	0	0
■ %Interested	0	23	23	36	5	0	0	14
☐ %Not intersted	0	0	0	0	0	33	0	0

FIGURE 1.3 Agencies interested in implementing social media.

trends in emergency management, engaging other emergency management professionals, and "making a few friends along the way."

It is important to note some of the barriers identified by respondents when asked why they were not using social media. Included amongst the responses were lack of trained personnel (both IT and operational), resources required to set up and maintain, need for corporate policy and strategic communications plan prior to implementing, lack of need, technical problems associated with remote area usage, and, perhaps the most frequently mentioned, security concerns.

As emergency management in Canada and the United States moves away from the historic command and control model to one that recognizes the importance of community engagement, social media, now firmly entrenched in the public domain, will need to play a more dominant role in communication and collaboration. The results of the above survey demonstrate that emergency managers in Canada recognize this. The power of social media to provide real-time, accurate information, as evidenced in the recent mayoralty election in Calgary, is likely to propel agencies into this arena with increasing speed. As a group, we must support each other by sharing information, successes, and mistakes to make the most of this opportunity.

WHAT IS SOCIAL MEDIA?

Social media are forms of electronic communication through which users create online communities to share information, ideas, personal messages and other content. Social media provides a way for people to connect to other people using the Internet and a host of services. Information can be exchanged, collected, aggregated, and disseminated in a split second. Social media is in its infancy and continues to grow and develop; this book aims to cover the critical foundations that should be considered during developing and utilizing social media for emergency management.

The social media and Web technologies covered in this book, for the most part, are free software solutions, although they may have some limitations due to their proprietary nature, which would require some nominal funding. However, for each of these technologies and systems, the author demonstrates that it is feasible to work within the limitations that coincide with the free versions.

WHO USES SOCIAL MEDIA?

Emergency management, on all levels and in all types of organizations, use social media. National, state, county, local, tribal, nongovernmental organizations (NGOs), volunteer groups, and the list continues to grow as more organizations realize the transformative power of social media (For-Mukwai, 2009). Each of these groups has a different set of goals and objectives where social media is leveraged as a set of solutions to fit the needs of that particular group.

The Obama administration launched a Transparency of Government campaign that created a social media blitz that supports all federal agencies in emergency management. The Department of Homeland Security uses Twitter, Facebook, and YouTube providing a host of services for citizens (www.dhs.gov) and first responders with their Gov2.0 philosophy (www.firstresponder.gov). The U.S. Secretary of Homeland Security, Janet Napolitano, conducted the Quadrennial Homeland Security Review as an unprecedented Web-based collaborative effort.

> Between July 16 and October 4, 2009, more than 20,000 stakeholders from all 50 U.S. states and the District of Columbia participated in the National Dialogue on the Quadrennial Homeland Security Review (QHSR). The valuable comments and ideas solicited were used directly to inform

the study groups tasked with writing the QHSR for the Department of Homeland Security (www.dhs.gov).

The director of the Federal Emergency Management Agency (FEMA), Craig Fugate, proactively uses Twitter with the pen name CraigAtFEMA and also has an organization account, FEMAinFocus, where they interact in a real-time engaging manner providing short messages with links to more information during time critical situations. They also tweet educational and informative information that is not time critical.

First responders use social media for a multitude of reasons. Firefighters embraced these technologies early as a professional emergency management/first responder group. During the California wildfires of 2007, firefighters and citizens leveraged social media not intentionally, but because communications between individuals had changed (Sutton, Palen, and Shklovski, 2008). There was and remains a growing trend of traditional channels of communications, such as land-based telephones, being replaced by cell phones, smartphones, and other wireless technology. This was realized by studies conducted by a behaviorist who carefully looked at the digital history of interactions that occur. Technology is driving how people interact and social media sites and Web 2.0 technologies provide ways for people to interact and exchange information in many new ways. The study concluded that "information practices by members of the public during the October 2007 Southern California wildfires suggest that community information resources and other backchannel communications activity enabled by social media are gaining prominence in the disaster arena, despite concern by officials about the legitimacy of information shared through such means" (Sutten, Palen, and Shklovski, 2008). In an August 5, 2010 report, the Red Cross confirmed this prediction and further stated that not only would people use social media, but that "many Web users would turn to social media to seek help for themselves or others during emergencies—and they expect first responders to be listening. In fact, 74 percent of those polled expected help to come less than an hour after their tweet or Facebook post" (incaseofemergencyblog.com). So, in essence, we—as a society—are changing the way we reach out, the way we communicate for help.

Change is difficult, especially for government supported entities, but these differences in behaviors and expectations from the public and younger generation are indicators that perhaps the traditional methods of crisis communications need to be modified to fit the needs of the public whom emergency managers are tasked to protect. It will be very difficult

10

for the government to provide rules and regulations that can coincide with the fast pace of this information and how it's supported. Trying to control the information flow from social media will prove fruitless over time as it is not under anyone's control initially. An alternative method of crisis support over the Internet will not meet the needs of everyone, nor will any of the traditional methods. The successful emergency agency will be able to be flexible and open to change where they explore and identify the best solutions to fit the demographics of their population. The organizations will need to provide a balancing act between the needs of those on both sides of the digital divide.

Citizen engagement is key to building and maintaining a resilient community. Determining how to best leverage all of these available and changing technologies can prove to be an overwhelming tasks. Emergency managers can disseminate information to the public about impending dangers, such as severe weather. They also can engage the public by offering educational videos on preparedness and evacuation routes and such. One very important task that social media seems to do well is to disseminate information fast, virally (see Chapter 5, Design Strategies). Important time critical information can be sent out through a variety of methods (e-mail, tweet, Post, blog) with a single click of a button.

NGOs realized early how to leverage and partner themselves in creative ways. For example, collecting donations directly and immediately can support greater fundraising for postdisaster recovery efforts. Texting a numeric code was one way the Red Cross raised money after the terrorist attacks of September 11, 2001, and more recently, 90999 was the charity code to text to donate funds toward the Haiti earthquake effort. Facebook recently supported CNN's Hero's Fundraising event by offering multiple ways to donate by providing a "donate" application that was integrated into the network's page and the Hero's pages. Twitter hosts a charity event, Twestival, to help raise funds in other ways for Concern, a humanitarian group. Volunteer organizations have been quick to tap into the potential of social media. The Red Cross has been pioneering efforts by implementing, creating, and leveraging the *art of partnering*, which is a critical component for emergency management using social media. Emergent volunteer groups pop up online and social media meets these spontaneous needs between group members.

Possibly the untapped gold mine remains to be citizen engagement. People enjoy tweeting the weather. Citizen involvement of novice meteorologists and storm chasers has been a passion of the community forever. This same activity occurs online and the National Weather Service (NWS) realizes the potential that such information can contribute to the forecasting and weather domain (http://www.weather.gov/stormreports/).

There is strength in numbers where individuals can provide information, filling in the gaps where no sensors or prior information can be sought. This "bridging of knowledge" could be one of the most powerful influences of how emergencies are managed and how communities work together. This is a way to give the power and responsibility back to the people. Neighbors are there to help one another immediately and already contribute by conducting iReports, storm tracking, and conducting damage assessment by posting pictures from smartphone technologies and such. *iReports, iWitness,* and such new terms are used to indicate that a citizen has basically freelanced information and passed it along to another credible source, like the Weather Channel for example. A lot of the footage videoed and presented on news stations is created by users who happen to be somewhere with the technology at the right time to capture events that would otherwise not be captured and reported at all. Many news stations solicit such reports as they understand the newscasters can't be everywhere the news is, but the chance that a citizen may be able to cover the information, and is present on the scene, may be a bit higher. It's this basic philosophy that is making social media such a powerful tool. This is not only for those with the technology, but for those without the technology. Many rural areas don't have the coverage and security systems in place that the more crowded metropolitan areas have. Social media can be used to help fill in such gaps in information.

WHAT CAN SOCIAL MEDIA DO FOR PRACTITIONERS?

A study was conducted where the possibilities of using social media, just for practitioners' personal needs, was explored. The question was asked: What benefits do you see from using social media? It was amazing the number of advantages that were foreseen utilizing such technology. The responses are provided below where they are loosely categorized into common ideas and suggestions.

One of the first comments provided a logical observation:

If it works for people outside of the emergency management domain, why wouldn't it work inside?

A popular area listed concerned **crisis communications.** This is one of the larger lists indicating that this may be perceived as one of the most beneficial areas to implement social media. The practitioners stated the benefits of **social media** as follows:

- Lots of people use them.
- It is a great way for information to be distributed.
- You can get more information to more people.
- It provides immediate responses to large numbers of people.
- You can distribute surveys anytime in a variety of ways in order to get quick feedback.
- If emergency managers could use all their resources, which include the Internet, then they can create almost boundless means of communication.

This directly related to the **information flow** where practitioners responded that social media are good for:

- Sharing data, comparing results of implemented plans, developing better programs to fit a wider group of EA programs.
- Reducing the amount of time it takes doing interviews face-to-face to provide media information; they could be given access to certain data. This would give good, accurate information and would reduce time wasted during a disaster.

Another popular category of responses centered on the **knowledge exchange between crisis management experts**.

- It would be an excellent medium for sharing and coordinating information in the event of an emergency.
- Video upload for first aid data in an emergency.
- Make the important video and files to a social network so that everyone can look at files in common and analyze them.
- If properly controlled, it could be very beneficial especially as a research repository for getting quick response and recovery information.
- Can be used as collaborative problem-solving technology.

Social media can help connect people and provide **human resource** functions. Some of the tasks presented by practitioners included:

- Help in job hunting.
- Career opportunities.

- We need to be connecting with known, trusted individuals whose identities and credentials are confirmed.
- It would enable people to contact other relevant people in the emergency domain and identify "useful" individuals.
- Forming teams.
- Direct younger emergency managers and give more practices to younger or professionals new to a field or particular area of expertise.

One participant said there was a need for a site domain specific to emergency management. Something like this certainly would be one way to help validate information confirming members' authenticity. Something like this may promote further networking given that such validity of information procedures are in place. This may make it where a practitioner will be more likely to reach out to another or accept another member's suggestion quicker. There are social sites specific to domains; TeacherTube.com is dedicated to education.

Another common theme in the responses concerned having the ability to form and utilize **domain-driven groups**. The idea of having a site designated for practitioners could be one method to support such an idea. However, limiting group membership can limit the good information that is available when it comes to focusing more on "information" versus validating the person/people from where it came. Practitioners saw collaborative opportunities using social media such as:

- It is an ideal medium to introduce dialogue on new or emerging issues.
- Know different kinds of people.
- It allows people to communicate with one another and allows other individuals to see what they are working on.

Networking can be difficult and maintaining those connections can be more difficult when encounters lessen. Practitioners indicated that social media could help them **connect and network with others**, listing examples of benefits such as:

- You could go straight to the source.
- Informal connections are made through new links with people meeting through social media due to common interests.
- It provides a good way for professionals to meet and a means for discussion.
- Helps to get people in touch with one another.

14

Not only do social media and Web technologies provide the ability to network more within your own domain, but practitioners listed the far reaching benefits linking themselves to the international community due to a **global reach**. Practitioners listed that:

- The network would serve as an immediate contact and reference point for those researchers and workers in the field of emergency management on a global scale.
- You can get more information about the world.
- Social media allows many people from many different areas across the world to contact each other quickly.
- It can bridge gaps when you need to reach out to an area in which otherwise you wouldn't know where to go or how to get information.

The obvious advantages of social media is a perception that can either attract or repel stakeholders. Most social media is **free and easy**. This is why kids use it and one reason for its popularity. Sometimes it's difficult for people to understand how something so much fun for kids also can be leveraged for very serious tasks. Practitioners listed that:

- It is a free, easy way for people in the emergency domain to connect and share ideas.
- It would enable emergency practitioners and scholars to exchange information and ideas in a time critical, cheap, and informal way.
- Better way to stay in contact with others.
- Networking—it's an easier way to keep contacts rather than business cards.

Practitioners quickly noted some **educational** opportunities with Web 2.0 technology:

- Could be used to explain why and how to prepare; it might help convince people to actually prepare, what they need to do, and what the government's role is.
- Training and research.
- Professional libraries.
- Best practice sharing.

When combing the right applications with the right tools available, many of these "benefits" can complement one another. For example, Best Practice Sharing could have a forum to support a discussion, ranking systems can be implemented, and a multitude of formats can be aggregated, from text to pictures and video to virtual real-world demonstrations.

Although a mass warning system to the public is an obvious function that social media can offer, it also can be utilized for practitioners to use as a **notification system** to one another.

- Issue warning and closures.
- Use as a mass warning tool.
- Allow ad hoc warning response and fault tolerant cross agency communications.

We've reviewed a lot of reasons for practitioners to use social media. Let the pendulum swing; now we cover what are the existing reasons that concern practitioners about using social media?

WHAT CONCERNS DO PRACTIONERS HAVE ABOUT USING SOCIAL MEDIA?

The question was asked, "**What concerns do practitioners have about using social media?**"

Some of the general concerns for all online transactions are the same for social media, such as privacy, security, and robustness. In addition, behavioral concerns were brought up, such as the rejection of technology, political correctness, and the ramification of verbalizing opinions. Social media reflects a real-world setting so many of the same "real-world" concerns will cross over to the online interactions.

Some of the **privacy** issues offered by the practitioners were about the information that transpires across the Internet highway. Some samples of this include:

- The fact that they are open to basically everyone.
- Confidentiality of information.
- One can give as much or as little of personal information as need be.
- Privacy might be compromised.
- Fear of being stalked or preyed upon.

Another big problem is from the people who reject technology. Worse, social media has a host of problems with perception from the stakeholders. Social media is something that kids do, not first responders. A general **distrust or lack of use of technology** was felt to be of concern to some stating that:

16

- Not everyone feels comfortable with using the Internet and there are always problems with connections, computers, and other stuff.
- There are people who do not have access to the Internet and there are others who don't check it as much.
- Some people don't want to be part of social media.
- People have to take it seriously and it has to be in the right setting.
- Most see it used for fun.

People can get into trouble for what they say or what information they provide to an online audience. There are **social ramifications** that were identified by the practitioners. Some were:

- Fear of ramifications of political views and other opinions that can now be viewed by potential employers.
- People flaming* others due to differing ideas or opinions.

The problem with social media is that, once something "politically incorrect" is posted online, there is no real getting it back. Once again, social media holds true to the same interactions and unwritten rules we have at any social gathering or environment; the same rules should be carried over.

One area of concern to practitioners is: Who has **accessibility** to the system? Reasons for this were:

- It is hard to limit who puts information on the system, which could lead to false information being provided.
- It might make practitioners too available.
- In times of crisis, people's main goals and objectives aren't to get on the computer and pull up the information and see what's going on.
- How do you plan on getting everything out there in a quick and informed fashion?

Another important concern noted by the practitioners concerned **information quality**. Responses ranged over a multitude of reasons:

- Information is easily changed by anyone, to just professionals making the data sometimes not very notable.
- A big concern would be someone uploading false or incorrect information.

---

* The act of posting deliberately hostile messages on the Internet used mainly by a troll.

- Hackers will steal information; identify theft.
- Information overload.
- Reliability and accuracy of information.
- Too much information that is unchallenged or quality controlled at critical life-saving times.
- Often attract wannabes with little or no expertise who will clutter the airways with useless or wrong information.

Security of information poses a constant threat in any online environment. Practitioners articulate a few concerns:

- There are some aspects of emergency management that require some degree of security, and these would require another avenue of communication.
- Fear viruses, Trojans and worms, etc., of the infecting system.
- People who pretend to be someone they are not; perpetration.

All communication systems and technology are vulnerable. In particular, given that so many of these sites are free, this poses an "accountability" issue, one that hasn't been observed to date where it concerns **robustness**. Practitioners' worries include:

- Technology can fail easily.
- It's not reliable.
- There are times, as well, when the Internet is down and not working, so access is unavailable.
- The system may be abused.
- Reliance for operational purposes.

One warning came from a well-noted response—the problem with **overreliance**. Of course, this is possible for anything, but the practitioner offered these words of wisdom, which will close this section:

> Social networks are not the end-all, be-all communication. Just because someone gets a text message does not mean they'll take it seriously. Just because someone gets a Facebook message does not mean they'll react to it. Social networking is something that may eliminate the middleman (the media) in reaching the people, but how we're perceive[d] in the "blogosphere" is still not as important as how we're perceived in the real world. We cannot allow our skills with managing the day-to-day media slip in favor of using online resources.

As noted, we can reiterate that there are many reasons for practitioners to use social media for their own professional needs. Many benefits were listed. However, there are many concerns when it comes to the idea of using social media. These are all valid concerns. Simply being online poses vulnerability problems of security, information integrity, and robustness. However, just as there will be many ways to demonstrate how the benefits listed can be actualized over the course of the book, so, too, will be some of the ways to minimize the negative consequences. As mentioned, social media is a reflection of what goes on in real-world interactions between people. The same norms, mores, and rules can be carried over to the "virtual" setting. Communications remain the same, only the way we give and receive them has changed.

WHAT DOES TOP MANAGEMENT THINK?

Chief nurse for the American Red Cross, Sharon Stanly, stated that "if national preparedness efforts do not acknowledge the need for a different type of nonscene-based mass-fatality management approach, our country will remain unprepared" (www.homeland1.com). Social media and Web technologies provide an avenue for team members to work together and manage events. These techniques are already used by some practitioners. Craig Fugate uses these technologies to manage events from afar. This next example demonstrates how, when used together, these Web technologies can bring the information to the decision maker versus the decision maker having to go to the location of the information. This greatly reduces the time and effort spent by emergency management officials during the more routine tasks where decisions can be made in minutes versus hours. Could this be extended to support the needs of a catastrophic event?

It's good to know that top management supports, even professes the benefits of, using social media. One person who has mastered some of the potential is Craig Fugate. At the International Association of Emergency Managers' conference in October 2010, Fugate preached the word. I found this example worthy of including here, as it demonstrates the power of leveraging the right technology the right way to get the information you need when you need it. And it's all very simple, very fast, and free.

A tale of social media represents FEMA chief's trust in public as a resource. Craig Fugate received an e-mail message from his office concerning a pipeline explosion in northern California in early September.

Fugate, the chief of the Federal Emergency Management Agency (FEMA), read e-mail references back to the California Emergency

Management Agency that painted an incomplete picture of a fire raging after an accident.

But, instead of tracing the e-mail back to its source and making phone calls in an attempt to discover more information, the FEMA administrator consulted Twitter.

"Sure enough, it starts tweeting out all of the people in that area that are putting out tweets on what is going on. A couple of them had links to the local TV station, which had live newsfeed coverage. So. I clicked on that. So, on my little phone, I am getting streaming video of this gas pipeline fire," Fugate recalled in a speech at the Emergency Management and Homeland Security Expo in San Antonio, Texas, Tuesday.

"I was a firefighter; I can tell the difference between an aircraft burning and a gas pipeline," he added.

Thus, using social media, Fugate made a rapid assessment. Although the fire was bad, its damage was limited. With his knowledge of California's resources, he projected that state and local authorities would handle the blaze, leaving FEMA's involvement to providing financial assistance.

Consulting the public via Twitter rather than waiting for official government responses, as Fugate illustrated, represented a change in thinking for FEMA. He would like to see FEMA adopt more of such methods to make use of the public as a resource in an emergency rather than viewing them as a liability—or worse, victims that only can do what they are told.

So FEMA launched a competition on Challenge.gov to collect the best ideas from the public on how to prepare communities for disasters.

"We are going to crowd-source preparedness," Fugate announced. "We are going to try something different."

The competition will run until the end of the year, after which FEMA will compile the best suggestions and publish them on the Website.

The principle of using the public as a resource must drive more emergency management operations at FEMA and state emergency agencies, Fugate told the crowd of emergency professionals gathered by the International Association of Emergency Managers. Neighbors and bystanders almost always will be the first on the scene of an accident like a car crash or a disaster like a tornado, and it's best that emergency managers and first responders make use of that fact.

"They are going to do it whether you give them permission or not. They are going to share information faster than your official sources will, whether you like it or not. And, they are going to beat you about 90 percent of the time and have the most accurate information about a disaster site, whether you like it or not. So it's either adjust to what the public is doing or continue to find yourselves more and more isolated as we try to help survivors," Fugate remarked. (From: http://www.hstoday.us/content/view/15288/149/http://www.hstoday.us/content/view/15288/149)

AN OUNCE OF PREVENTION IS
WORTH A POUND OF CURE

A good set of safety tips to review prior to using social media is provided by different groups and organizations all of the time. The excerpt from "Is Your Social Media Site Protected?" Defense.gov article, in particular, was a good brief list of safety tips that will be covered.

Six Safety Tips to Follow When Using Social Network Sites

1. **Don't just accept the default privacy and security settings.**
   Default settings may not suit your needs or the needs of your organization. Sometimes the defaults are set open to the public and this may not be what is desired from the group. Also, settings change, develop, and are modified by the sites automatically. It is always a good idea to brief over the options available. The more you learn about social media, the more you'll understand the most beneficial settings to meet the your needs and that of your organization. There are some basics that help filter and shape the flow of information provided in the next chapter (see "Is Your Social Media Site Protected?", www.defense.gov).

2. **Choose a complex and unique password for each of your accounts.**
   Although it can be difficult to keep up with, passwords should be unique, a bit complex, and should change every so often. It helps to include a capital letter with lower case letters, numbers, and a character or two if allowed.

3. **Watch out for third party applications.**
   Make sure to pay close attention to any applications that come your way through a friend or service. Sometimes these applications ask for access to all of your information and, worse, all of your friend's information. This may not be desirable and until you understand the ramifications of such acceptance, it's best to avoid this sort of invite.

4. **Only accept friend requests from people or organizations you know directly.**
   Marketers, spammers, and other threats can come in the form of groups having access to your account and information.

5. **Carefully read the privacy policies and terms of service.**

All of these social sites and services come with policies that you must agree to prior to having an account successfully created. Policies will not be covered here as the subject matter is out of the scope of this book; however, every business and organization should carefully review the privacy policies and terms of service for the applications used. You will need to design the social media to adhere to the goals of the organization.

6. **Be careful what you post**.

For emergency management, this should be taken into account for both private and public sites. Many emergency managements have an official site and a private site. These two different sites have different purposes, friends, and information posted. This is one way to separate work from home, too. Also, a certain amount of netiquette should be used when writing a blog or on to anyone's Wall, including your own. Personal information should not be distributed; phone numbers, addresses, and *tweeting* your location may not be a good idea at certain times. In the next chapter, design issues are addressed providing guidance to what information should go where and when. This is all a result of the goals and objectives that need to be met in order to achieve those goals.

TRASH IN, TRASH OUT

It is important to create a network of links connecting yourself or your organization to credible and reliable information links. If people are networking in a professional sense, you will need to carefully choose the people you subscribe to (i.e., are *Friends within Facebook*, or *Follow in Twitter*). Social media and Web 2.0 technology opens people to all of the information on the Internet in both formal (digital libraries, electronic magazines) and informal (blogs, posts) sources. The network that you create will influence the information both received and disseminated. Therefore, it's important to include all of the stakeholders and sources of information needed while using your human network of connections as intelligence gathering mechanisms. It is important to use credible sources of information like the local emergency management and volunteer organizations, but it is equally important to determine other individuals and groups who may provide useful and unique information that is deemed important and reliable.

The remainder of this chapter will cover the following information in a chapter-by-chapter sequence. It is suggested that these chapters be covered in order as the information from one is a foundation for the next chapter to build upon and integrate. There is no one-all solution and once a team has designed a system, it's important to know what's available, what types of systems to look for, and how these can fulfill the needs as identified by the persons creating such systems.

Chapter 2: Designing Social Media Sites for Emergency Management—Back to Basics

Social media is exciting and like any new toy, people want to jump in with both feet forward. A common mistake is for an organization or group to blindly create a site, such as Facebook or Twitter, without first identifying the goals and creating a design that will support these needs. There are unfortunate consequences of these mistakes that are difficult to recover from. There are many considerations that should be made prior to any group launching Web 2.0 technologies for crisis communications. The objective of Chapter 2 is to cover the basics and help organizations create a sound foundation given the considerations that should be taken into account when developing successful social media for emergency management and crisis communications.

Chapter 3: Social Sites for Group Support Using Facebook

The objective of Chapter 3 is to introduce the concepts learned in Chapter 2 by creating an interactive collaborative site using Facebook. Facebook offers many ways for emergency management to use their system by providing a host of applications for individual accounts, then more applications for communicating to or within a group. Different types of group pages exist. Each offers a set of benefits and drawbacks. Although Facebook is covered, the issues reviewed in the chapter can be carried over to other Web-based social networks that support groups. Presently, there are two major group types supported by Facebook. One is called a "Like" page and the other is a "Group" page, although the group pages are evolving at this point. One key issue to address is "citizen engagement" and determining where and when this is a productive idea. Some basics will be covered through the use of Facebook demonstrating the variety of ways groups can be created allowing a variety of roles to be supported. Different ways of leveraging Facebook with other media is explored.

Chapter 4: Introduction to Microblogging Using Twitter

There are different reasons to use the various social medias and technologies available. Twitter offers a simple yet very powerful tool in which to microblog, e.g., tweet messages. Twitter is introduced and explained. Partnering is a critical component for organizations; this is especially true in the Twitterverse. Citizen engagement is important and provides a tool to help fill information gaps. Techniques are covered and ideas are offered on how you can partner with others to leverage your information needs. What you tweet is important and how much you tweet is something to be analyzed. The author covers topics that an Emergency Management Agency (EMA) wants to consider and some best practices concerning frequency of tweets. With a restriction of 140 characters per tweet, an art and technique to put more bang into your tweets is offered. GeoLocation devices in equipment provide an additional tool that can further map information onto a site as a visual interpretation of data. This chapter ends by presenting a case showing how surfing the net and networking can provide invaluable information during an ongoing crisis.

Chapter 5: Relationships—Twitter for Teams and Information Exchange

Twitter is powerful and is presently used a number of ways. However, the group support dynamics of Twitter are untapped and largely unexplored. Relationships linking users on the various social media types are covered. This explains why one site may best support a need or objective versus another alternative site. This chapter demonstrates creative ways organizations can further benefit from microblogging by developing frameworks of group interactions that offer an alternative to present crisis communications. A case study is provided from a team of storm chasers where their radio communications are diagrammed over and supported by Twitter. This method also can be used for search and rescue and other situations where groups of subteams are working together. A diagram is provided indicating how strategic designs can support complex group decision making and direct information flow.

Chapter 6: Collaboration and Documentation

Chapter 6 introduces the concept of online collaboration and collective intelligence (i.e., intelligence of the masses) to help support the various needs of emergency management agencies, organizations, and individuals. One might expect social media to create more 'information overload' for the end user; however, it's quite the opposite. Social media filters large amounts of data using both human and nonhuman techniques. It is all in how one networks. Web 2.0 cradles the transformative thinking that Web-based applications and technology support and nurture. Many theme-based Web applications are introduced providing solutions for a large number of the tasks that agencies are confronted with on a day-to-day basis. Online and offline, free open source software for document management (presentations, forms, spreadsheets, sites, wikis) is covered. This is both for the nonurgent day-to-day needs supporting communication and documentation needs as well as the ad hoc, time-critical situations when some unexpected event has occurred.

Chapter 7: Mapping and Open Source Disaster Management Systems

Chapter 7 covers three primary areas that all have a common thread of community and volunteerism. Each area will provide examples of a variety of the applications available and how they may be used. First, Web-based maps are surfacing one after another providing emergency officials with a host of tools that can be used before, during, and after an event has occurred. Second, humanitarian efforts occur in an online environment in many forms. These are covered in their many forms from existing organized efforts to ad hoc efforts during times of need. Community members from around the world create global communities of practice where groups form, participate, and work together to help with a variety of technology-based disaster support needs. Individuals can offer aid by populating information into a database, by providing a "pin" or "bubble" of information on a map in a collaborative, real-time effort or by going to the scene and setting up wireless communications. Third, disaster management systems are created and supported by a dedicated and devoted team of software designers and developers. Systems that have been built, used, and are ready to use are covered in this chapter. The Haiti earthquake is used as a case study providing the event from which open source disaster management systems were deployed and also some newer developing trends of volunteerism utilized to leverage the global community.

Chapter 8: Open Source Software—The Building Blocks of Customization

Chapter 8 is a bit more advanced, showing how complex systems can be created and shared between organizations using a free and open source platform. Many free and open source software applications are available and can be used as modules to build a customizable system that can be used for complex problems costing the organization much less than the proprietary equivalent. Although these systems require more technical expertise in the initial stages of development and deployment, they are available for a much lower cost and are traditionally more integratable and interoperable with other open-source systems making them easier and cheaper to maintain. This *philosophy* is catching on as more systems are created and tested, then shared proving the applicability. A case study is provided by border security showcasing the power of such a system along with leveraging a community, in order to collaboratively report illegal activity through a common surveillance system that was provided online and tested by a global audience.

Chapter 9: Launching and Testing Social Media

Social media sites are created, but then should be tested in exercises like any emergency plan. Challenges arise in how these systems are to be adequately tested and by whom. The systems need to be tested to ensure that they will work as expected and analyzed to determine if they satisfy the objectives laid out in the initial design by the stakeholders. Social media is not the end-all of crisis communications and it is crucial to best determine where and when it will work best, if at all. Not everyone uses social media and social media will not work everywhere. Other challenges arise in debuting new media to the target market. There can be strong opposition against social media and barriers to stakeholder acceptance, which can be difficult to manage and overcome. Having multiple social identities can be confusing where aggregating data and information can prove more of a challenge for both the agency and the user. Strategies are covered to help minimize these confusing aspects that are best managed by applications that bring together other applications. The chapter ends by providing basic guidelines of best practices, considerations, and other observations that help get an organization off to a good start.

ONSITE CONTRIBUTIONS

Each chapter has a segment that is provided from a practitioner's perspective in the field. Each contribution is unique given the expert's background and focus. The practitioners were solicited for their expertise in a given domain and the contribution that could be gained from their insight into how these technologies can be further leveraged. More contributions are provided by practitioners throughout the book in order to keep the "real–world" focus of application and implementation. It is the intent of the editor of the book that what is presented in this work can be taken over and implemented in a real-world setting and utilized immediately. This strategy was taken with the hope that the "rubber will hit the road" where experts can provide the real-world details that connect the dots between the lessons presented before you and their real-world application.

CASE STUDIES

Case studies are offered throughout the text and are based on real world implementation of Web 2.0 technologies. Case studies will be a component of the text for two primary reasons. First, cases provide an example from which others can identify commonalities and modify the considerations and implementations as needed. They give the reader an example to go by. Second, the cases will synthesize the information that has been presented prior to the case. This will demonstrate how concepts and components are integrated into real-world situations in emergency management. The cases provide a situation along with a threat assessment. A scenario is provided to demonstrate the system's use by covering situations. These cases cover the natural, manmade, and terroristic, and have been created by practitioners in the field from the United States.

EXERCISES

Exercises will be provided to help the novice create accounts and administer initial settings. Problems are provided to help the user gain a better understanding of what to consider while also trying to teach a skill set to help the user better understand the environment and how to work in it. This book can be used to teach both undergraduate and graduate courses.

Basic requirements can be covered along with test cases for undergraduate exercises. A more rigorous team approach can be driven by pushing graduate level groups to create frameworks, new ideas, and solutions, and to apply these techniques to discover the newest ways to implement tasks as this is a rapidly evolving environment.

TECHNICAL NOTES

Technical notes will be provided indicating methods and hardware being used. So much technology can be used to create videos, prepare educational slides, and such. Although it is not social media, it is free software that helps you create media for your needs. I am not promoting any software or hardware, just indicating what I use and why.

FIVE-MINUTE TUTORIALS

A series of tutorials are available from the authors' Website created to support this text, http://smembook.com.

SUMMARY

This book has been written with the intent to teach emergency managers how to leverage social media. The goal is to create a new mindset and provide the skill set needed to help manage the needs of an organization or individual within the emergency domain. This will be conducted by introducing concepts and then by exposing the user to a host of the free social sites and Web 2.0 technologies available. This book is by no means a comprehensive review of the available technologies out there, but rather tries to teach the professional a different way of thinking that includes using different types of applications together to aggregate and direct information. An important lesson is to teach you how to effectively search for and implement applications that will fit your needs. It can be used by the individual as a means to learn how to build, create, and launch sites as a textbook in an undergraduate or graduate course covering social media for emergency management. This is a straightforward, hands-on book with the main objective of putting the power of the technology in the hands of the people who need it most.

One of the goals of the book is to cover the most important foundational issues that should be considered when designing social media to fit the needs of an organization. The capabilities of social media and the information provided in this text is best implemented when the chapters are covered in sequence as all material is related, interlinked, and should be synthesized together so that the best solutions can be generated by you, the creator. There are many ways solutions can be created using social media. Problems change and so, too, does social media, so it's important to develop a "way of thinking" and not get too comfortable with any Web 2.0 solution as this is a volatile, dynamic environment the Internet has provided.

Chapter 2 begins by introducing basic concepts that are common to all social systems. The first well-known social media was MySpace, next came Facebook, and now Twitter has the spotlight. These sites may come and go, but the elements that are the building blocks of these sites remain the same. Core concepts that influence design and productivity will be covered first. It's important that you understand how implementing certain selections available to dictate security and privacy can greatly affect the outcome of the overall effort.

2

Designing Social Media Sites
for Emergency Management
Back to Basics

INTRODUCTION

Social media sites, such as Facebook and Twitter, are free, quick, and easy to set up. The instant gratification tempts us to jump right in and create a site. As simple as it may seem initially (and it is), social media is a complex set of tools that needs to be carefully coordinated aligning the site's design to meet the goals and objectives of an organization. Early mistakes from poor or no design at all can cause a host of problems that can threaten successful implementation. Social media and Web 2.0 technologies can help get the right information to the right people at the right time. One must first identify who the decision maker is, what the problem will be, and then identify the set of tools available that can be put together such that they can create an optimum solution.

The purpose of this chapter is to cover foundational materials that should be considered when creating social media sites for emergency management and crisis communications. Important design issues should be outlined and identified prior to launching any media. Establish who is the decision maker and what is the sensitivity level of the information

that will be exchanged, and, thus, the security required for that information. A critical step in using social media for crisis communications is to
build a sound foundation upon which to support the organization while
at the same time keeping the design flexible and agile enough so that it
can cater to the particular needs required to accomplish a task (Harrald,
2009). Considerations also will need to be made so that the design can
evolve with the fast changing pace that is characteristic of the Internet.

As with any plan, all of the stakeholders of an organization wanting to use social media should collaborate by creating a list of goals they
desire from this technology. A list of objectives and desired outcomes
should be created so that the goals of the organization can be evaluated
and measured after the system is created and launched. A system will
need to be tweaked and fine tuned as the organization learns how to use
the applications and technologies that together implement the optimal
solutions available with the present environment. There are no hard rules
of guaranteed success when a group begins to build and connect their
sites. Social media is exploding in growth and usage. Web technology is
rapidly evolving and maturing to fit the needs of the user within a set of
space restrictions.

A set of guidelines for creating successful information systems using
social media for crisis communications will be covered. This material is
foundational and should be covered prior to any other chapter. Like any
foundation, the decisions made at the administrative levels influence the
use and information that will be exchanged. The information covered in
this chapter will help emergency managers, dispatchers, volunteer organizations, and other agencies manage their crisis communications needs.

FUNCTIONS OF SOCIAL MEDIA

Popular social media and Web 2.0 technology are currently used to simply provide an easy way to share information and communicate with
each other, for free. However, social media is, for the most part, an
untapped gold mine. Social media needs to be organized such that it
meets the objectives and goals for an agency. More beneficial, however,
is when groups work together outlining common goals. This produces a
synergistic effect that has the potential to further support the way emergency organizations work and learn. If these groups work as virtual communities together, then massive amounts of training materials could be
aggregated and used by everyone. For example, if one fire department

ONSITE WITH HAL GRIEB

I never dreamed I would become a source of information for emerging technologies and their future implications in emergency management. Heck, I never planned on being in the field of emergency management. I have a BS/BA in economics and always thought I would end up in the corporate world. I usually tell people, "I didn't find emergency management, it found me." I fell in love with emergency management after multiple activations in my time with the Florida Army National Guard through working at Florida National Guard Joint Force Headquarters Emergency Operations Center for Hurricanes Katrina, Rita, and Wilma, along with the 2007 Bugaboo Fires. I was hooked and eventually found my way into the civilian profession with the Seminole Tribe of Florida's Office of Emergency Management prior to landing in Plano, Texas.

In regard to Web-based applications and social media as tools for emergency management, I stumbled into that as well. Not to date myself, but I was on MySpace before it was cool. I am part of

FIGURE 2.1 Hal Grieb, Senior Emergency Management Specialist, Plano, Texas Department of Emergency Management.

the generation that lived through each new update and version of a site and soon found myself beta testing the newest shiny online toy. As my experience in emergency management increased, so did my personal knowledge and use of Web-based and social media technologies. One day, I mused, "Wouldn't it be cool for my professional world to merge with my social world?" The end result is Prepared in Plano (a social media initiative).

I realize Prepared in Plano was not the first government organization to utilize social media. However, it was *one* of the first. I messed up multiple times in how to correctly utilize the multitude of platforms to facilitate the phases of emergency management. In fact, Prepared in Plano was booted for violating terms and conditions on one particular site because it was a faceless government user and not a "real person." So, through my years of learning and failing, I have tried to maintain an edge by keeping my eyes on the social media horizon and testing the newest tools and techniques to help the citizens and stakeholders of my jurisdiction mitigate, prevent, prepare, respond, and recover from any disasters they may face.

We are witnessing the emergence of a community-drive, streamlined world of technological advances more adept at helping those in need faster than ever before. We are witnessing the burgeoning increase in the "high-tech humanitarian" community. Prior to this point in time, only dot com moguls and philanthropic billionaires have had the resources to really affect the world with technological ventures showcased at venues like the Technology, Entertainment, Design (TED) conferences. Now, through how-to videos on multimedia social sites, small organizations are able to recruit individuals with advanced computer skills sets from all over the world to collaborate on a unified project and produce solutions to help their fellow man. We have seen these major strides in community open-source projects, such as Ushahidi, Sahana, Innovative Support to Emergencies, Diseases, and Disasters (INSTEDD), and CrisisCommons in aiding disasters throughout the globe.

Now, with the accessibility of smaller, sleeker tablet computers and smart phones, real-time information, instant requests for resources, and real-time common operational pictures are not unrealistic. In fact, society now expects this as well as real-time actionable information and resource coordination from authorities during times of crisis. As we move into the future, the line between unrealistic expectation and actual government implementation is blurring. We can now tap into the collective societal needs by crowd-sourcing information using Web-based technologies not only for the times immediately following a disaster, but, in the prevention and mitigation phases of the emergency management cycle, these technologies can be used in forecasting epidemic outbreaks or tracking the effect of projected weather events through satellite monitoring systems.

The United States has been a place that emphasizes the power of the people. Now more than ever, we see this statement in a new light. Social media and other Web-based technologies allow emergency management to utilize the individual as a refined node of information. Through location-based games, real-time online posting of information, and multimedia and semantic aggregation, we will soon be able to verify the impacts of incidents such as severe weather and effectively project the forecasted resource needs for a population after impacts within minutes, if not seconds.

Many technologies that have no direct correlation to emergency management still possess major benefits. Take, for instance the social sites that allow users to post recent purchases of goods. Gathered from an individual user, this data is not relevant, but when combined with users of a particular impacted area or region, emergency managers will be able to develop a clearer picture of the point at which economic recovery is happening by comparing it to past consumer data.

Augmented reality is another technology that will have enormous impact on emergency management and first responders. Augmented reality allows the ability for GIS specific and other types of data to be overlaid onto an image viewed through a smartphone's camera screen. Imagine the day when a first responder arriving to an apartment complex call can pull out his/her smartphone and (through the viewing screen) have the blueprints and tenant information laid out to the actual building's image. One may even take this a step farther; imagine a Bluetooth-enabled helmet shield or glasses that project the information to a responder in a smoke filled or damaged structure, giving the responder the ability to know where each room is (or should be), saving precious time in rescuing trapped individuals.

With so many fantastic technologies beginning to emerge, there also are many hurdles to confront. Individual rights of privacy, fear of "big brother," ability to comply with Freedom of Information Laws, as well as cyber threats, worry many impacted by this new realm of technology. Unfortunately, the problems will never truly be solved. Moreover, the tension of each prospective barrier will need to be mitigated effectively to the best possible compromise. What needs to be understood by those that embrace or despise these many convergences of technologies is that both sides need to understand the issues concerning the opposing view and work toward the common goal of helping others in emergencies.

We are bearing witness to a new future of possibilities in emergency management. While no technology is 100 percent reliable, we must continue to explore new technological innovations and be willing to combine our desire to help others with our outside stakeholders and community. By constantly battling organizational silo development, we can soon bring to fruition more open and collaborative emergency management tools and platforms, thus unifying governments' ability to merge with outside citizens and worldwide stakeholders. Open minds are the start in beginning to open collaborative opportunities for fostering a better future.

concentrated on making a few good training videos and then offered those to others on YouTube (or some other video sharing application), and then other departments around the country or world also did the same, then imagine how quickly a library of training videos could be developed. If for every time an emergency official creates some digital media they offered it to others, imagine how quickly video tutorials and other shared documentation could be leveraged for others to use. This would lessen the burden of the costs of educational materials, but also provide sets of Best Practices in education used by others. These materials could be ranked. Nothing would be mandated, but groups would be free to view the materials available, then pick and choose the ones that best fit the needs of the organization. Organizations could build a huge repository of information dedicated to helping one another and, basically, create online libraries full of a variety of types of information to use, share, and implement as needed.

Social media can do so much that it may be difficult to try to implement a manageable set of solution sites that can be built upon as needed as the needs of the organization are met and the site matures to meet more goals. It is important to plan a social media strategy carefully and to keep the design flexible. New smartphone applications and other technologies are being developed at the speed of light. Some sites, such as Facebook, change features and functions throughout the year to keep up with the demands of the users.

LEVEL OF GOVERNMENT

Before you begin creating a site, it is important to identify who the target user and population are. This should be laid out in the goals of the design. Your user population should be in the list of objectives. You may need more than one Facebook or Twitter site given that you may have more than one target population with whom you are communicating, e.g., public versus professional groups. It may do some good to do a bit of research on the local community and group of professionals for whom you will be creating these sites/using these applications. For local-level emergency management agencies, it may consist of looking at the demographics of the community. This will help identify the ages, languages, and educational levels of the user population. A rule of thumb is that the younger populations are more likely to use social media and embrace it. If there is a rich culture in the area, multilingual considerations will need to be taken into account and implemented. Social media, to a great degree, is a reflection of the social groups around you. However, you have the ability to connect to people with whom you may have a common interest. This ability to both use Web technology on the local level for emergency management needs and, on the global level, extending the reach of expertise is just one example of the synergy that is a byproduct of social media.

Preexisting relationships and partnerships should be created and maintained where these groups create a virtual community. This doesn't replace the existing relationships, but provides other ways to stay connected and communicate during times where groups or individuals don't interact. The virtual community should consist of the normal players in the emergency domain: the local police, emergency medical services (EMSs), firefighters, Red Cross chapters, churches, neighboring emergency management agencies, state level agencies, community emergency response teams (CERTs), and the many other players who will interact at some time

37

over the course of the year in some capacity related to an emergency or disaster. It is by keeping connected through these times of separation that information is still shared and communications are still ongoing. This element of consistency helps maintain these relationships, making times of reengagement more beneficial. Time is not spent catching up on things, people remember names better and, unlike with most e-mail, a name is given a face or at least some sort of picture. This simply makes it such that interactions will be more productive as everyone is more likely to be on the same track from the prior information exchanges and interactions. This also helps people manage information as information can be disseminated over time, in many different formats, and anytime, so people aren't bombarded with information when they do get together for a meeting or to respond to an event.

IDENTIFY GOALS

It is important that the group or organization creates a list of goals that they desire from social media and Web 2.0 technologies. The design is driven by the tasks that need to be performed in order to meet the goals of the group.

Educate yourself on what can be accomplished by using a variety of applications and social media. When a technology works for something outside of emergency management, consider using it to help accomplish some task inside the emergency domain. Always be on the lookout for new ideas and keep updated with emergency management technology news-driven information. These ideas should always be updated and evolving. A few ideas include:

- Damage assessment and disaster intelligence.
- Collaborative problem solving.
- Consultation for real-time decision making.
- Planning or exchanges of planning materials.
- Training or exchange of training materials.
- Collaborative exercise design and development.
- Citizen engagement or citizen input.
- Peer exchanges among and with CERT members.
- Best practice exchange.
- Border security video surveillance.

- Fast and cheap mass distribution of communications that can be used for announcements, emergency notifications, and to share best practices and lessons learned.
- Enhance networking with others.
- Educational tools for public and practitioners.
- Solicit community volunteers to monitor online activity.
- Have competitions between first responders to create the best videos for education.
- Help coordinate and manage response and recovery efforts.
- Match employment opportunities with candidates.
- Locate experts for real-time consulting and to mentor new emergency managers.

The information that will be exchanged and its security level should be evaluated. This will drive the user permissions and group types that will need to be created to match the security needs of the group. For many situations, organizations may want to consider two different sets of requirements, one for the public that is more open and another for emergency personnel and administrators that will need to be more secure. It is only once the goals have been identified that matching solutions can be networked to fulfill these needs.

USER ROLES AND PERMISSIONS

Roles are created to provide particular users specific functions. This helps to manage information. Some systems are more collaborative than others, but normally there is a structure supporting a variety of privileges. When an account is created, the creator of the account is commonly deemed the *administrator*. This role can be shared with others, but it is the governing role that creates other roles that help define the organization and who is privy to what information. Basically, by defining roles, the administrator is defining "who can do what." There is no set number of roles that can be defined for users and no hard core set of categories that are used by all systems. These sorts of implementations are based on the design of the application and what it is meant to do. Figure 2.2 is an example screenshot from Facebook. In Facebook, the available roles are defined by the group type that you create. This will be explained more in the next chapter, but for now, this figure shows you an example of what roles are available for a certain group type.

FIGURE 2.2 An example of a screen shot from Facebook.

Roles can be changed anytime. For example, someone can be allowed to Accept New Users to a group for a certain length of time. The role of that person can then be changed to any other available role, an officer, administrator, or participant. This is the same in Google Documents, any document can be Shared with another person. That person can be given the ability to edit the work or just view it depending on the role they are given.

There are a variety of roles. Some of the more common roles and a list of their privileges are explained below.

Administrators

Administrators are normally the people who initially create the account. This role holds the greatest amount of power and accountability. Once a site has been created, things can be modified, such as if the group is open or closed (covered next) and users can be added automatically or requests to join the group approved by the administrator. For some groups, users can request to join the group if the group is not open for anyone to join. This is a security measure and the security check can be minimal to ensure that a hacker isn't getting access or it could be to ensure the credentials of a user for greater information assurance. The general rule of thumb is that "the more open a group is, the easier it is to be a member, and the more closed a group is, the more difficult it is to obtain membership and access."

Guests

Guests can normally view information, but cannot contribute in anyway. Also, guests will be able to view only the information allowed to be viewed, so other information can be cut off from their view. Guest will not be able to post information on a Wall or in a Discussion Forum nor will they be able to participate in other activities.

Participants

Participants of social media have control over some of the information accessibility, etc. as a member. Participants can contribute, post on Walls, interact in Discussion Forums, vote and interact in a variety of other activities, and have access to other priority information. The roles can be unique to the application and defined differently dependant on the system being used.

Officers

Officers is a new role and can be seen on Facebook. Many organizations and councils consist of organizations that have the normal structures that reflect an organization (secretary, treasurer, president, etc.). Roles are created to fit the needs of the group type, so a variety of "roles" can be available and different, depending on the group type. This was not part of the original roles supported by Facebook, but was added later. Facebook and other systems are constantly changing to fit the needs of the user, conform to emerging rules, and to set restrictions so that functionality will not be compromised. For example, you can post a link to a YouTube video, but uploading a huge picture may not be allowed because it will take up too much space. Posts are limited, as well, in some forums. This is to help manage the huge amount of information being contributed.

Roles are simply a set of permissions used to define a person's abilities on a system. Any word can be used and a combination of permissions can be used to uniquely define participants in an organization. Many more roles are sure to be created as social media matures.

GROUPS

Some social media support collaboration between members of groups. Depending on the needs of the group, along with target populations and

Table 2.1 Group permissions

Group Type	Who Can Join?	Restrictions
Open or Public	Anybody	There are no restrictions; people can search and find the group
Closed or Private	Members can be added or invited to join; members can also request membership that must be approved and either accepted or denied	Restrictions of any type can be created and defined by the administrator; people can find the group and put in a request to join
Secret	Members can be added by administrators or others with privileges to add	There are greater restrictions on membership; the group cannot be detected through a search, hence, *Secret*

the security level of information, groups need to have the ability to accommodate to the needs based on the tasks that will be performed by the group. This is illustrated in Table 2.1.

Groups will vary given the needs of the groups using the system. Social systems evolve and are modified to meet the demands of the groups now and in the future.

First responders and emergency management officials wear two hats: one for the public and another that is private and is associated with the professional where interactions and the information exchanged should remain secure, i.e., not for the public. Therefore, it seems logical for organizations to create two primary categories of social media, one for the pubic and interaction between the citizens, and a second one that is closed and/or secret including only those groups that are officially affiliated with emergency management including nongovernmental organizations (NGOs), government, private, humanitarian, volunteer organizations, etc. All systems should remain flexible so that modifications can be made if new or emergent groups need to be added

KEYWORDS AND HASHTAGS

It is critical for the correct keywords and hashtags to be used when creating social media. Keywords describe content and are regular words used in everyday speech and written normally for the most part. Hashtags help direct information to those searching for it in an organized, sometimes ad hoc, manner and can be cryptic as they are a single word that can consist of many characters as long as the first one is the # (pound) symbol. YouTube videos, tweets, and online documents require particular words to be used, ones that best describe the content of the media being created and stored. Keywords are critical for searching and directly affect retrievability. This refers to when a user is on a search engine such as Google (www.google.com) and types keywords into the search engine. The way the search engine knows information is related to some particular subject or area is from these keywords. An example of some keywords that I would use to describe this book would be:

Social
media
crisis
communications
emergency
management
education
facebook
twitter
mapping
case
studies

Note that no word is repeated. When you repeat keywords, they are ignored by the search engine so they are just taking up precious space. Sometimes the number of keywords may be limited, so you will need to try to use the words that are a best fit to describe whatever it is you are uploading.

When creating accounts in most of these sites, either on the initial setup or when an information object is created, like a video or presentation or Twitter account, others searching for these objects will be able to find them and get to them easily. This is covered in a number of other ways that will be discussed later in the book, but it is important for the organization to understand and to not underestimate the power of keywords and their importance to the World Wide Web and your user population.

Hashtags will be covered more in Chapter 4, Microblogging with Twitter. A hashtag is a keyword with the pound symbol (#) in front of it, #Keyword. Hashtags are keywords in that the word represents a meaning, but hashtags should be created with care so that information can be directed where need be. Also, hashtags should be kept as small as possible. This reduces the human error potential in entering the word and, during a disaster, it may be difficult to enter lengthy descriptive hashtags. The hashtag should be logical and represent the entity itself, but there may be a tradeoff between logic and length. Hashtags and keywords are entered differently depending on the social application being used. In a YouTube Video, there is a form requesting information that is used to provide the user a description of the video. These descriptions, along with keywords and hashtags are used to search for and direct information throughout multiple applications on the Internet. Twitter includes keywords and hashtags as part of the tweet where each counts toward the 140 character limit (*microblog*). Figure 2.3 demonstrates a common template used for some sites. These forms are also user friendly, which is good when people are learning new skills under time-critical situations.

If I were going to tweet something about this book, I would include both keywords as presented earlier and I would also use hashtags to direct it to groups like #SMEM (Social Media for Emergency Management) and #sm4r (Social Media for 1st Responders) so that anyone filtering those two hashtags (to keep up on the subject) would have my tweet appear (be retrieved). For example, some hashtags I could use would be

#fema
#social
#media
#socialmedia
#SMEM
#CERT SMEM
#dhs
#sahana
#crisismappers

The hashtag used would depend on the tweet information being disseminated. When using a hashtag, make sure that it's used only when the information pertains to that hashtag. For example, sometimes during an event, hashtags are created in an ad hoc manner. This is quickly picked up by anyone following the event. For example, from the recent fires in Boulder, Colorado, of 2010, #boulderfire emerged (#BoulderFire—not case sensitive). If you go to Twitter now and type in #boulderfire, you will

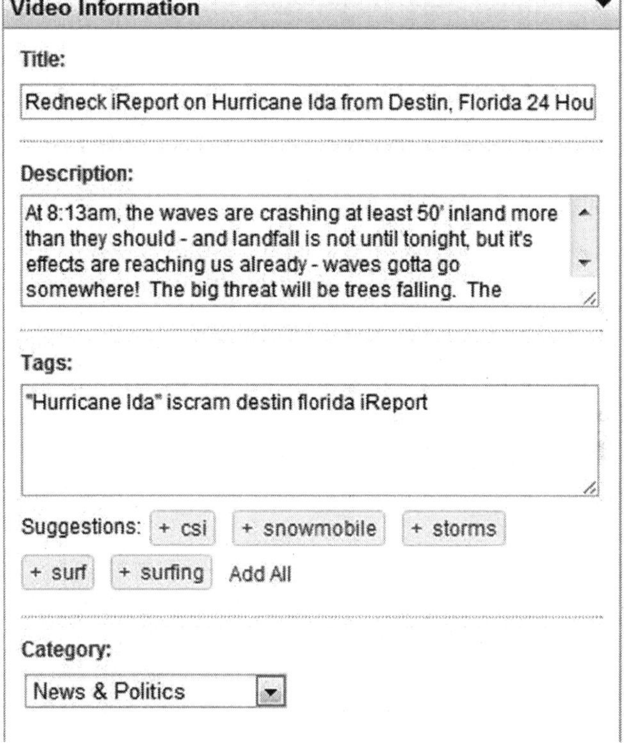

FIGURE 2.3 Common template used for materials posted.

retrieve a list of information. The information tweeted will be a reflection of the ongoing event in most cases.

Keywords and hashtags may be changed or modified anytime during the use of the social media. However, for some cases, during response efforts, using a hashtag in a tweet, for example, may be time-critical and used for a quick viral dissemination for a fast response due to some urgent need. On the other hand, a keyword or hashtag may be used to describe a training exercise video on YouTube. If the owner of the account finds that other terms better describe the keywords, then these modifications can be made and are encouraged. The better the description accurately reflects the contents of the media, the easier it can be retrieved and used by others. This also pertains to hashtags, these can be changed so that they are directed to a new area or an additional area. Hashtags and keywords can be changed normally with no major consequences.

It is important for organizations to create hashtags ahead of time. They need to be short and make sense. A few hashtags can be created, but too many may cause confusion. It is good to create conformity where common groups may interact. For example, the hashtag used by the National Oceanic and Atmospheric Administration (NOAA) to tweet severe weather is #wxreport where each state is identified by #wx[state abbreviation]. Therefore, for Georgia, one would tweet #wxGA. Each state can create its own way to direct information, #wxGAcherokee for Cherokee County. This is only an example, but, even in this example, take into consideration how difficult the hashtag may be for someone to enter. Human error can erode the entire microblog.

DISABILITIES AND VULNERABLE POPULATIONS

It is important that the design of such systems includes and identifies ways to meet the needs of the disabled. It is easier to design such sites when thinking that a younger, technologically savvy user group is at the other end. Social media can be leveraged equally as well to protect our vulnerable populations. Techniques will be covered in the text, but it is critical for the people designing the system to consider these alternative needs during all phases of designing, implementing, and launching such technologies. The Department of Homeland Security (DHS) began including text scrolling along the bottom of its YouTube videos. It's important that verbal messages include all of the information required for the user to make the best decision possible or to best understand the material.

COMPREHENSIVE EMERGENCY
MANAGEMENT APPROACH

Social media should be used for a comprehensive emergency approach. Identifying users and partnering with other organizations prior to any event helps build relationships and networks groups that will prove useful for other needs.

Below is a list with some examples of how social media can prove useful within the four phases of the disaster cycle.

Mitigation:
- Risk assessment
- Documentation management
- Collaborative generation of policy/procedure
- Collaborative decision analysis tools
- Exercise creation

Preparedness:
- Prepare to take in donations.
- Conduct exercises testing the system and determining if the stakeholders are reaching the goals identified in the exercises.
- Videos can be created for training.
- Risk analysis.

Response:
- Quick information, more people required to monitor/filter/disseminate. It may be difficult to get information out due to a suppressed situation.
- Capability to take photographs, video events, and disseminate over a variety of methods (e-mail, Facebook, Twitter, Blog) by using a hand-held smart device, such as a Droid or iPhone.
- Mapping information by the victims onto a site with bubbles providing GeoData.

Recovery:
- Resource allocation, mapping visualizations
- Donations: texting phone and FB links, tweets
- Damage assessment through pics, videos, geodata geo locations
- Geomapping routes open

CITIZEN ENGAGEMENT: TO USE OR NOT TO USE

Citizens are the greatest resource of untapped information right now as far as social media and emergency management goes. There is great debate on if and when citizen participation should be integrated. Some argue that allowing citizens to participate on emergency management social sites compromises the integrity of the management group. The argument is that the information cannot be controlled and that it's easy for a civilian to post something that could be detrimental to the agency and position it to "lose face" with its intended audience. It also raises the possibility of presenting false or intentionally nefarious and endangering information. On the other hand, citizen engagement is considered proprietary. Citizens are everywhere and can report information that only they are privy to due to geographic location and such. Citizens could help in response and recovery efforts and are already used and solicited by news organizations (Belblidia, 2010). The Weather Channel has the *iWitness Weather* with their *"See it. Send it. Share it."* campaign (http://iwitness.weather.com/) and other useful information on a daily basis. During extreme events where information is scarce, they solicit the public for information. Their site provides a user friendly interface where the information can be easily uploaded to the system.

The Texas Border Security Operations Center built a surveillance system on an open source platform. The system was built and Texas launched a test pilot over a 28-day period. The site had over 27.5 million hits. Over the duration, security officials monitored and observed the interactions of the public, validated reports, and generated information based on the interactions and information provided by the public. A very interesting set of rules surfaced that are described and presented along with a case providing details of creating and implementing such systems in Chapter 8, Free and Open Software.

APPLICATIONS

Applications, better known as "Apps" on the Internet, are software products that are built to perform some task that may be a function or a service offered on the Internet. Apps can be simple or complex. At present, there are over 10,000 applications that can be used with the Driod smartphone (operating system) and over 100,000 applications that can be used with the iPhone. They can be something altogether on their own or built to enhance the abilities of an existing application. For example, Twitter has many apps built for it to help manage the information and to add other abilities (like including an image) to the allotted 140 character limit. There's one application that makes it such that you can tweet longer messages, Twitlonger. These are easy to find if you use the right key words. For example, "longer tweet" typed into a search engine instantly retrieves "Twitlonger is a simple service that lets you post those tricky messages that really do need more than 140 characters and send them to Twitter" (www.twitlonger.com). There are many smaller apps that can be used together to build custom sites. This is covered more in Chapter 6, Collaboration and Document Management, where we cover sites. There are hundreds of applications created for social media to aid in crisis communications utilizing Web 2.0 technology. Some are used on a laptop, some are created for mobile phones, others for smartphones, some online, some off, others can be either. If one needs anything, they should simply do a search online. You will be amazed at how much is out there, most of which is free or can be purchased for a nominal fee. There are hundreds of thousands of applications available. Seek and ye shall find.

LOGINS AND PASSWORDS

All sites require that you register with at least a login name and a password. Passwords need to be a bit complex so that they are not easily hacked. For example, one good rule of thumb is to include a capital letter with lower case letters, and use a number and another symbol if the system allows it. Try to change your password every few months and don't use something someone might guess, such as a birthday or street address. Try to use different passwords for different sites. Try to make your login name something that reflects you and not something cryptic like cmp4 that was actually my e-mail name at one time. Logins and passwords are easily forgotten especially when we do not log onto an account for a while or let the computer do it for us. If you don't remember a password, don't fret, this is normal and the sites will have some way for you to either retrieve your login or password information or they will e-mail you information. Figure 2.4 demonstrates Twitter's present Forgot Your Password screenshot.

FIGURE 2.4   Twitter's present Forgot Your Password screenshot.

CASE: AMBULANCE STRIKE TEAM

Keith Noble

Noble inquires about using social media as an alternative way to support the crisis communications of his group. The theme of his scenario is a common one to those new to social media – Will it work for my group?

I want to use social media for our ambulance strike team. It is a team of about 50 people consisting of 3 teams that get deployed for disasters when requested. I have started a test Facebook site for our team. I also have a test twitter and uStream. I have presented this to my command. They really like the idea and I'm moving forward with it right now; I will be testing it soon. In addition, one of the supervisors has been playing devil's advocate and has brought up a lot of points. He liked the idea very much, though. My goals are listed below and also some issues that we both had. What solutions can be provided?

> You are to consider solutions to this problem and continue to develop solutions over the course of the text.
>
> You are to build solutions you will learn in this text and by practicing the concepts learned using these technologies in real life settings.

Goals

- Provide up to the date information to deployed teams and department leaders
- Obtain up to date information from deployed teams, text, video, and pictures
- Provide information to family members and other team members or those deployed
- Be able to link social media networks in one spot
- Video (recorded and live) for training and up-to-date deployment information
- Training: documents, video, checklists, state level plans
- Up-to-date weather and maps on deployment areas
- Team rotation/deployment status

50

- Links to department resources (checklists, phone numbers, repair manuals, etc.)
- Chat
- Able to view on BlackBerry, iPhone, and Android mobile phones and computers with Internet
- Provide news reports from local area, both video and print

Issues:

- **Security**: How open or closed should a site be? Should the site be open to employees, family, or the public? If site is department-sponsored, does it have to be open to the public?
- **False or misleading information posted onto a site**: The purpose of the social media is to obtain a lot of information from different sources. How much power should an administrator of a site have to delete or alter that information?
- **Possible users will be too focused on using social media and not focusing on the event**: Too much time on the computer when responders should be doing assigned work. There were reports that during the Austin plane crash, responders had statements and photos on Facebook before responders were even on scene.
- **Issues on responder morale**: How does social media affect morale if a user is posting negative items on a site? For example, if someone is deployed for a week and on the second day they are bored, tired, and hate living in a tent and eating MREs (meal ready-to-eat). They post that on Facebook; how does that look for the team, department, and to the public?
- **Family issues**: If social media is shared with family, that also means they can send information to those in the field. For example, information on sick family members, especially children. Spouses may post that they miss responders and want them to come home. How does this affect those responders? Will they want to go home? There is a domino effect when this starts. Once one person on a team goes home, there may be more that follow. How does this affect deployment?

- **Technical issues with these sites**: Most are down at some point or very slow every day. How will sites react when there is a disaster and there are even more users? Often you can't rely on the site too much.
- **Limited access for some employees**: Not everyone has a smartphone or access to a computer while deployed.

CONCLUSION

Social media is easy to use, especially when leveraged with the right tools. It is imperative that time be put into the design and foundation of such a system if an agency wants to see real results. Decision makers need to identify their goals and create a list of objectives they would like to see met by social media and Web 2.0 technology. Separate groups along with stakeholders (roles) should be created to match the groups presently existing. Once a model of the agencies and groups interacting with them is built, the respective tasks that can be performed by technology can be identified and matched to meet the objectives listed. Only then can the full potential be reached and measured to determine if the needs of the community are being met.

EXERCISES

A preliminary case study is provided to get you thinking about using social media for a real-world case. The main objective here is to demonstrate how a group may evaluate using social media by identifying the needs of the group as well as listing any concerns the members may have. This case originates from a graduate student who was taking a class of mine where we were exploring the uses of social media for a variety of emergency management needs through scenarios used as projects. However, this was a real situation as it pertained directly to the student's position with an ambulance strike team. It is presented to you as a case study to help integrate the lessons and applications covered throughout the text with the real-world goals and needs of a disaster response team. Without further ado, the first case study.

This information should be considered during the reading of this book and afterwards. Try to come up with solutions as various media are introduced and explored for practitioner benefit. Evaluate the media being covered and analyze it against the needs described in the case. See what alternatives exist as solutions and conduct a comparative analysis, prioritizing the ones that are most likely to be a best fit to meet the objectives of the organization.

A *BIG* tip to help you understand how social media can be used *is to use it.* We learn by doing and this was never any more true than when implementing technology-based concepts/applications. If you have needed an excuse to buy a smartphone, to get a new NetBook, or iPad, here it is. It is important to use social media in order to truly understand how to implement it and benefit from its power. Lessons can be covered and tips can be provided, but for a user to truly build a skill set such that he/she understands how to best leverage these technologies and applications, is an art form at best, under development and constantly evolving. Read everything you can, consider going to any workshop that is offered, participate in Webinars. There is a lot of information, advice, best practices, and opinions on social media and emergency management.

SUMMARY

Social media is changing quickly. Not only is one site more popular than another from one year to the next, the sites themselves are constantly being updated and modified to meet the demands of the user. Whether you want this change or not is not up to you, it just happens because you don't own the software. However, there are foundational elements that remain common to the social sites no matter what user interface changes are made. By identifying a set of goals that remain common to the needs of particular disaster types and the areas in which they occur, the best solution set available on the Web can be selected and implemented, knowing that certain administrative group and individual settings can be made to better fit the information needs of the individual, agency, or organization. One untapped gold mine is to be leveraging the public by engaging them as part of the comprehensive emergency management strategy. This idea is put before you and will be further discussed over the course of this text. Implementation of such citizen engagement will be discussed from a low to high input level where real-world case studies are provided, demonstrating what is presently emerging with collaborative behavior and collective intelligence of the masses.

The next chapter will be the first where you will get your hands dirty creating a profile in Facebook. This is not a chapter that teaches you about Facebook, but is a chapter that covers many concepts that are found in Facebook. Therefore, this social site was used as a way to help put the "rubber to the road" in teaching you how to use group's social sites for the needs of emergency management and crisis communications. LinkedIn is another site that supports groups of people in one place. Many more exist now and something is likely to replace Facebook; however, the same foundational information covered in Chapter 3 will be common to most group support social sites as such. It will be important to keep up with the changing technology to ensure the best fit in order to best reach the goals set forth by the organization.

3

Social Sites for Group Support
Facebook

INTRODUCTION

Social networking sites and applications support a variety of communications and information needs. Communications can take place a number of ways in order to satisfy the need to exchange information. Communications are supported by linking accounts together. Throughout this book, people, organizations, agencies, and accounts will be used interchangeably to satisfy the need of the theme. However, these are all used synonymously and actually refer to "an account" that has been created and is being used on a social network. An account can be created for a person, place, or thing. Each application has policies governing what is allowable within the definition of an account.

The relationships between accounts can be one-to-many, where one person can send information to many at once; can be many-to-one, where many people can direct information to one account; or can be many-to-many, where one organization can send information to many people at once and, in return, many people can send that one organization information. Figure 3.1 provides an example of a one-to-many communication relationship where one person can send information to many people. This could be in a tweet, a blog, or an e-mail, for example.

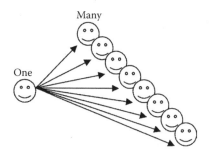

FIGURE 3.1 A diagram demonstrating a one-to-many relationship.

In social networking, people "subscribe" to each other, which is what links one person to another creating a network. Subscribers are *followers* in Twitter, *friends* in Facebook, and *connections* in LinkedIn. Each application has its own term, but they all have the same meaning. Links have a directional flow of information from one account to another.

A one-to-many relationship is satisfied by microblogging using something like Twitter. A tweet is sent to all of the people and organizations subscribed to, or *following* that Twitter account. In Facebook, a person's or organization's post will be disseminated to that person's network, which consists of other registered Facebook members referred to as *friends*. Links between people can only be made to other people with accounts registered to that social network. In Twitter, someone can *follow* you, but you don't have to *follow* them. The information flow is one way. Of course, you can also *follow* the person *following* you and then you will each receive one another's microblog, better known as *tweets*. This sort of back and forth interaction works great for some of the needs supporting the exchange of information. However, it is not so good where people and organizations need more support for group interaction, where a history of the interactions is maintained.

In Facebook, information between accounts is two-way. Both parties have to agree to network. For example, in Facebook, an invitation between entities must be initiated. An invitation is sent where the invitee can accept or reject the member. This provides control over who is networked with whom. A many-to-many relationship is satisfied by offering group support. This is accomplished by many social sites like Facebook and LinkedIn. LinkedIn is a job-oriented social network that connects professionals looking to strengthen their "career network." Although friends must be directly linked to one another, groups can be created where members of the same social network (members of Facebook, for example) can be formed and not have to be friends (i.e., directly connected). This is a common concept found in social sites. For example, groups also can be created in LinkedIn where people can be brought together in an open or closed setting, and not have to be formally or primarily linked. Group support application provides emergency personnel with a set of tools that practitioners and the community can benefit from in a number of ways. These accounts, relationships, and the information exchanged will be the focus of this chapter demonstrating how these are structured, but agile knowledge exchange systems.

This chapter will cover some of the characteristics common to group support sites. Facebook will be employed as the real-world application to use while covering the foundational concepts. Hence, this is not a chapter on Facebook, but will use this application as the social site to demonstrate the capabilities that can be leveraged by many Web 2.0 technologies that can support groups. Group sites are a great way to share and disseminate information by providing ways to connect videos, pictures, Websites and schedule events with others. They are maturing and constantly evolving, modifying policies, functions, and security features. Facebook is presently the most popular social networking site. It is used by a large and growing percentage of the population for not only people, but for groups, organizations and causes, support groups, and ways to express opinion by "Liking" a site. Social media like Twitter, YouTube, and Facebook give an organization a face and provide groups a variety of ways to engage the public and user population. This chapter will cover the common set of functions that are available for group support. These characteristics should be critically evaluated when designing and using social media.

WHAT CAN SOCIAL SITES DO TO SUPPORT GROUP COMMUNICATIONS AND INFORMATION SHARING?

Facebook has a number of ways to manage groups and the information transferred between them. Many of these features are found in one form or another in applications that support groups. When creating a group, for example, members can be assigned a number of different roles. Each role has with it privileges, a set of functions that define the role. Roles help restrict or provide access to information in a number of ways. Privileges can range from someone being able to:

ONSITE WITH JACK "ROBBY" WESTBROOK

Effective communications during all phases of emergency management are critical for any emergency management program to be successful. Historically, emergency managers have stayed with the established methods of delivering risk communications to the program's stakeholders to include outdoor warning sirens, local media, and reverse 911 to landline phones. Each of these risk communication methods are expensive to install and require a great deal of time and money to maintain. While all of these methods have merit, society's growing need for instant two-way communications around the clock opens the door for a new and exciting method of communicating across the entire community. Most people from teenagers to grandparents insist on having a method of communications with

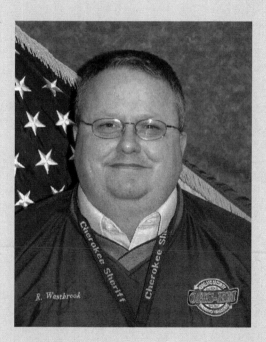

FIGURE 3.2 Jack "Robby" Westbrook, director of the Cherokee County, Georgia, Sheriff's Office of Homeland Security—Emergency Management.

them at all times. Often these cell phones are linked to social networks, such as Twitter and Facebook, connecting a single person to hundreds of friends and family members almost instantly. Finding ways of leveraging these new methods of communication to interact with our citizens in near real time may be one of the most important communications issues facing emergency managers today.

When one first thinks of using social networks in the emergency management environment, we, of course, look at ways to deliver risk communications to large numbers of people. By simply establishing an emergency management program Twitter or Facebook page and then advertising those pages to the community, emergency managers can quickly gain a very large audience. Applications also have been developed that allow Emergency Alert System (EAS) messages, including tornado, severe thunderstorm, and flood warnings, to be automatically posted to the emergency management program's social site. In addition to providing time-critical warnings and emergency information, emergency managers can use these social sites to deliver preparedness information for both home and business. While the delivery of emergency information may be an important aspect of leveraging social sites, it is not the only one.

Situational awareness is vital for effective decision making and, for this reason, practicing emergency managers are always looking for information. So, many times what happens after the initial event impact during the response and recovery phases is remembered much longer than the actual event. A review of past disasters finds that the lack of a clear operational picture not only slows the deployment of effective resources into the disaster area, but delays the overall recovery as well. Allowing citizens to communicate what they are seeing through existing social media channels could assist emergency managers in gaining a true picture across the community. Emergency managers with any amount of experience know that a certain percentage of information received from the public via the 911 system is exaggerated or just plain wrong. This same issue will have to be accounted for when evaluating information received via social media as well. However, if the information obtained from the public, whether it is received through the 911 system or social media applications, is juxtaposed with reports from trained first responders, a much improved operating picture can be obtained.

- Add information to a site
- Remove information from a site
- Only view the information
- Vote or rank alternatives
- Invite or accept new members
- Post information

Just like in any real organization's social environment, roles provide the set of rules that accompany what someone is allowed to do or not do. This helps manage the information and controls/restricts what members are allowed to do. Roles are provided so that more than one person can be in control of administering permissions to the group users. Groups are supported by more than just roles, though. Groups can be open, closed, or even secret to the public so that they are not searchable and only known to a select few. Membership is obtained through a number of ways, each dependant on the type of group that was created. For example, in an Open group, members can either freely register or ask for permission to be added to a group. Closed groups are good to support departments, businesses, and other such agencies where the employees/practitioners can interact more freely and have a place to support further networking. For more security and privacy, a secret group can be created where membership is by invitation only. Figure 3.3 is a screenshot of the members of a group. This is the view of the Administrator's Role where I had the ability to change other member's roles. For example, I could click Make Admin under any of the members' profile pictures and then that member would

FIGURE 3.3 A screenshot of Facebook group members.

have the ability to manage the members of the group, too, along with any other privileges that are available to that role.

Group sites, such as Facebook, can be very powerful if used correctly. At present, Facebook is the most popular social site with over 500 million active users, half of which log on daily. Given that it already has such an enormous number of users, supports so many languages, and hosts a great number of media types (video, music, links, pictures), it makes the perfect application both for the public as a way to interact with the community, and for personnel to further support the communication needs of practitioners. Table 3.1 provides some stats reflecting where Facebook presently stands. Of course, this will possibly change over the next year as does all social media.

WHAT CAN FACEBOOK DO FOR PRACTITIONERS?

It may prove beneficial at times to create more than one site to fulfill the needs of an organization. Two sites could be created such that one is for the public sector and another is for the private sector. At present, two types of group support exist: one is in the form of a Fan page, the other is in the form of a Group page. These sorts of alternatives will be common in group applications. Groups have particular needs that should be evaluated such that the best choice is made for an agency. Also, it's very important to identify any limitations that the application may have that will prove a problem in the future. For example, when considering a Group versus Fan page, Facebook has a restriction on the number of members a Group can have (5,000 now), but no limit on the number of Fans a Fan page can have. An agency would need to evaluate the number of potential members it will have. This would be good to support a department or organization, maybe even smaller communities. However, federal- and state-level agencies would have to default to Fan pages in this case, otherwise, they would not be able to accept all of the member requests. At present, the Federal Emergency Management Agency (FEMA) has almost 22,000 Fans. Obviously, a Group page would not be an option.

Both Fan and Group pages are a wonderful way to engage with others. On the public site, postings of impending danger can be disseminated, educational videos can be uploaded, and other events can be scheduled through the site. Facebook can really be used as a tool for the private needs of the organization. Videos can be created on YouTube, documents can be created on g-mail and linked to the site. After a disaster has occurred,

Table 3.1   Who uses Facebook? Some stats

Statistics

People on Facebook

More than 500 million active users
50 percent of our active users log on to Facebook in any given day
Average user has 130 friends
People spend over 700 billion minutes per month on Facebook

Activity on Facebook

There are over 900 million objects that people interact with (pages, groups,
  events, and community pages)
Average user is connected to 80 community pages, groups, and events
Average user creates 90 pieces of content each month
More than 30 billion pieces of content (Web links, news stories, blog posts,
  notes, photo albums, etc.) shared each month

Global Reach

More than 70 translations available on the site
About 70 percent of Facebook users are outside the United States
Over 300,000 users helped translate the site through the translations application

Platform

More than 1 million developers and entrepreneurs from more than 180
  countries
Every month, more than 70 percent of Facebook users engage with Platform
  applications
More than 550,000 active applications currently on Facebook Platform
More than 1 million Websites have integrated with Facebook Platform
More than 150 million people engage with Facebook on external Websites
  every month
Two-thirds of comScore's U.S. Top 100 Websites and half of comScore's Global
  Top 100 Websites have integrated with Facebook

Mobile

There are more than 200 million active users currently accessing Facebook
  through their mobile devices
People that use Facebook on their mobile devices are twice as active on
  Facebook than nonmobile users
There are more than 200 mobile operators in 60 countries working to deploy
  and promote Facebook mobile products
http://www.facebook.com/press/info.php?statistics (accessed November 25,
  2010)

pictures can be uploaded with only a few touches to a smartphone, taking a picture and then uploading it to a Facebook site such that responders can get the real-time information that may be needed for a rapid response. People who may be in need of help can post information to their walls (there are documented instances where this has already occurred) and this can then be "shared" and linked to the proper site so that the information can be taken in and responders can be dispatched.

COMMUNICATION

Social networks allow agencies to interact more with their extended network of response support agencies. Facebook connects emergency managers with emergency managers. This creates a learning environment where best practices and lessons learned can be informally shared virally between those with common interests and needs in the emergency domain. Facebook supports a learning environment that can contribute to fill some of the needs of an agency. A study was conducted on using Facebook for college education. I will cover these results, adapting the classroom situation to parallel how such implementation might meet some of the needs of an emergency management agency (Munoz and Towner, 2009).

1. **Profile Page**: By creating a profile page, a practitioner can build a living, breathing business card with capabilities that far exceed that of the traditional form. A profile page provides one with the ability to offer as much information as one pleases. The next screenshot in Figure 3.4 provides an image of Facebook showing how easy it is to create a new account. Also note in the figure that the application states that "it's free, and always will be." This is a concern that comes up often—these sites are free now, but what about later. Facebook has provided its members comfort with such a statement on the homepage. To begin using Facebook, the first thing you must do is create an account. Go to www.facebook.com. You will need to provide your social sites with an e-mail address. This is so you and the application have a way to interact. E-mail is used to verify information, to provide you someplace to get your "password" when you have forgotten it, and provides another way for notices to be provided to you. For reasons explained later in Chapter 6 (Collaboration and Document

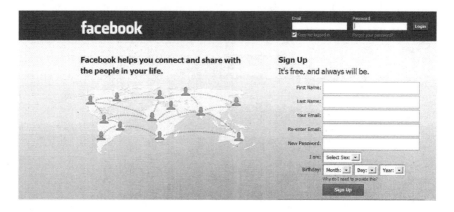

FIGURE 3.4   Creating an account on Facebook is easy.

Management), it is best to create an e-mail account with Google Mail at www.gmail.com. This is a free service; however, you can wait until later to create a g-mail account if you prefer to use your current e-mail account.

One word of advice: Keep a personal profile separate from an organizational page unless you want the public to associate the name with the position. Some people are so well known to the community that they may intermingle the ability to use their name and profile account in the same manner as an agency would.

2. **Creating a Group Page for an Organization:** Creating a page to support an effort is easy enough to do. Figure 3.5 provides a screenshot demonstrating what is required. An official site can be created for organizations. Group sites can be created by one person, but many people can have administrative powers by simply providing the member with the role.

Groups are created from the pool of available members using the application. Through a group page, members learn more about one another and communicate in a variety of ways. This makes it such that people can get to know one another better. More information can be shared when it is needed most. Mass announcements can be made to the group using an e-mail system and invitations can be sent to the group informing them of upcoming training events, meetings, or opportunities. People can share links of information and post on the group wall and do a

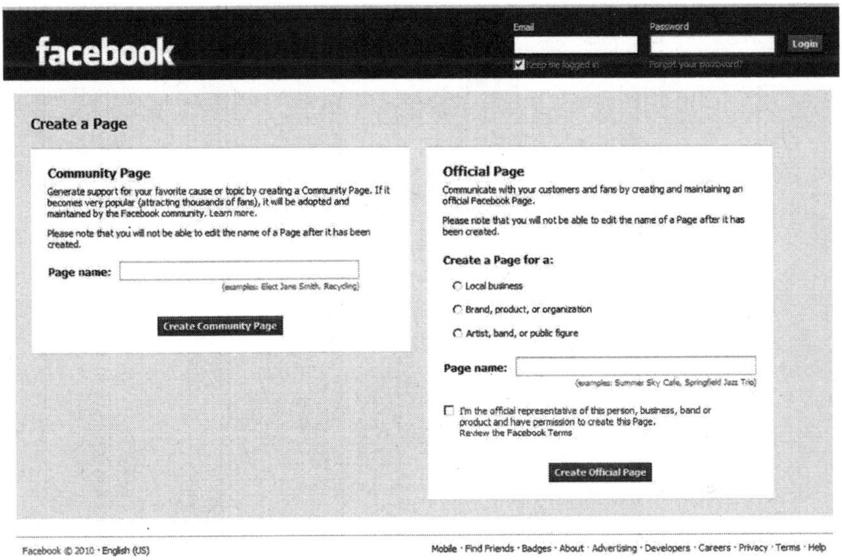

FIGURE 3.5 Shown is the Facebook Community page and Official page creation.

variety of other things that creates a tighter network of specialty subgroups.

Once a group page has been created, information can be added to seed and populate the site before new members are added. Discussion forums can be created, videos can be uploaded, and pictures can be added. New ways of creating groups and the functionalities offered are evolving to fit the needs of the user population. Figure 3.6 is a screenshot of a group, Online Social Network for Emergency Management Research, which demonstrates what a populated site can look like.

3. **Replacing/duplicating online functions on Facebook**: Facebook provides tools and functions that are available elsewhere, but in one location. For example, there is a forum discussion, chat and e-mail. Additional ways to communicate are a good back-up when other systems fail. Some groups may not have any discussion forum at all, thus, a good, free system may be a good solution. Chatting is offered and this can replace other antiquated systems that are not integrated into one user interface. Many of

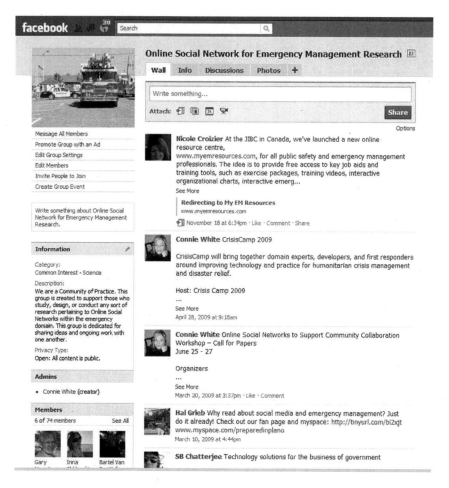

FIGURE 3.6 Facebook Group populated with members and information is illustrated.

these older systems were created before social media existed and they are cumbersome to use in comparison with the ease of most social sites. Members can post information and documents that others can download and use elsewhere. This frees up many of the size restrictions that are on organizational systems.

Facebook has its own e-mail and chat functionality. A list of online members is provided indicating which members are currently on

Facebook and are available to chat. Their profile *pics* (short for pictures) are visible along with a little square on the corner with colors to indicate if someone is busy (red) or not (green).

On the page, media-rich information is added by:

- Attaching links to news articles, documents, and other Websites
- Uploading pictures and video
- Photographing and recording video live to post instantly as a discussion component

This brings information directly to the group members. Members are exposed to other relevant and emergency management groups.

Documents will be covered in Chapter 6. Using collaborative and free software, such as what the Google Suite offers with Google Docs, provides users with alternative ways of sharing information.

TYPES OF GROUP SUPPORT

In Chapter 2, we covered a variety of group memberships that could be supported. This is likely to change over the years as other social sites will appear with their own groups supporting a variety of membership restrictions.

LinkedIn has Huddle Groups where they state that "with Huddle Workspaces, you can get your teams working together in seconds. Create different workspaces for different groups of connections—you decide who sees what. Keep your documents private and secure; you can access them from anywhere, anytime." LinkedIn targets professionals who want to "link" together to promote their careers and to keep in touch with other professionals. This is why there is, and will continue to be, more social networking sites; they cater to the particular needs of the group. At present, many features cost money where Facebook groups are free. Sometimes, that's the key ingredient to success of a social site, the fact that they are free, flexible, and open platforms.

Social sites have to manage the space they have available because it is limited. They are designed to optimize a need. So, where Facebook allows participants to easily share posts, upload pictures, and create videos live to the site, LinkedIn allows users to share documents and other text-based information. One common element that you will find between all of the group-supported social sites is the ability to have open or closed groups, or even something in between where, depending on the role of the user, certain privileges of "viewing" but not "posting" may be given.

Let's cover three group permission types that are offered in Facebook that can be used in three separate ways for emergency management and crisis communications: open, closed, and secret.

Open Groups

Open groups mean just that, that the group is open to anybody. Although Open groups may be able to block certain users if needed, the group is open for anyone to join and fully participate in the allowable activities. Open groups can have users who can view contents or participate. In Facebook, Fan pages give the person who joins the permission to only view the information where Group pages allow the members to engage and interact with the site. A special note: There will be a host of privileges and settings of security and privacy that people will need to take upon themselves in the initial setup of an account. This applies to all social media. Almost all settings can be modified, especially when it pertains to the personal profile.

When a Group Facebook account is created, the creator can allow the members to have the ability to do or not do a host of things. These capabilities are changed every so often by Facebook and are modified to fit new needs such that the creator needs to be aware of what is available and what is not. At a certain point, the goals of the organization may be met. However, technology and the Internet are changing at an incredible rate. As soon as you learn something, it's changed or something else is out there cheaper and that can do it better. Also, sites are enhancing the available functions to meet the needs of the user base. So, where an application may be needed to add an image to a tweet, Twitter incorporates adding images as part of the tools available.

Closed Groups

If an agency wants to restrict membership to the pool of available members, a closed group may be best. This means that people have to either be invited to join a group or they have to get permission to join the group. Group access can either be accepted or denied. Figure 3.7 provides a screenshot showing how easy these options are to implement.

There are many reasons for an agency to have a closed site. First, a site may be created just for official emergency management (EM) use where local fire, police, emergency medical services, and other responders

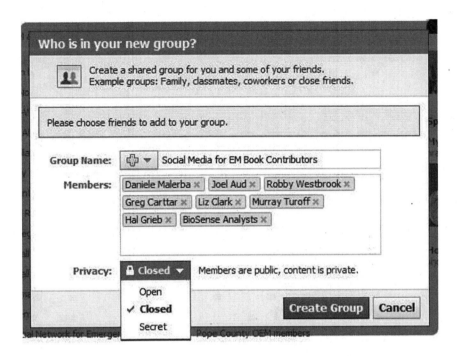

FIGURE 3.7 Privacy settings for groups in Facebook.

interact. Training exercises would be available to one another and notices of events would be posted. Depending on the phase of emergency management, different information could be posted that could prove beneficial and support the comprehensive approach. This could prove beneficial in that information can be more discrete and directly provide responders the information they need. A closed group will be retrieved on a list if a user searches for a group, but in order to be a member of the group and be able to be privy to the information, the administrator, or whatever role has the power to accept/reject requests, would have to issue approval. And, thus, this person can control the user population.

Secret Groups

A Secret group is a closed group. The difference is that the group is not searchable. The group will not be retrieved on a list by a search engine, not outside the site, such as on Google or from within the site, like searching for groups on Facebook. There are obvious reasons for this. Groups may be very restrictive in their membership and this adds one more layer of protection. The sensitivity of the information should be weighed against its security threat of exposure prior to any communication method being selected. I would never suggest putting any pic or document on one of these sites that would compromise a severe situation or expose the public to questionable scenes. I'm sure over time other services will surface to support these much-needed security measures, but for now, it's best to utilize these tools in a logical and responsible manner. It is important to remember that the information can go viral and once it is posted on a social site, it's there (and maybe somewhere else) forever.

In addition to creating the right kind of group to fit the goals outlined by the agency, it's important to identify and foresee any problematic areas that may occur and be difficult to reverse. For example, Group pages have restrictions and characteristics different from that of a Fan page. This will always be the case no matter the social media being used. When there is a variety of ways to do the same thing (group support), then it is critical to identify the differences in each to promote a successful launch. There are reasons and design issues that are the basis behind the varieties offered. If they all did the same thing, then there would be these higher level options upon creation. A common pitfall is for a group to create one sort of site to support a need that would have been better supported using another alternative. Once you get a group of followers, fans, or members, it's difficult to switch over to another group and take the information and people with you. Of course, that's why they call it hindsight or perhaps *hindsite* in this case.

ONE-WAY OR TWO-WAY COMMUNICATIONS?

One-Way

Group social sites can have many members, but the site can be created to have information flow out as in Fan pages (or Like pages as they are now called), which supports information flow one way. This is a more controlled environment where the agency can disseminate information to the Fans. Fans on Facebook are people who subscribe to the group by clicking a Like button on an organization's page. The Fan now will receive information from that agency. Some social sites may allow the posted information to be Shared with others. This is a built-in function to social media where options are available providing very simple ways to promote information going viral and passed on to other members of their network or other social media sites. For example, if someone has an interesting article link on Facebook, I can Share it with my Friends. If I take a picture on my Android smartphone, I can Share it on a variety of applications like Facebook, e-mail, Twitter, YouTube, Picasa, Seesmic, etc. Other sites may not allow the information to be shared, especially if it is also a closed group. This can include information being redisseminated through the same social networking site or it can be sent to other social sites. This is one of the reasons it is suggested that the reader of this book read every chapter in the order in which they are presented. So much information from one area is integrated with another area, hence, leveraging each other producing a synergistic effect.

Two-Way

Depending on the goals set forth by the organization, two way communications may be needed. It is important to note that your agency may need to set up more than one account per social medium available. For example, it may be beneficial to have a Fan site for a state-level EMA (EM agency); however, to engage the community and others, two-way communications is necessary. There is a lot of research that supports engaging the community and other participants in social media. People are able to interact with the agency and contribute to the needs of the community. This may promote people using the site and building a trust with emergency officials. When people interact with each other on social networks, they get to know one another better. This is no different when it's a person interacting with an organization. Two-Way would also be beneficial in closed sites where emergency agencies are partnering. People need to be able to offer resources and let others know about important information. The lack of information sharing is one of the biggest problems between agencies, and social media offers one more avenue in which officials can better communicate and be better prepared to respond to a situation.

CHAT

Chat features can be built into a system in a number of ways. In Facebook, there is a wonderful way to chat. When you are in the account, you are able to see a list of your Friends online. In the case of an emergency agency, this lets you know which other organizations and agency representatives may be online. At present, this list represents Profiles, not to be confused with Group pages. People, (i.e., profiles) can create Groups and Fan (Like) pages. Back to the wonderful chat feature, this list lets you know who you can chat with immediately. There is a list with colors that have an understood meaning. Green is for "available," yellow means that the user has been inactive, but is logged in, and red means that someone is "busy" and asks not to be disturbed. These colors are used in g-mail, Skype, Facebook, and other social media. You can click the person on the list and a chat box comes up immediately. This is a very user friendly, easy, and a quick way to interact. I would imagine video interaction soon will be incorporated into Facebook as another means of communication. One will observe that, if the users need another way to communicate and it is fulfilled by another service, Skype in this case, the media will update their system to provide this additional feature. However, we know in emergency management that if it can fail, it will fail. So, try to keep a number of systems available to communicate through if one should happen to go down. And, as always, always keep the amateur (ham) radio ready.

Chat can be incorporated as a separate functionality where all of the users have to go to the "chat" feature in order to use it. Moodle is a wonderful educational course delivery system. However, it is just great for group support as well. Moodle is a free and open source, which means you can use it for free. Educators can even have it hosted for free. This sort of service is free when you buy a domain. Domains cost around $7 to $12 depending on your needs. That's not a bad price considering you can have a large variety of free and open source software installed on your account. Moodle has one Chat system where the users go to the Chat area. Once in the area, the user's profile pic is listed and many people can interact with one another. The design is nice and easy to use and easy to read. This is beneficial for groups who want to have a meeting using chat. Chat is a good feature to use when systems are compromised and not running at full speed, especially if run as a single system. XChat, for example, has good group support for more complex needs of groups who must communicate this way. We will cover more sophisticated chat software available later in the book.

Chat is a good feature that is also integrated into cell phones and smartphones. A notification can be triggered where the phone will vibrate, ring, or do something else to make the person aware that a new message has been received.

A word of caution, though. Sometimes it may look like someone is available to chat, but they may not be physically at the computer or device at the other end of the account. People have a tendency to walk away and are perceived by others to be available when they are not.

CATEGORIZING

A lot of the social group support sites allow information to be categorized in a number of ways upon creation. This helps further with search strategies, not only for you, but for those looking for you. This helps bring up categories of educational versus recreational groups. This categorization also may define the set of Roles that will be available for the new site being created. For example, a Facebook group supporting a university class will have different roles available for its participants where a non-profit or official group may have Officer roles offered upon the creation of a site. Be careful when naming a social group site. You may not be able to change the name once it is created and this can cause confusion to the target population.

WHAT SORT INFORMATION DO YOU SHARE?

Social media provides ways for group members to interact in a discussion. They also offer ways for one person to share information with many people. On Facebook, this is accomplished by posting information on your site's Wall or on another site's Wall. A Wall means that everyone can see it and it goes out to all the Friends' or Members' home page. For a single user account, your Wall is updated with information posted by others. For any kind of Group page, the post is listed on the group's site.

It is very important to post the right kind of information and to identify the information needs of the target population in order to best meet the goals and objectives of the agency. All kinds of information can be posted on Walls and in Discussion Forums. People love to use social media to share information about the weather. This is no different for EMAs and other sites reporting crisis information. However, make sure to be aware that there is much more useful information out there that should be shared with the target population. Links and locations should be added to help the person on the ground be aware of the situation. The "decision maker," i.e., the target population, is what should be guiding the information being posted. For example, a site created for community engagement will post different information from a site created to network local

73

responders. Responders have conferences, workshops to give, classes they are teaching, grants available, and other information that will prove useful to share. And, of course, another determining factor of the information being exchanged is the "state" of the environment phase-wise: mitigation, response, recovery, preparedness. In emergency management, the information disseminated and aggregated will be influenced by the phase of an emergency.

Social media may prove most useful managing an ongoing event. During a flood, civilians can upload pics when they run into a road that is flooded, which will make officials and other drivers aware of this impending danger. This lets officials know that they need to block the road and let other community members or those in the area know to avoid this road. Of course, this same logic can be applied to any group evacuating from any disaster be it flood, fire, earthquake, volcanic eruption, or hurricane.

WHAT CAN YOU DO AND HOW DO YOU DO IT?

I want to demonstrate some of the basic and powerful features presently used by Facebook Groups. As you can see, Figure 3.8 provides an example from which I'll explain the features and how to use them. One very powerful tool is having the ability to include links to other Websites, services, or other information. This also can be a good way to share photos, events, and videos.

Figure 3.9 provides a screenshot of what a link looks like when included in a post on a Wall. Also, this shows one of the most underutilized features: video. With the video feature, not only can you upload videos, but you can record one as well. This could be used a number of ways and as an alternative if typing is out of the question. It also could be

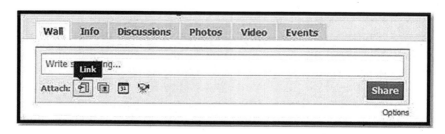

FIGURE 3.8 Functions available for groups in Facebook.

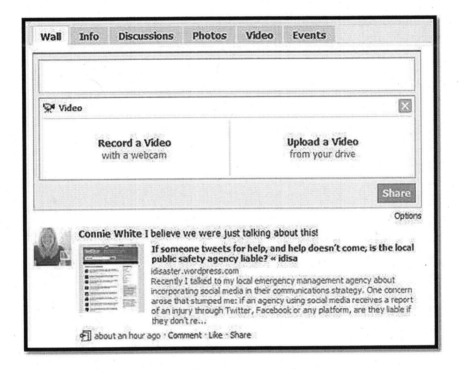

FIGURE 3.9 Capabilities available in Wall Post on Facebook.

used to record damages and upload them immediately to a closed group to aid in damage assessment.

Across the top of the window, you see Wall Info Discussions Photos Video Events. There are other functions that can be added or not used. More are sure to develop, so know to explore all functions available when you create a Group page. Info simply describes the group.

Basic information is provided including the Name, Category, Description, and Privacy type. Notice that these features can be changed. This is accomplished through the Edit Information tool that appears in the upper-right corner of the screen. Contact information is provided along with a home page. This is very important information. "Discussions" is a newer feature and still has room for improvement. They basically have a blog where there's no Reply function (at present) to associate or link a stream of thought. However, there is a pic that accompanies the user's name, and links and such can be included in the

75

post. Photos, Videos, and Events aggregate all of the photos, videos, and events in one place. This helps organize the information.

GET DONATIONS

Social media provides multiple ways to solicit donations. After the terrorist attacks on the United States on September 11, 2001, people could use their cell phones to contribute donations. This convenience and great method of ease, provided people an simple way to donate to the victim fund. People are more apt to donate when emotions are running high and the event is fresh in one's memory. However, just like with the Red Cross and other not-for-profit relief agencies, contributions are welcome anytime. This is being reflected in the digital world where many options are being provided to the contributor, to make a donation. Websites can have links, the link can be tweeted, and arrangements can be made with the application providers. This occurred during the 2010 CNN Hero awards. CNN got together with Facebook and asked Facebook to create a way for the online members to contribute donations, but available on their Facebook page. CNN leveraged Facebook by creating a page for their Heroes event, a special honoring 10 individual humanitarians selected from all over the world, who have made a big difference to society. CNN had the advantage to let their television viewing audience know about the site and promoted its use throughout the airing of the show, which was later rerun. CNN highly integrated Facebook's capabilities and Facebook stood up to the challenge by providing a DONATE NOW tab on the group page, which is seen in Figure 3.10.

Then they added the Donate Now button on every Heroes Facebook page for each of the 10 Heroes who also had a Facebook page that allowed them to provide more information to the viewer. Each Hero had the special video focusing on his/her work, links to his/her Websites, and other affiliated information. Figure 3.11 demonstrates how this further helped CNN and the humanitarians reach their own goals and objectives.

News agencies have embraced social media like no other. It is important to develop a partnership with your local agencies and others so that eminent and valuable information can be disseminated using a number of avenues. By working together with traditional media, social media can get the exposure needed to help support public information needs.

FIGURE 3.10   The Donation tab on the Facebook page.

Many radio stations also use social media along with other Web technologies. Most have a Website and many stream their radio shows live. Although social media can be used to leverage the needs of crisis communications, it's critical to remember those who do not use social media. By combining multiple methods of media (television and radio), a larger audience can be reached.

FIGURE 3.11 This shows the Donate Now tab on Facebook profile page.

HOW MUCH IS ENOUGH?

One question is: How often should information be disseminated? This goes for any agency providing information. How much information is too much or are there certain situations that call for more information to be posted at times versus others? Certainly, during an emergency, a site or sites will be more active. However, it is important to keep the public actively engaged with the site and information on it so that there is an on-going interest. Also, it's important for people to remember how to use the site so that in the event of a disaster, using the system will be second nature (Turoff et al., 2004). This can be accomplished in a number of ways. One way is by engaging the public in a conversation by posting a question on the Wall. One question could be: "Are you prepared for hurricane season?" Of course, the question would have to be adapted to the risks to the area. However, there are many educational opportunities that can be delivered during nonemergent times. Sites will be more active when an event is occurring. This could be anything from a large-scale exercise to a real-world event. When a hurricane is approaching an area (or any such imminent threat), more information should be provided to the user. This could be through any social media available. An educated public is a safer public. Maps can be provided showing evacuation routes and indicate stations with gasoline available along the route. Hotels with vacancies can be identified, along with shelters and other time-critical information. (Mapping is covered in Chapter 7.) Many other Web applications can be used to provide the public the information they need. Links to videos, pictures, Websites, and news regarding the incident can be shared, not only by emergency management officials, but also by the citizens of the community. During an event, members of the general public are the first ones able to report the happenings, and this can never be utilized enough.

SMART TECHNOLOGY

You can hardly go to any article or site on the Internet and not see a way to connect that information directly to your site. This is functionality that is now cross-linking many of the more popular sites to one another. It's important to identify what types of hardware have applications that can be used in cohort with these sites so that, with a single click, one can get the most bang for their click. For example, I have a Droid. Figure 3.12 provides a picture of the Android providing a view of the screen. Icons are available for each application and the touch-based screen makes maneuverability easy.

There are many other smartphones like BlackBerries and iPhones. Their numbers will only increase as they decrease in price. You may hear of these referred to as smartphones, but they are a far cry from being a phone. It's more like you have a handheld computer device with phone capability, along with a geographic information system (GIS) that can give

FIGURE 3.12 A photo of the screen on the Android smartphone.

you a map of your location, send and receive e-mail, shop for goods, play music, YouTube, and provide you with the ability to take pictures and videos. There are thousands of little specialty programs available for these smartphones, called *applications*, a lot of which are free. Applications (or apps) are Web-based software products that do just about anything you can imagine.

What makes smartphones so powerful is their ability to integrate functionality. For example, on my Droid, if I'm reading an e-mail and someone puts a phone number in the message, my Droid recognizes that this is a phone number. I can touch the phone number and it will activate my phone functionality providing me the ability to call that number in a single click. This sort of integrating capability, called Sharing, has great potential for emergency management. For example, someone can be driving to work during a storm and come upon a flooded street. A picture can be taken, the *Share* button can be triggered, and the information can be uploaded to the EMA or tweeted or posted to a Facebook Wall, among a number of other things, places, etc.

Social media used with smart technology is proving a most powerful tool for practitioners. They work like a personal assistant notifying users when new e-mails arrive, when someone has called, provide you with status updates of actions taken, and provide you with the ability to Share information with the greatest of ease. For example, I can video a tornado, then upload it directly to Facebook, or tweet it or e-mail it, all with a few touches. E-mail is easier to check as multiple accounts can be managed. Smart technology provides notifications where, with one swift move across the display with your finger, e-mail is open and the new message is available to view. This occurs with no login or anything, just setting up the mail application within the phone. The power these tools offer is incredible, especially during response and recovery efforts. Smart tools as such can revolutionize the way emergency officials conduct damage assessment. By using the community members, along with specialized technology teams (those sent in with the tools and know-how to record the required information), information can be provided more quickly and accurately than before. This provides decision makers the capability to respond and react in a more timely fashion.

PARTNERING

It is important to partner with the right groups that can help keep you connected together both during nonemergency as well as time-critical situations. Partnering with the right groups helps information that is related to your group's interest stay connected and time relevant. You basically partner with the same groups you normally partner with offline. Who do you work with to manage crisis on a day-to-day basis? What about on the state level? Who do you work with when a disaster occurs? The Red Cross, Humane Society, and other volunteer organizations have embraced these powerful free tools leading the way for others to learn as well.

WITH WHOM TO PARTNER?

You should partner with anybody you may think you may need to associate with. There are so many different reasons to partner, but, of course, information overload is the enemy for any decision maker. By strategically selecting who you Follow and Friend, relevant information can be channeled to specific individuals versus the poorly planned site where information can bombard personnel, which creates more problems than solutions.

Agencies with which the EM needs to network:

- Volunteer Organizations: The Red Cross, community emergency response teams (CERTs), churches, aid groups, eCitizen Corps
- Businesses: Restaurants, local general stores, big box stores, transportation, campgrounds, hotels, schools, gas stations
- Officials: Mayor, fire, police, state governor, neighboring county and state-level EMAs, National Guard, other military groups, DHS, senators and other elected officials, CraigatFEMA, healthcare groups, and local hospitals
- Information: Domain-specific news groups, health (CDC), weather, Environmental Protection Agency (EPA), National Association of Emergency Managers (IAEM)

Partnering is very important and can be used as a powerful tool when groups make an effort to work together. Once you have identified groups that use social media, it may be good to actually speak to the person in charge of the information and others and work out strategies that help the group reach their overall goals and objectives. This is especially true where one group may not have the authority to do something while another group does. This helps certain tasks get accomplished more quickly so that the group can move on to tackling and solving new problems.

PAVLOV AND NOTIFICATIONS

Social media integrate sounds as a way to notify the user that something has occurred. Instead of having to repeatedly look at one's device to see if any activity has happened your device will alert you. It does this by using various tones and sounds that have associated meanings to them such as a new e-mail or tweet arriving, or that a new voice mail exists. There are a zillion different ring tones. This can be created to indicate a song per specific caller. For example, you can make the phone ring with a particular song if it's your boss. This can allow you the ability to recognize people before you look or even answer the phone. Of course, phones vibrate. We've all sat in a meeting before where someone's cell or smartphone vibrated across the table, scaring half the group to death. However, it's the notifications of updated information that is sent through a variety of tones that makes me wonder how many sounds I can hear and know what media has received new information. This allows me the ability to walk around the office or even into another part of the building and know instantly when someone has responded to a mail of mine, a post has been made to my Wall, a reply has been made to a conversation that I'm a part of, a new tweet has come in, someone wants to chat, or someone has replied to a chat. One can't help but laugh after awhile and recognize as we react to these sounds, how proud Pavlov would be knowing how this original experiment evolved into a way to trigger such human behavior to stimulus response information reception.

CASE STUDY

Sometimes a disaster occurs quickly, so quickly that the news media cannot report it until a fair amount of time has passed. The Internet makes it such that status reports can be posted and streamed as live video from any smartphone and available for anyone on the Internet to see. This reflects a near real-time news report, given you know where to look, know how to search, use a good search engine, and have a bit of luck on your side. This is the premise behind this next case study. The objective here is to provide a scenario where a catastrophic event has occurred and to demonstrate techniques and strategies that could be used when surfing the net (i.e., looking for information on the Internet).

TALLADEGA NATIONAL SUPERSPEEDWAY

Larger sporting and recreational events challenge emergency officials in a number of ways. Manmade and natural disasters along with terrorist threats can pose a number of risks. One case in particular holds a number of threats that could be detrimental and most difficult to manage if the worst case scenario occurred. If you consider a rural area temporarily populated with an enormous amount of people, then combine this with the misfortune of major disaster occurring, then you have a situation where an enormous number of people will need communication to support a variety of needs, ingoing as well as outgoing.

Talladega Superspeedway fans have grown accustomed to the severe weather that occurs annually during the September races. North Alabama gets what's referred to as "straight-line" winds where severe storms blaze across the state causing wind and hail damage. Tornados are produced and

Alabama gets hit often. However, Talladega fans are not easily deterred and when severe weather does occur, they simply hunker down and *ride the storm out* in their makeshift homes of tents, campers, and recreational vehicles (RVs). There are acres and acres of fans who call this open pasture home for a few days, where over 200,000 will gather for the big race on Sunday.

As anyone can imagine, this situation can challenge officials as the event is located in a nonpopulated area—fields really—and the people attending the event are in pop-up campers, tents, and RVs. The one good aspect to this scenario is that they are located right along a major interstate highway. The racetrack is located between Birmingham, Alabama, and Atlanta, Georgia, but no other facilities around the area could hold the numbers of potential victims requiring medical attention should a tornado or terror attack occur. Another potential hazard is the Anniston Army Depot. This houses 7.3 percent of the world's biochemical weapons. Although they are being destroyed, leaks do occur. The threat of a tornado is bad enough, but combine the additional harm that could occur from a chemical plume that could challenge surrounding agencies and then you would have a broadening and more complex crisis to manage.

Social media needs to be used together in order to fully leverage its abilities to be most useful. Information gathering, dissemination, input, warnings, and damage assessments can all be provided with ease in a very fast pace if used together. This case was inspired by the severe storms that occurred through the central southeastern states on April 24, 2010. Forecasts were provided to the public and an aggressive warning campaign began two days earlier. The weather channel and its site were used along with other traditional methods in order to aggressively warn the public. Major events were occurring in these areas. In particular was the Talladega Superspeedway Race where a large number of fans congregate twice per year. At the same time, New Orleans, still in the long-term recovery phase from Hurricane Katrina of 2005, was in harm's way with thousands of attendees for the Jazz and Heritage Festival. Severe weather was nothing new to either of the events. However, The New Orleans Jazz and Heritage Festival still had a strong memory from Katrina and was used to dealing with tropical storms during the festivities whereas Talladega had experienced strong storms, but had not experienced a catastrophic event to date.

In order to stay abreast of the situation given ample warnings were given, anyone can turn to The Weather Channel's site, www.weather.com, and view a variety of images provided. Also, video is provided showing the past few hours of activity, which can provide a directional pattern and

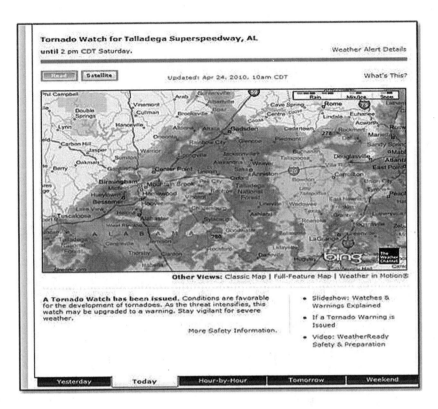

FIGURE 3.13   Weather alert details provided by the Weather Channel site.

intensity. From this site, other links are provided with "official warnings" and more specific information. Figure 3.13 provides a screenshot from the Weather Channel's site. This provides detailed information of the ongoing storm showing the storm activity.

Twitter

Although the visual map of the severe weather is very useful, there is other information that could be gathered when none is available. Twitter is especially good for real-time information when there is nothing being reported. If something has happened and a number of people were present, there's probably a tweet floating around somewhere about it. This is because of the way the social site is structured.

Facebook may have someone post on a Wall that something happened and others can Share that information, but the information cannot spread as quickly as a tweet. This is because people *Follow* one another and this brings information to people's attention. Also, hashtags and keywords can be used. This is very powerful for directing information and also for searching for information. For example, in this case, on April 24, 2010, the Talladega Superspeedway race was in progress. Severe weather had been predicted from the prior Thursday and all predictions became a reality. The races were cancelled for Friday and Saturday as campers huddled together in the stronger structures. So, the question is: How do you know what is going on? On one hand, being present at the event would provide the best source of information, especially when very large groups are gathered. Reports are generated and can be confirmed by multiple accounts of the same incident being reported.

On the other hand, when the Fort Hood mass killing took place, it was reported on the news because this was not a place where people normally tweet given the event, but then thousands of people started tweeting the information. There were 50,000 tweets per hour recorded as the event unfolded. Most of this information was repetitive and redundant (retweets) and would not provide much useful new information. Also, those tweeting the information were not on location where the event was unfolding. So, this was tweeting by users through information already being reported versus tweeting by observation. Twitter can easily cause information overload when many people are reporting and retweeting the same information. So, it's important to filter out retweets.

Confirmation of information is provided when many people report the same instance of an occurrence. For example, once some unique information is tweeted by observation at the Talladega Superspeedway, the information can be confirmed by a number of ways, but if management is solely using Twitter, multiple tweets from different individuals can be a method of confirming an event took place. Emergency management and other public information officials need to require that a team of people surf the Internet for useful information not only to receive, but to provide to citizens. Over time, humans and computers will need to be used to filter through such information and provide it in a useful format beneficial to those who need it the most.

Dissemination of Useful Information from Experts

Former director of the Florida Division of Emergency Management (FDEM) and current FEMA director Craig Fugate tweets. During serious weather, he uses this platform as a means to connect directly with the population. In order to ask for more specific information, Twitter name CraigatFEMA can be used where his dedicated team *may* respond and provide very timely and useful information that can, again, be retweeted. I say *may* because, at present, there is no official policy stating that an emergency management agency *will* be responding or be available through their official social media sites. On this occasion, I had made a comment on Twitter (mentioning @CraigatFEMA) that although we knew the tornado was coming, there was nothing we could do. As shown in Figure 3.14, CraigatFEMA responded with a link that provided much useful information.

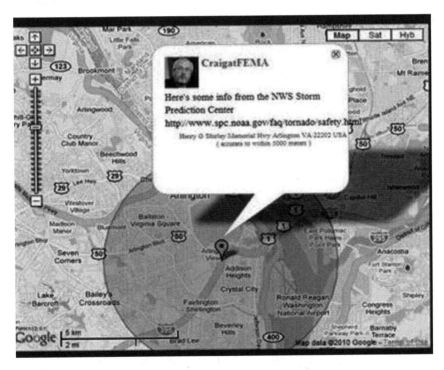

FIGURE 3.14 Engaging with individuals and providing useful information.

To help you find information using Twitter in another way, you could use the Search box. To do this, you only need go to the Twitter site at www.twitter.com and put keywords in the search box. You don't have to login or even have an account to use it. For example, if you were trying to find out what was going on and if anything dangerous had occurred at the race, you would go to Twitter's search box and type in the keyword "talladega" and that would probably bring up the information you were looking for. Many times I will see people post information on Facebook asking if someone knows about some emergency that has just occurred. The rule of thumb for now is to go to Twitter, just go to the search box and use the least amount of keywords that describe what you are looking for. You may need to change out words if there are multiple words that can be used with the same meaning. If you get too many tweets retrieved, then a strategy is to try using more words to be more descriptive and filter out what you're looking for. If you get too few tweets or no tweets retrieved, then you may want to reduce the number of keywords you are using in your search.

Facebook

Along with the other methods being used, Facebook can be used to reach those who do not use Twitter. Many people who use Facebook do not Tweet and vice versa. Facebook may be cluttered with other information where Twitter is straightforward and quicker to disseminate a particular warning. However, as there is no one solution to reach the entire population, all methods available should be used. In an ongoing Facebook Wall discussion, a friend, Greg Carttar, posted other information on maps. Facebook is a useful tool as it brings together local people and/or those sharing the same interest. When extreme weather is occurring or a disastrous event is ongoing, different pieces of information can be shared, and the information goes viral. People can have interests in common with people, or groups of interests. It's through this variety of connections that information is further exploited. Figure 3.15 shows the interactions between Friends on Facebook. The Wall allows people to have a short discussion that focuses on a particular object (link, video, picture, or status message).

E-mail

Although e-mailing lists can be used for mass dissemination, they also are used in cohort with other social media available. For example, Twitter

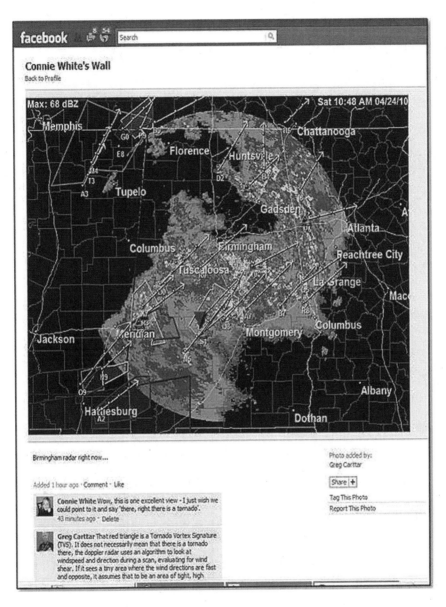

FIGURE 3.15 Informative discussion on Wall between Friends.

allows Direct Messages to be sent, which are then notified also through an e-mail indicating not only that the user has been contacted through Twitter, but that an e-mail has been sent to the user's primary e-mail account. This also occurs with other social sites (like Facebook) in attempts to let people know that some activity is going on in the social site. This is just a back-up method to ensure that people get the information. So, if someone knows that I'm looking for information on the Talladega Superspeedway, they can add the @connie.m.white on a tweet and an e-mail will be sent to me notifying me that information has arrived. In the prior figure, every time a reply is made on that particular set of interactions posted on the Wall object (link, video, pic, or status), I will receive an e-mail letting me know. When someone comments to a post of a particular user, the others who have replied to the same post are now connected information-wise as a group where each is now indicated that other posts are being made. This information is also notified via e-mail to the user to know that something specific that directly relates to them is available. This helps reduce information overload as only those things identified as of particular interest are indicated to someone. A direct link to the information is provided also in an e-mail. This greatly reduces the time it takes to find the "new posts" in discussions.

Mapping Information through Social Media

Validation of the information being reported from the user is available through a link. Storm chasers are verified and the information is more valid given it is provided to the public or those using the information. Mapping information is a very useful tool. Information can be interpreted quickly and accurately. More information is provided through links and such. The information in the prior figure is a way that people can collaborate and disseminate information on a map where a bubble is placed over the geographic location of concern. Videos and pictures can be implemented along with maps identifying evacuation routes, buildings, and other useful visuals. In Figure 3.16, you can also see where these storm chasers also have made Sharing this information possible. There are counters included with these Sharing functions showing how often the information has been shared and how. This helps the creator of such sites to determine how useful his/her site may be to the given situation or to others.

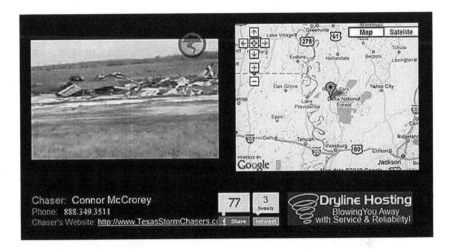

FIGURE 3.16 Information can be mapped.

YouTube

From the storm chaser's Website or through any of the other social media used (Twitter, Facebook, etc.), a direct link to YouTube is provided such that the video and other visuals are available for damage assessment. A video can be taken using a smartphone where it is then immediately shared through a variety of available medias (Facebook, Twitter, G-mail, Bluetooth, Picasa, Messaging) or embedded directly into the storm chaser's site with ease. Figure 3.17 demonstrates the functionality that is available just through this one application. There are many ways the social medias can be cross referenced and linked to other sites.

Google provides free space for users to develop their own sites. It also has a lot of applications and functions making this sort of creation easily developed. By searching YouTube and other search engines, more information is provided through more media avenues. This case of following severe weather demonstrated that many of the social media can provide information when someone is surfing the Internet looking for information concerning a severe situation such as a tornado hitting the Talladega Superspeedway during a big race. Figure 3.18 is a screenshot showing the results generated in a search on YouTube for information on 'Storm April 24, 2010' as an example of 'how to' further use social media to find information about an ongoing event.

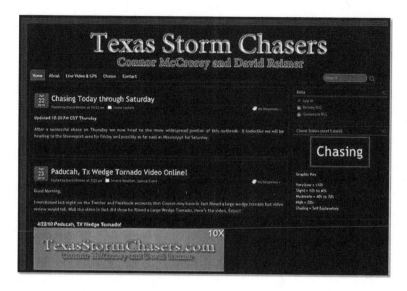

FIGURE 3.17 A screenshot of YouTube.

FIGURE 3.18 YouTube search.

Nothing bad happened that Sunday and the race went as expected; all fans returned home safe and sound. However, had an F3 or F4 touched down on the field, how would the information be best handled given the use of social media?

CASE QUESTIONS

Go online and search for information so that you can conduct a risk assessment of the Talladega Superspeedway Race and then answer the following questions:

What are some possible threats where crisis communications will be needed?
Who is the decision maker (i.e., the target population)?
What sort of information do they need?
How will information be exchanged?
How will the information be managed by the EMA?

Can you come up with a list of goals and objectives that will be used to measure the success of the site?

SUMMARY

Different social media sites support different types of communication needs. Sites such as Facebook can support individuals and groups where a history of the interactions and information objects exchanged are maintained. The roles of the members of organizations along with the types of organizations created can help groups customize these group support social sites to best fit the needs and goals of the individual, agency, or organization. These systems are forever changing without our request and so too must we adapt and evolve along with them. These group sites have a variety of functions that can help support crisis communications. People can communicate directly to one another by sending messages or posting a message on another person's site. You can chat, have discussions, post pictures, record videos, post videos, create an event, and link news articles, documents, and other sites that provide an abstract, direct link, and sometimes a thumbnail as an image to accompany them. This adds media richness that enhances the information that can be exchanged.

The next chapter covers a different type of communication relationship where information is brief and timely. This fits another niche in crisis communications and is why it, too, is popular. Twitter also can be used for group support, but it does not maintain a history or the organization of objects of Facebook, but holds a powerful place with emergency management. Microblogging techniques and strategies are introduced and covered using Twitter in the next chapter.

TUTORIAL

There are five-minute videos showing how to use Facebook. These are not perfect, but I do hope that they prove beneficial. Where one video may leave off unexpectedly, just move on to the next video as each is only five minutes long. This is Jing software (www.techsmith.com/jing) that I am using to record the screen on my computer. The free version only allows five minutes to be recorded at a time. I may break down later and get the full version, but for now, five minutes at a time. This can be used as a teaching tool also for all at your work. The one good thing about the five-minute cutoff is that you learn to try to keep things short.

Technical Notes: I am on a Dell Vostro laptop that has a built-in camera, microphone, and speakers. I used the laptop's microphone to record this. I also have a great Snowball microphone that has three area setting levels, all of high quality output and sound control for (1) a single voice, (2) group area removing noise beyond a limit, and then (3) group area with indefinite intake/input. There is a trade-off between the sound of the quality and ability to deliver online. The larger the file (the better the quality), the more difficult it is to upload, stream, or download. Given we are using a good bit of free software, there are naturally limits. In order to leverage the video, quality compromises must be made in trade for an effective delivery. People do not want to wait on the video, have it break up and buffer, and also want the ability to see it on smaller devices, such as smartphones. This trade-off is with all media we cover: images, video, sound, etc., with respect to using it for emergency management purposes. More consideration would have to be given during emergent times where communication systems are extended past capacity. The emergency manager needs to stay goal driven; know what needs to be used to accomplish the task. So, although you would prefer better sound quality and a higher resolution (video quality), where these things may be required for a good cinema experience, that level isn't required to conduct tasks that need to be given provided there is some need. For example, after a disastrous event has occurred, individuals can upload pictures to a site for EM to use in damage assessment. However, the information coming across on the screen should be clear and obvious so that EM officials can detect information and utilize it effectively.

These next videos provide you some basic information showing you how to do the individual assignment. It is important that you dedicate time to play around with this system (and all of the systems). So, where you would normally read in a course, you will play around and learn how to do things on the system. You don't really learn a system but learn what systems can do. This way, when you are introduced to a new system, you will know how to navigate it, or at least have a better chance to find what you want. These systems are very social so try to think of ways to leverage the abilities for emergency management. Make sure to take into account the four phases and different group types.

Video 1

http://www.screencast.com/users/connie.m.white/folders/Jing/media/7a590563-ee72-4d8a-b8c0-7e9e410a3c15

Video 2 (stops short, but close enough)

http://www.screencast.com/users/connie.m.white/folders/Jing/media/e3e1cb5d-68e8-4caf-8c17-faf3a0041de8

EXERCISES

1. Compare and contrast three emergency management agencies using Facebook. Any three on any level: federal, state, county/parish, city, or tribal.
2. See what commonalities they have and identify what kinds of information they post (weather, educational, conference, etc.).
3. In addition to anything you come up with, make sure to answer the following:
   a. What kind of information are they posting?
   b. How often do they post? Is that good or bad? Actually count how many posts, the hour intervals, etc., over a past week for example, but make it a calculation. Don't just say, "some

or a lot." And, if you discover any other interesting patterns (weather at 8, 12, 5) etc., include that as well.

4. Which is best for an emergency management agency to use: Fan page or Group page? Explain why and use examples to justify your answers.
5. Identify five new ideas on how Facebook can be used in more ways for emergency management purposes. Look at information from an article assigned this week. Provide a hard example on how this can be implemented.
6. What Friends or Fans would you recommend an EMA have?
7. What is partnering and how can this be accomplished on Facebook?
8. List specific examples of agencies that a local EMA would be good to partner with and explain why this would be beneficial.

4

Twitter and Microblogging
The Basics

INTRODUCTION

There are hundreds of different social media sites available. DandyID (www.dandyid.org), an application that brings social identities together in one place, supports over 330 alone. All of the available sites differ in a number of ways based on the needs of the user population. The available ways that people will be allowed to communicate will vary from one application to another. We covered "group support" social sites in the prior chapter where people could interact and exchange or post information and a history was maintained in an organized manner. Now, we move on to another popular social site being used by emergency management, but where the communication structures are much different. It's this dichotomy between these two, very popular social sites, Facebook and Twitter, that makes them desirable and beneficial to so many organizations.

Twitter is an enigma to many people; we all hear about it, but what is it? This chapter will begin by providing some basic information on Twitter. Some of the terms may sound foreign to you at first, but just keep on reading, the concepts will come together quickly. We begin by first defining some of the concepts and continue by covering what you should know to get your agency receiving the benefits that a good microblogging strategy can provide!

Twitter is a simple way for people to send and receive short messages with the 140-character limit (i.e., a tweet). A person creates a Twitter account (www.twitter.com) and then can subscribe to other individuals or organizations with accounts. By the same token, a person with an account can subscribe to receive any information you may send out. It is by subscribing to others and others subscribing to you that a network of information is created. A Twitter account can represent a person, place, or thing. Some examples include the Red Cross; CERT (community emergency response team) Pope County, Arkansas; PreparedInPlano, ReadyGov, NorthLandFox, AlabamaBeaches, and CraigatFEMA. It can represent a group, but only one person (or one login/pw) can be used per account.

DEFINITIONS

Twitter: A social network and microblogging system where one person can enter text and it is sent out to anyone following that account or anyone who views that account's page. So, either the information comes to you automatically or you go to the information directly. Anybody can view any page. You do not have to have an account to go to Twitter.com and look at Twitter pages or to use the Search tool and search for information that has been tweeted.

Private versus Public: As noted in Chapter 2, an account can be open to the public or closed, i.e., private. *Public is the preferred option for optimal engagement.*

Tweet: A message of no more than 140 characters. It can include a link.

Following: Any person can receive any tweets from another twitterer (entity account) by following it. This is accomplished by going to the entity's account and clicking Follow.

UnFollow: The option that removes the link between you and an account you are Following.

Follower: Just as you or anyone can follow any Twitter account, so, too, can your account (or your entity's account) be followed.

Block Follower: This is the option that allows you to remove someone from following you and then further blocks the entity from "linking" to you and Following your account.

ReTweet: When a tweet is deemed important enough by an entity to send it out to those Following them. This is a mass communication technique that can be directed toward a group. For example, the Centers for Disease Control and Prevention (CDC) is followed by many Red Cross groups, which in turn are followed by the communities in which they reside; thus, there is a directional flow of information to those who need it most or desire to receive it. If the CDC were to send a tweet out that should be sent to others, the Red Cross groups could then immediately ReTweet the information by clicking that option.

Mention @AccountName: @ is used and attached to the beginning of an account name to "mention" a tweet personally to another entity's account, e.g., @conniemwhite. This brings the message (i.e., the tweet) to the attention of the person with that account. This is very beneficial if the entity is using a Twitter management system like TweetDeck (covered later in this chapter) that actually will filter the "mention" out into its own column. Anyone looking at the Twitter Account page can see the tweet. Anyone can "mention" another entity in a tweet.

Direct Mention D AccountName: By placing a capital D at the beginning of a tweet, a "direct" tweet is sent to another entity account. This is a one-to-one communication that is private and only viewable by the person who sent it and by the person who received it. Both people or entity accounts must be Following one another in order to be able to communication this way.

YOU HAVE CREATED AN ACCOUNT, NOW WHAT?

Once you create an account, the first thing you may want to do is to find the Twitter account people with whom you can partner. One way to do this is through the Find People option available on Twitter (that will be available on most sites; a member search tool). For example, you may want to partner with other emergency management agencies that tweet so that you can learn by observation and ReTweet important information. You would go to the Find Friends box and type in "emergency management." Next, a list is retrieved and presented. You can go down the list and confirm whether the groups are indeed emergency management agencies or something you find of interest; if so, simply click the

ONSITE WITH TIM BRICE

For over 15 years, I have forecast the weather across southern New Mexico and far west Texas for the National Weather Service (NWS). This weather can vary in intensity from wind storms in the spring to flash floods and hail in the summer to snow in the winter. Many times it can be challenging to forecast the weather, but, thankfully, I get to use the latest computer technologies and digital weather models along with satellites and Doppler weather radar. But, even with all this equipment and information, challenges remain, especially with regard to forecasting severe weather.

To help me better know what is happening underneath a thunderstorm on the ground, I work with trained weather spotters and area county emergency managers (EMs). These spotters and EMs are my eyes and ears out in the field. They can tell me how big the hail is that is falling, how much rain has fallen in the past 30 minutes, or how strong the winds are blowing. These trained volunteers are invaluable, but even they have limits. For example, trained spotters do not exist on every mile of road in our NWS office's area of responsibility (or anywhere for that matter), so it is possible for

FIGURE 4.1   Tim Brice, National Weather Service.

severe weather to affect people without me knowing about it. This is where social media can help out.

With over 500 million Facebook users and over 100 million Twitter users, people who use social media are everywhere. Lots of people like to complain or comment about the weather in their Twitter or Facebook posts. Now, with millions of people moving around with Internet-connected smartphones, they can instantaneously make their weather-related posts, where and when the weather is happening. The National Weather Service has started a test program to try and leverage these weather posts, specifically weather-related tweets. We ask Twitter users to use a certain key word (hashtag) in their Twitter posts and identify their location when they tweet about the weather. Then, we are able to harvest these tweets from Twitter and, with the location information provided by the users, we are able to plot them on a map. We can use these tweets to update and adjust forecasts and warnings in real time. We also can use them to help verify some of the warnings after the storms have passed.

Crowd sourcing (a method of outsourcing a job to a large available pool of volunteers or employees) of weather observations has the potential to revolutionize how the NWS monitors and disseminates severe weather information. In just the next few years, the majority of the people with cell phones will not only be able to instantly post weather-related comments and observations, but they will be able to stream live video feeds of the weather as it is happening. Imagine being able to watch live as a tornado touches down or when the golf ball-sized hail starts denting a car. In addition to the NWS being able to receive weather data, in the not too distant future, we will be able to send out warnings and advisories to every person with a smartphone in a specific or regional area. People will be able to receive weather warnings via Twitter, Facebook, or other phone applications immediately and regardless of where they are or if the TV or radio is turned on.

The science of meteorology will always be challenging. In the next few years, with the aid of social media technologies, we will be able to better react to a changing weather situation and more quickly and efficiently transmit important life-saving information to the public.

Follow button that is provided and located right by them. Figure 4.2 provides a screen shot of the present options provided by Twitter that might help you link up to the best information available to fit your needs.

Later, if you don't like following these groups, you can always select the option to not follow them anymore. This is a common function in social medias. You can "un" anything you do, normally. Friends on Facebook can

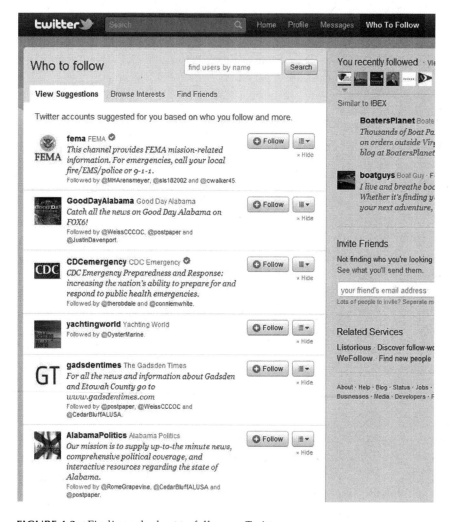

FIGURE 4.2 Finding who best to follow on Twitter.

be UnFriended and people and groups can actually be blocked. You will find marketers following you. If you are doing analysis evaluating your social sites, marketers can mess up statistics. Also, porn is everywhere online, including social media sites; unfortunately, you may see porn groups following you trying to advertise. I have even seen porn tweeted during the Iranian Protest after the Iranian presidential election in 2009. It's good to block and report spam to help keep bandwidth available for important communications.

Another way to find groups who you may want to follow is to go to a group that you know you want to Follow. From them, you can see who they Follow and who's Following them. This may identify other groups that you may wish to Follow. A good way to get ideas on good tweet syntax is to view the tweets of a group you admire. This will give you ideas of things to tweet about and how to best deliver the messages. For example, it's good to post brief tweets and include a link to more information. Make sure to shorten the URL so that you can get more words typed into the allotted 140 characters presently allowed. Of course, there are applications that allow you to have larger tweets. Remember, if you have an idea, something you need, just search for it … and make sure to include the word "Free" in your search. There will be accompanying evaluations and opinions from people. Good apps (applications) will have good reviews.

Once you Partner with people, it is an unwritten rule that the person you just Followed, in return, now Follows you. When someone follows you, and this is true for a lot of social media, you are sent an e-mail that notifies you of this as soon as it happens. This helps you control who Follows you and helps keeps your site professional.

Another way to motivate groups to follow you is to mention them in tweets. This is accomplished by adding the @ sign before the name of the site name. This is called a Mention and can be used as a filter to see who mentions you.

WHAT TO TWEET ABOUT?

Now you have set up your Twitter account and have a list of Followers, what do you tweet about? How often do you tweet? Like any communications system, the rate of speed of information flow depends on the "state" of events. If there is a crisis ongoing, obviously more tweets and information will need to be provided. More will be needed and it will be needed at a greater frequency. But, what about when there's no crisis occurring?

Crises occur on many levels where some disasters' effects are more obvious than others. This is the case with how tourists perceived the Panhandle of the Gulf Coast region during the BP oil spill that occurred through the spring and summer of 2010. It was estimated that 205.8 million gallons of crude oil gushed from the Earth during the three months the well was not capped (http://en.wikipedia.org/wiki/Deepwater_ Horizon_oil_spill). Video was streamed live 24 hours a day, 7 days a week. The tourist industry was already hurting due to the poor economy. Fishing trips and family vacations to such resort areas just weren't in the average American's budget. However, there was a fair amount of tourism still ongoing. The BP oil spill couldn't have occurred at a worse time—at the beginning of the summer vacation. Public perception prevailed over what was actually occurring. Although the oil spill did come ashore a few places, there was no oil indicated in most of the beach areas. It was this perception, nonetheless, that kept people from coming to the white beaches of resort areas, such as Destin, Florida. However, it wasn't terribly far down the beach that huge globs of oil did come ashore.

Social media can be used to fight these perceptions and help overcome the secondary financial catastrophe that can follow a primary event. @AlabamaBeaches used Twitter to fight this perception in an unprecedented way. They used Twitter as an avenue to keep the community updated on what was going on, providing daily reports during the most critical times when the oil carried much uncertainty with it. They created videos and marketed other businesses and events to get the message across that Alabama beaches were fine and safe to come and visit.

WHAT TO TWEET ABOUT FROM A PRACTITIONER'S POINT OF VIEW

What kind of information can be tweeted by an agency or ReTweeted through another? So much depends on who you are tweeting and the circumstances under which communications are occurring. Practitioners were solicited and responded with this list of useful things to tweet about.

- Personal preparedness.
- Severe weather alerts.
- Major road closings.
- Exercise notifications.

- Messages linking other messages related through different media, such as YouTube, Blog, News Post, Facebook, live streaming show.
- Political issues that have an impact on the safety of the community.
- Emergency affiliated information that may impact the local community.
- Announcements concerning officials within the jurisdiction of the agency.
- New programs that impact the safety of the community.
- Employment opportunities.
- Warnings of any nature.
- Preparedness and education.
- Brief message linking to another media, such as YouTube, Flickr, or Website enabling the user to obtain more information.
- School, university, and business closings.
- Follow local television stations.
- Follow neighboring emergency management agencies.
- Follow and ReTweet other relevant information from other emergency agencies, such as the Red Cross, CERT, public safety, Homeland Security, FEMA, and the Centers for Disease Control.
- The public can tweet nonemergent information, such as downed power lines, trees, damaged buildings, and road hazards, reducing the load on emergency communications. If the public utilities department had a Twitter account, the public could be used to report damage, which would lessen the time it takes for the utility assessors to tour an area and reduce the load on personnel answering the phone and taking the reports.
- Damage reports, weather situations, disaster news, and community events.
- Flash flood warnings, earthquakes, hurricanes, wildfires, and snowstorms.
- Amber Alerts.
- Search and rescue.
- Location of shelters provided with a link to a map.
- New policies in place.
- Resources that are available to the public.
- Self promote activities and good deeds. If groups can quickly show how they are interacting and improving the community's welfare, the citizens may be more supportive and involved.
- Family disaster plans and various types of emergency kit lists.

- Evacuation routes, ferry closing, bridges flooded, and other traffic hindering efforts.
- Hotels and gas stations with vacancies and gas along evacuation routes.
- Make the language fit the population/demographics.
- Promoting community festivities.
- Animal emergency agencies.
- Kid-specific emergency information from dedicated kits for kids to the FEMA kid's link.
- Pass along calls for assistance from the Red Cross or Salvation Army during times of need.
- Request donations.
- Promote CPR, CERT, and other community educational programs offered by partnering agencies.

Tweets are posted in chronological order. This differs from Facebook and Wall posts (right now). This is a good feature with Twitter because it keeps one abreast of the most current information with respect to both real time and to the most recent tweet from an agency, which may not be but every 4, 12, 24 hours or so.

It's important to ReTweet other organizations' information so that the public is exposed to more information in which they may be interested. This is accomplished by selectively choosing other tweets from partners to ReTweet.

Agencies should take advantage of trends. For example, during National Preparedness Month, post information that the public and private sector need.

Engage the community by asking questions that challenge their level of preparedness and education concerning potential threats.

Not everyone uses Twitter, but by using other ways to communicate information, both new and old methods are certain to reach more people. A tweet can be sent to many other places and then that information can be transmitted through more traditional avenues, such as word-of-mouth, a phone call, or an e-mail.

BEST PRACTICES
Too Much Tweeting Is a Turn Off

Learn by watching the mistakes others make and try not to make them. If an agency tweets a lot, people will select to ignore or not follow them. If there are too many tweets from an agency, then information overload occurs and people will not read the information. So, the whole reason behind tweeting is lost for that agency. When I check my Twitter account and my entire page is dominated by one group, I remove them. If you have got that much to say, then another Web solution may prove more beneficial. If there is a crisis, then a large number of tweets is acceptable, but when a group just tweets and tweets and tweets, well, it's just too much tweeting and takes over any other agency's ability to provide me information in a feasible manner. You want to have a variety of people you follow so that you will have a variety of information.

Too Little Tweeting

Sometimes you come across accounts where someone tweets once or twice a month, or even less frequently. This may indicate you don't have much going on or anything to say. People may elect to unsubscribe, not Follow or Unfollow you based on this. Interestingly, this is almost a less egregious offense than too much. If you have occasional tweets, that certainly isn't as obtrusive as too many.

Same Subject

Another mistake I see is where an EMA will just tweet about the weather. People like to see information they can't find elsewhere; it's what keeps them coming back or suggesting you to others. If the same type of information is tweeted all the time, users may lose interest. This is especially true if the message is full of acronyms and abbreviations. However, if the message is going to another group of trained professionals and meant for that target market (subgroup), then messages with more obscure or specific references may be fine to use.

Agencies are about much more than just one topic. Emergency management and public information officers can tweet about ongoing local CERT courses or provide information on closed roads and so forth. It's important to work at providing a wide variety of information that will satisfy all of the different types of Followers a group may have. We provide a variety of ideas that outline some of the different types of information that can be distributed by microblogging. Refer to the list of "What to Tweet About" found earlier in this chapter.

Organizing Tweets

Free Web-based software exists that can help you manage and get the most "chirp out of your tweet." This is accomplished by using keywords and hashtags in conjunction with aggregation software. TweetDeck is such a product; it's free at www.tweetdeck.com and installs on your hard drive. TweetDeck sets up columns where each column filters specific information. Once you launch it, columns are automatically created by default. A column is automatically set up to show all the activity in your site; this is followed by a column that filters out any Mentions to you. When someone mentions you, everyone sees it. This is followed by Direct Mentions that are private messages sent to only you. No one else can see these. However, you can customize the columns to follow whatever you want and you can arrange the columns in any order you wish. Figure 4.3 shows a screen shot of TweetDeck showing how information is filtered and presented in columns to the user.

From the previous screen shot of TweetDeck, one can see how the information is divided into four columns. The last two columns are set up to follow particular hashtags. The hashtags indicate some event is ongoing. This is good to use when something "active" is taking place. It is good to add and delete columns that filter information to best fit the real-time needs. For example, after Hurricane X has come and gone, you may not want to get information on it anymore, as it no longer poses a threat. A new hurricane is surely to take its place and will need to be "filtered" out by using other hashtags. New hashtags evolve as a situation occurs. They may have temporary or permanent meanings and they may only be used for a certain amount of time, as needed. They are dynamic and can reflect a volatile ongoing situation changing as the events unfold.

ReTweeting

Retweeting is a function found in most Twitter apps and is the same thing as sharing. It is how tweets go viral. Viral just means that they spread or have the potential to spread with an enormous capacity given the number of people following you and others who may ReTweet the information or message. You can ask for your tweet to be distributed this way by putting RT in the beginning of the tweet. For example,

RT @*EM* Fire on Mount Vernon, I65 closed, for more information http://website.shorten.url

108

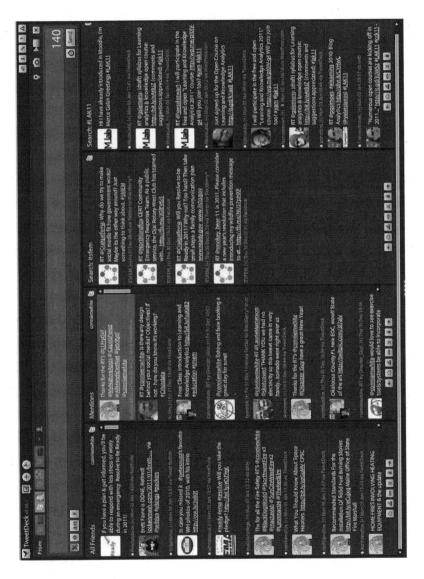

FIGURE 4.3 TweetDeck organizing tweets.

One reason to Follow people is to see what they are tweeting about; to discover what is going on. Sometimes you will read a tweet that is informative to those who are Following you. When I first set up an account, it was just to play around and see what all this Twitter stuff was about. Before long, people were following me. However, I didn't really tweet. Once people and agencies started following me, I felt compelled to tweet something. After all, why else were people following me? Well, as I mentioned earlier, all sorts of groups follow you for all types of reasons.

Technique for Reducing Tweets

Many times you will go to post a tweet and will find that you have way too many characters. As mentioned earlier, one way to provide information is to provide a link to more information and use a "shorten URL" function provided by Twitter and TweetDeck and other applications, such as http://bit.ly/. Of course, there is the TwitLonger application found at www.twitlonger.com

There are many ways these messages can be reduced, it just takes learning a few strategies and being creative—less is more. This is a great way to reduce information overload, too.

I want to present you with an example of the strategies on how to reduce the number of characters in a tweet without losing any of the meaning of the message. It's important to learn strategies that will be second nature to you in the event that a disaster occurs. You don't want to be trying to learn strategies while posting time-critical information. On the other hand, make sure that your tweet makes sense to your target population.

This is an example where I am presenting a workshop on Leveraging Social Media for Emergency Management. I am promoting this a number of ways and am trying to market it through using Twitter. There is a lot of information that needs to be conveyed, but I am restricted to 140 characters. How can someone get the most *bang for their buck* in a tweet? Here are some suggestions on how to aggregate information in a tweet and use this as an example to show the methods used to reduce a tweet to fit the allotted character space. One thing you will discover over time, you can say a lot in a single tweet.

One way is to simply tweet a title with the keywords directly including the link to the Website that provides more information, maybe including the date and cost. Another way is to read the Tweets of those target groups you have chosen to Follow and then Direct (i.e., use the @ before the Twitter account name) to a group using the information from their tweet.

Tip: I Follow many emergency management groups. I first went to their sites and looked at who was Following them and also looked at who they were Following. This provided me another way to find people who I would like to target and partner with eventually. FEMA has thousands following them and is a good source of information. This provides the user an alternative way to find groups other than by Searching with the search tool using keywords.

A group tweeted a link providing groups information on how to secure their documents. The workshop I was conducting covered this from another standpoint and was enough to inspire me to create a tweet that related this message. So, I listed some of the topics of documents that would be covered. I wanted to include a description of what was going to occur and direct it to some groups using both hashtags and target group names. The initial tweet is provided in the next box.

Google docs, Slideshare.com, wiki's, sites, bookmarking, Learn how to Manage Documents for Emergency Management needs, Leverage Social Media http://ITSFEM.com (-19)

I make the initial tweet including a description of what's going on. Once I've written this, the software indicates that I am at (–19) characters over the allowed 140. Now the question is: How do you change your tweet to make it fit? Read over the tweet and remove anything that can be taken away without changing the meaning. You will be surprised at how much you write that is unnecessary. This is great for crisis communications because it keeps messages brief and direct.

1. Remove the .com from Slideshare.com (–15).
2. The word *needs* can be removed with the space by it, and it doesn't change the meaning of the tweet (–9)

Google docs, Slideshare, wiki's, sites, bookmarking, Learn how to Manage Documents for Emergency management, Leverage Social media http://ITSFEM.com (–9)

---

3. Change the word *for* to 4, saves 4 characters when you include the space (–6).
4. Change the word *to* to 2, saves 3 more characters (–3).

111

> Google docs, Slideshare, wiki's, sites, bookmarking, Learn how 2Manage Documents 4Emergency Management, Leverage Social Media http://ITSFEM.com (-4)

5. Remove the comma between Management and Leverage, adding & and removing the spaces between the words, creating Management&Leverage (–2).

At this point, you could do a variety of things and, of course, you could have done different things all along. For example, you could abbreviate the word Management to Mgt. I thought about changing Managing Documents to Managing Docs, but was afraid that this may be ambiguous and people may misinterpret it to mean only Google docs or something, but I needed to make sure that they understood that it meant "all of your document needs," so, I changed it back. You could also remove all of the commas, but then this could be ambiguous again. The word *how* could be removed at this point; this would save 4 characters and put you at 0, but, for this example, I want to direct this to any group searching for social media who is also emergency management affiliated. Some of these groups are #gov20, #egov, #sm4r, and #fema. Government 2.0 is the new way the government is trying to harness the benefits of social media, egov also addresses "electronic" government. #sm4r is Social Media for Responders, and, of course, #fema is the Federal Emergency Management Agency. Remember, by adding hashtags, people or groups who filter and search for information using these hashtags will get your tweet.

I also want to send this to a target market, emergency managers in Florida and the southeast who could attend this workshop that is going to be held in the panhandle of Florida. I know from partnering that there is a FEMA Region IV group, so I will add @femaregion4.

6. At this point, I abbreviate Management, and remove all spaces after any comma. I made a few more modifications and got it all in and down to zero.

> Google docs,Slideshare,wiki's,sites,bookmarking,How2ManageDocuments4EmrgcyMgt&Leverage Social media http://ITSFEM.com #fema (0)

If you are lucky enough that someone ReTweets your message, you may want to thank them for the RT. If they follow you, you can send this as a direct message where nobody but the person who ReTweeted your message will read it. This can only happen to people who are following you. If they don't follow you, then you can use the @ and thank them, and anyone following you also will see it.

If this were deemed critical information that could not be further reduced, which, in this case, it is not, you could use some application that allowed longer tweets. Remember, there are free applications you can search for that can do anything you most likely can think of. Some applications may require some form of payment. This is up to the user to determine it the fee is worth the need. I pay extra to have the additional benefits that go along with an online survey software system QuestionPro. For free, you can create and maintain three surveys. This may change and other services could change, but, at present, they allow a few surveys each with 10 questions each. Only a few types of questions can be created and these normally cover most questionnaire needs. However, in my case, I do a lot of research and like keeping the data and the results. I enjoy that they maintain my information and it's protected. I can download anything to my computer, but, otherwise, the company takes care of it and that is worth the $15 per month that I am presently charged.

Here is one more example demonstrating effective ways to reduce characters in a tweet.

From:
Options for citizens to report damage and to tweet GeoData to officials so they can map for situation awareness and damage assessment http://ITSFEM.com

Technique here is to use numbers anywhere you see a word that sounds like a number, remove the spaces in between the number and the word, replace *and* with a comma or & and remove spaces before and after. It almost turns into a game and is fun to conquer.

To:
Options 4citizens 2report damage,2Tweet GeoData 2officials 2map 4situation awareness& damage assessment http://ITSFEM.com

A word of caution as we build skills. Do beware that Twitter goes down a lot at the moment. It can get overloaded, but is back up quickly. Other alternative communication methods should always be maintained as in any case.

GEOLOCATION DEVICES

Tweets now have the ability for the hardware source of the tweet to have its longitude/latitude identified and accompany a tweet. This is a much desired feature for obvious reasons. It provides the user a very powerful tool that, when combined with mapping, can be extremely powerful in a number of ways. We next provide an example with an unofficial experiment that was conducted by the National Oceanic and Atmospheric Administration (NOAA). In this case, other ways are described in which locations can be attached and deciphered to map. For example, NOAA had people type in their zip codes or street addresses along with the city and state. This was parsed by a system that identified this information by seeing a WW in a tweet followed by the location. The WW is a way for a computer program to detect that the information is there, it doesn't necessarily have any other meaning other than to provide a function. This was really powerful because it allowed the locations to be entered in a number of ways and, of course, if your geolocation device was activated in your Twitter settings, then your information was automatically sent without including any further information in the tweet.

What NOAA did was really clever and is something a handful of others are presently doing. They would have the user type WW followed by the location, then another WW followed by the weather report. Keywords were used to interpret the meanings. For example, *hot, wind, rain,* were some of the many keywords made available to users. Another part that will probably become common practice is how a tweet could be passed along to other officials in a state. There was a format created of #wx__ followed by the abbreviation of the state. Of course, putting hashtags in the tweet directs the tweet to a group who is looking to aggregate information pertaining to the weather in that particular geographic area. This way, more information is sent to the state's weather center so that they can have greater input. A case describing the specifics is presented below.

NOAA TWITTER CASE

Some other keywords are offered that can be used in your weather tweets. These are the official words and icons that are mapped with the NWS mapping tool (Figure 4.4).

Twitter Storm Reports

You can now submit your significant weather observations to the National Weather Service (NWS) via Twitter.

Thanks to the new Geotagging feature available through Twitter, individual tweets can be tagged with the location in which it was sent. This will help to enhance and increase timely & accurate online weather reporting and communications between the public and their local weather forecast offices.

How to Submit a Report:

1. Sign up for a Twitter account at Twitter.com
2. Send report via Web or Mobile Phone using the 'hash tag' #wxreport to group your message in a specific searchable category

- **With** Geotagging on a 3rd party Twitter Application (i.e. not using Twitter.com, m.Twitter.com (mobile) or via text messages):

    1. Make sure Geotagging is turned on for your 3rd party application
    2. Make sure Geotagging is enabled on your Twitter account (see Twitter.com/account/settings)
    3. Submit report using the 3rd party application in the following Format

#wxreport <your significant weather>

- **Without** Geotagging on a 3rd party Twitter application or on Twitter.com

    1. Log on to your Twitter Account via the web or a mobile device
    2. Submit your report in the following Format

#wxreport WW *<your location>* WW <your significant weather>

Examples of how to code *<your location>*

1. **A City Name:**
   WW Winfield, KS WW
2. **A zip code**
   WW 67209 WW
3. **An Address**
   WW 683 W. 184th Rd. Chase, KS 67580 WW

4. **An Airport Identifier**
   WW HUT WW
5. **A Street Intersection:**
   WW 21st St. N and Maize Rd., Wichita, KS WW
6. **A Latitude and Longitude:**
   WW 38.043, -97.344 WW

115

Twitter Storm Reports

Examples of Properly Coded Significant Weather Tweets

- **With Geotagging**

  #wxreport Tornado on ground 3 miles south of my location at 5:34pm

  #wxreport 3.4 inches of Rain in the past 2 hours

  #wxreport Golfball sized hail at 7:54pm

- **Without Geotagging**

  #wxreport WW 378 W. 156th Rd. Anthony, KS WW Wind Gusts estimated at 60mph

  #wxreport WW McPherson, KS WW 4 inches of snow from 3pm-7am

  #wxreport WW 67201 WW Quarter sized Hail at 5:34pm

Best Practices for Writing your Significant Storm Reports

1. Use a City, State or Zip code as the preferred method to code a non geo-tagged report.

2. While any weather can be tweeted, the NWS is most interested in Significant Weather Reports. (see below)

What Significant Weather to Report
(Report the time that the event occurred and how much or size as appropriate)

- Snowfall during an event and storm total
- Freezing Rain and Freezing Drizzle
- Dense Fog and reduced visibility
- Damage from Winds

- Hail
- Tornadoes or Funnel clouds
- Flooding

General Guidelines	Troubleshooting and Questions about Tweets
• The purpose of this project is to allow people to submit reports. Please be responsible and respectful of the purpose.	1. Be sure to put the "WW"s around <your location> in your tweet if you do not have geotagging on a 3rd party application. The "WW"'s are used to help computer software mark your location to plot on a map
• A valid Twitter user account is required to submit reports. As such, use of this service constitutes an agreement to the Terms of Service (ToS) of the provider. Go to http://Twitter.com/tos for more information.	2. A 3rd party application is something you have to download separately on either your phone or Personal Computer that will send out and geocode the Tweets
• This project is in an experimental state and may not always be seen or the message may get stuck in twitter-space, don't rely on Twitter for reporting life threatening reports.	3. A hash tag is the <#wxreport> part of the tweet, and it is used to identify the tweet as a weather report and can be found and plotted on a map.
• If report is life threatening, please use Original reporting methods	4. See Twitter Help FAQ for more information if you are new to Twitter : http:// help.twitter.com/forums/10711/entries/13920-frequently-asked-questions
• Official Representatives of the NWS will not respond to any Tweet to confirm its receipt.	

FIGURE 4.4 Icons and Keywords for Mapping Weather.

Case Example Exercise

Based from the NWS Twitter experiment, another experiment launched: Tweet the Heat. This is a good assignment to implement when you have a lot of people participating. It can be altered to better reflect the characteristics of an area. For example, inches in snow, rainfall, and other information could be the focus.

Tweet the Heat: A Collaborative Tracking Project

This is a research project where we will track heat waves that occur over the summer months. This research is an extension of the present ongoing experiment by the National Weather Service. Background information

117

can be located at the following (recommended that you view http://www.srh.noaa.gov/media/epz/Twitter/TwitterStormReportProgram.wmv). For Winter environments, modify for 'Severe Winter Weather' or 'Cold Fronts'.

Turn Geo-tagging on in Twitter under Settings, check Tweet Location. Three primary hashtags

- For tweeting the heat:
  - #heatcw
  - Our keywords: hot, humid
  - Example: #heatcw hot 98 humid 65
  - Other weather reports go to #wxob and #wxreport
- Nonsignificant weather:
  - #wxob
- Severe weather:
  - #wxreport
  - Only temperatures over 100 degrees or 105 heat index are considered severe weather
- If heat is considered severe, tweet using both #wxreport and #heatcw

Watch as your posting is mapped http://mybrowncouch.com/codenoobs/examples/NWSTwitter/

Rules
1. Do not ReTweet any other person's Weather Tweet; this causes redundancy in data entry and causes the system to be inefficient.
2. Letters are case sensitive on Twitter; WW is different from ww and Ww. This will cause the system to be inefficient because the information is not formatted correctly and will not post to map. So, if you do not have Geo-Location ability, WW <your location> WW <your weather report>.
   a. Example: #heatcw WW Cedar Bluff, AL WW hot 87 humid 45
3. Make sure to enter only information that is required. Post precisely for effectiveness and efficiency.

EXERCISES

Create a Twitter account if you don't already have one at www.twitter.com

Compare/contrast/analyze three emergency management agencies using Twitter.

1. What kind of information do they tweet?
2. Do they also send pics, links, and leverage other Twitter capabilities?
3. What is the tweet rate? Too fast or slow? Identify cons of doing either.
4. In this week's article reading, analyze two particular areas discussed in the report:
   a. How does the EMA leverage community participation?
      i. Provide an example on how each EMA can further use the community as if you were a consultant.
   b. How does the EMA leverage their partnerships?
      i. Identify a partner for each EMA describing how this would benefit each group as if you were a consultant.
   c. Use two more of any concepts discussed in the article in which to compare/contrast the three EMA groups.
5. Tweet an article link about some Twitter- and EM-related news; have it such that this tweet is automatically posted to your Facebook account (*not afterward, but when one happens, so it does the other, i.e., automatically*).
6. Tweet a pic of some picture you have taken of severe weather or any other emergency management-related image and have it such that it automatically goes over to Facebook and posts it. Understand that once you tweet or post any picture to the Internet, it is there for life. There is no way that you can ever really remove it, especially once you tweet it.

5

Design Strategies
Twitter for Teams and Information Exchange

INTRODUCTION

Twitter is growing in unprecedented popularity and usage. One only needs to watch the news to hear about Twitter and its present use with the news media. iReports are common in the news and crowdsourcing is catching on, creating virtual organizations that work expeditiously together on time-critical missions. Given all this, there is enormous potential that remains untapped. The Twitterverse is exploding at the seams and many are exploring a variety of ways in which to tame the beast. However, for the most part, there's no real effort by organizations to implement a structure or design that directs information in a strategic manner. There are ways to implement Twitter, for example, that can support emergency groups in ways not yet utilized.

The objective of this chapter is to demonstrate how directed design efforts can harness a much greater capacity and channel the collective intelligence while reducing information overload. These sorts of ideas should be explored for any given social media. An exercise is presented to demonstrate how microblogging using Twitter, in this particular case, can be leveraged for crisis communications between members of a team and

ONSITE WITH MATTHEW MILLER

SOCIAL MEDIA: THE NEW FACE (BOOK?) OF PUBLIC HEALTH PREPAREDNESS

Social media is currently riding a surging wave of popularity that seems highly unlikely to crest any time in the foreseeable future. Services such as Facebook, MySpace, YouTube, and Twitter have, in the last few years, become household names and terms such as Tweets and Facebook Friends have become a part of the national vocabulary. The use of such services to rapidly share information and also to find out "the latest" about, well, nearly anything, has, in a short time, woven itself seemingly inextricably into the very fabric of American and global culture. The number of users for these services

FIGURE 5.1 BIOSENSE Analyst/User Administrator/Application Trainer

is skyrocketing, as is the amount of time people are spending using them, sharing everything from the mundane (the latest pictures of their cat "Bobo") to the potentially earthshattering and life-changing (up to the minute pictures and first-hand information from the scene of a tornado strike). The meteoric rise of these services has had both a positive impact as well as a negative side. On the positive side, it is bringing an already highly "connected" world (thanks to the quantum leaps in communications technology over the last few decades) even closer, by allowing thoughts, experiences, and information to be shared on a near real-time basis. On the negative side, it has brought with it new social problems, particularly among teenagers and young adults, such as cyber bullying and the use of social networks as a tool for stalkers and sexual predators. Another downside of sorts is that some studies are finding that the use of social networking sites is costing businesses billions of dollars in worker productivity. This may possibly be inaccurate, however, as other studies show that limited use of social networking during the workday may actually increase worker productivity.

Whether one is a proponent or an opponent of this social media revolution, one thing appears to be exceedingly clear: these sites and services are not going anywhere. In fact, they are very likely to continue to grow and expand in their reach and influence in our everyday lives over the coming years. A recent, pretty amazing example of the power of social media was found in the attempted uprising against the Iranian government by young, technologically savvy college students in summer 2009. Following some questionable activities by the Iranian ruling theocracy relating to a presidential election, there was a significant anti-government uprising led largely by the university students mentioned above. The Iranian government moved swiftly to prevent the media from broadcasting the brutal details of the crackdown launched in response to the uprising. The students, however, employed other means to broadcast the truth. They took to various social networking outlets including YouTube and Twitter. Numerous short videos of brutality by the Iranian Revolutionary Guard on protestors quickly appeared on YouTube for the world at large to peruse and be shocked and horrified by. One video that emerged from the maelstrom, that of the murder of a student named Neda Agha-Soltan by Iranian militiamen, became, to a great extent the face of the event. Iranians also heavily utilized Twitter, reporting the rapidly changing events in real-time. The Iranian government struggled desperately to try to stem the flow of information, but without much success as new servers, proxies, and auto-forwarders were set up nearly as rapidly as they were being dismantled by pro-theocracy forces. Ultimately, the Iranian government was successful in crushing the uprising, but this event did much to continue to usher in the age of social networking as a legitimate means of communication during a crisis situation or disaster and as a force of positive change in the world.

If the power of social media could be leveraged to make a difference in an unstable, violent political situation such as the Iranian uprising, it can certainly be leveraged in a positive way in other important areas. One of these areas is that of global public health, the ongoing high-stakes chess game that medical practitioners and epidemiologists play against diseases, both ancient and newly emerging. It is a game that mankind must endeavor to keep the upper hand in. Our very survival as a species may depend upon it. I have worked in the healthcare and public health industry in one aspect or another for over 20 years. I began my career as a firefighter/paramedic in various jurisdictions in the state of Georgia, working in the field from 1990 to late 2002. In December, 2002, I came to work at the Centers for Disease Control as a watch officer in the Director's Emergency Operations Center. The DEOC job gave me a great introduction to public health and much perspective as to how my previous work as a paramedic had played a part in it. In June of 2004, I accepted a position as an analyst with the CDC's BioSense program. BioSense is a national, web-based syndromic surveillance system which allows users to examine trends of chief complaints and final diagnoses in a variety of syndromes and subsyndromes in selected emergency departments and outpatient clinics around the country. Statistical anomalies in the data could potentially be indicative of a seasonal trend, such as influenza, an outbreak, or, potentially, a bioterrorism event. Over the six-plus years I have been with the program, I have inherited a number of "hats" with the program, including application user administrator and trainer, situational awareness lead, GIS officer, and, recently, social networking

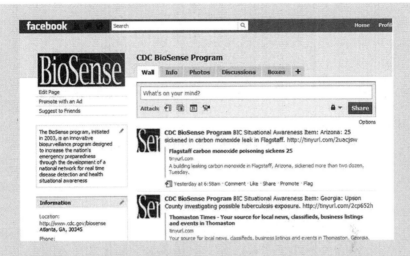

FIGURE 5.2 CDC BioSense Facebook Page

lead. Figure 5.2 demonstrates how we are using Facebook to share information.

The use of social networking and social media as an outreach of the BioSense program is something comparatively new. A Twitter account for BioSense was established over a year ago, but not much was done with it at the time. Prior to beginning to maintain the Twitter account about five months ago and setting up the Facebook account for the program around the same time, I was largely indifferent to social networking. My wife has a Facebook account and enjoys communicating with her friends on it, but, at the risk of sounding like a crotchety old man ("Hey---get off my lawn!"), I had thought it was largely a fad, a phenomenon for teenagers, with little in the way of practical application in the area of emergency/crisis preparedness and response. Some recent global events in conjunction with my several months of heavy engagement as the social networking "voice" of the BioSense program have convinced me otherwise. I am now seeking new and better ways to leverage available technology and to be a part of molding the future of social media in public health preparedness initiatives at the CDC and perhaps beyond.

FIGURE 5.3   CDC BioSense Twitter Page

The BioSense program at the Centers for Disease Control currently utilizes both Twitter, see Figure 5.3 (http://www.twitter.com/cdc_biosense) and Facebook, see Figure 5.2 (http://www.facebook.com/biosense.analysts) as a tool for routine communication and also as a means of working toward building more of a user community for the application. On a daily basis, these services are employed to send out national public health situational awareness updates. These updates are based upon open-source news items gleaned from monitoring RSS news feeds. There have been several instances during the time we have been offering the situational awareness updates where we have been able to detect an event that we have found in the news feeds in the syndromic data contained in the BioSense application. These instances of convergence between situational awareness and syndromic surveillance are extremely exciting and let us know that our efforts are continuing to bear fruit and that the BioSense application is truly useful as a situational awareness tool. The social networking outlets are also being employed to disseminate training announcements and other important news regarding the BioSense program. In the future, we are hoping to offer custom-tailored content for interested parties or jurisdictions.

I think the future for the use of social media as a means of emergency and disaster communication is extremely bright. Social media provides yet another way for those on the scene of a disaster to begin to rapidly distribute information and intelligence regarding the nature and scope of the disaster to those on the outside, allowing those preparing the disaster response to get ahead of the curve earlier and perhaps better tailor their efforts based upon the most current information available. The beauty of this is that the information flow can literally begin from the moment the disaster strikes. Thanks to the boom in both the popularity and affordability of the smartphone, one does not even need to have a PC or a laptop on hand to begin to share their experience. Just grab the phone and start typing, start snapping pictures with the cameraphone, and start uploading. It's easy enough to do that even someone who is not particularly adept technologically can be a source of valuable first-hand information.

Another great benefit that could be reaped by skillful leveraging of social media by public health practitioners is the ability to reach audiences that it might be difficult to communicate to effectively through more traditional means. Let's face it-social media outlets are where much of the youth of America congregate and also where some of the disaffected individuals that exist on the fringes of society may be found. Clever use of this new technology can allow public health to disseminate messages encouraging healthy practices such as hand washing and safe sex and discouraging destructive practices such as the use of illicit drugs and abuse of alcohol. Receiving messages of this sort in this format may make the audience more receptive as the messages will be sent through a medium that they are very comfortable with. This could result in an improvement in health statistics and outcomes in areas such as STDs, drug overdoses, and alcoholism.

The recent H1N1 pandemic was an excellent proving ground for the use of social media to quickly get the latest information out to the public quickly. "The World Health Organization used Twitter during the influenza A (H1N1) pandemicand, at time of writing, had more than 11,700 'followers.' One account from the Centers for

Disease Control in the United States has more than 420,000." (McNab, Christine. "What Social Media Offers to Health Professionals and Citizens." Bulletin of the World Health Organization (online). 2009, vol. 87, pp. 566-568. http://www.scielosp.org/pdf/bwho/v87n8/v87n8a02.pdf) In July 2009, researchers at the University of Edinburgh published an interesting study in which they used prediction markets and Twitter activity shortly after H1N1 was announced in April 2009 but before a pandemic was declared in June of that year to model an early opinion/forecast that H1N1 would indeed result in a pandemic.

I think the future of such technologies may include such innovations as more and more advanced algorithms being run against trending keywords or topics as a means of attempting to mathematically or statistically predict public health or preparedness needs that will have to be met or geographic areas that may require further assistance during an outbreak or similar disaster. An idea would be perhaps a Facebook app that allows users to do a short daily inventory of their health, listing symptoms of any illnesses they may be experiencing. The data from this app could then be ported into a geospatial display by ZIP code, city, or state. Something like this could act very much as a cyber "canary in the coalmine", perhaps giving the first sign of clusters of illness in a given geographic area. This could potentially allow emergency departments, physicians' offices, or emergency medical services to better allocate staff and resources, knowing that they may potentially see an upswing in patient volume based upon an increase of symptomatic patients in their area. It could also give local pharmacies a heads-up to consider ordering additional over the counter or prescription medications again based upon an increase in people reporting symptoms in their immediate area.

Another potential area that effective use of social networking could be of tremendous benefit would be for individuals who are under isolation or quarantine restrictions during an outbreak of disease. Such a scenario actually occurred to a reporter named Mike Su who was detained by Chinese authorities after he had the misfortune of sitting two rows away from someone on an airplane who actually had H1N1. "Since he needed no real medical attention whatsoever, Mike was left to sit alone in a hotel room for days on end with just his thoughts and a computer. Finding nothing mean-ingful to do, he decided to blog his entire experience for the rest of us to enjoy...He describes how he was able to use Twitter to interact with the outside world and live vicariously through the rest of the GeeksOnAPlane group. Skype and other live streaming services helped him tap remotely into the events we were attending. And blogging, of course, helped him pass the time and ensure that his experience wasn't for naught." (2009. Hendrickson, Mark. "Leave It to Chinese Quarantine to Reinforce the Value of Social Media." http://techcrunch.com/2009/06/18/leave-it-to-chinese-quarantine-to-reinforce-the-value-of-social-media/)

More importantly than just giving those quarantined or isolated something to do, social media could be a means of communication between healthcare professionals and quarantined patients, allow-ing some level of interaction and assessment to occur without physi-cal contact having to be made, thereby potentially lessening the risk of additional exposure to the disease in question. It would also allow the quarantined patients to have interaction with their families via webcam or Twitter.

Another growth area of technology and study that is extremely likely to have a tremendous impact on social networking in general and its application in the area of preparedness in particular is that of natural language processing. NLP is a hybrid field of computer sci-ence and linguistic study that is chiefly concerned with interaction between computer systems and human languages. The growth of this type of processing will allow free text such as would be found on most social networking sites to be processed into potentially use-ful and usable data more quickly, regardless of the language or dia-lect the text is written in. Such processing will allow information and trends to be studied and acted upon more quickly. It is an area of study that is still relatively in its infancy and the ability to consis-tently suss out such subtleties as tone in a block of free text is very likely some time away. As our capabilities in this area grow, though, its usefulness undoubtedly will too.

The last 20 years in particular have seen quantum leaps in the capabilities of the personal computer. This has brought with it the internet and the world wide web coming into its own as a means of every day information gathering and communication. It has also brought with it the personal computer as a part of over 80% of American homes. As Apple's Ipad and similar products are ushering in a new era of touchscreen-based tablet computing and as smartphones are growing in their capabilities while dropping in price, social networking is also becoming more portable. As so-called "mega disasters" seem to be increasing in both frequency and impact and as outbreaks of various diseases continue to occur at a very regular pace globally, social media should also continue to increase in its prominence as one of the tools of choice for the modern emergency manager or public health professional. These are exciting times indeed for those of us presently using these tools and are likely to become more exciting as social networking continues to expand its reach.

designated points of fusion to pass along pertinent information to expeditiously facilitate the knowledge that is exchanged between a group and its members. Tweets are good for dynamic situations where the teams are in the field and smartphone technology is utilized.

In this chapter, a model is presented to show you how smaller groups can intentionally connect to one another to model the needs of the group. This model for small groups is dynamic, flexible, and scalable. Subgroups can act as smaller networks linking important information in a strategic manner to meet the needs of very large organizations.

CASE STUDY

We present here a case study in which to demonstrate the details of how Twitter members can be linked up—strategically, ahead of time, and with a common goal—to work together under a time-critical situation where crisis communications are at the core of the event and result in success or failure. By using Twitter to pass information along with photos, news links, hashtags, and geolocation (just to name a few), ambiguity can be minimized and uncertainty can be reduced (especially when using Mapping; see Chapter 7, Visuals, Mapping, and Disaster Management Systems). This can support better decision making for the people on the ground and for those needing to predict the next move to make in order to reach the desired target. The objective of this case is to demonstrate that, when analyzed properly, information flow diagrams can be created and then implemented in Twitter, to provide an alternative way to communicate for traditional team problems. A step-by-step process is taken with the original communications record to demonstrate how each communication from each team member is "linked" up and directed so that information goes where it's supposed to go. After analyzing this one "exchange of information" by one group, then combining the idea with other efforts ongoing with the National Weather Service, larger networks were created and presented. This sort of goal-oriented group can be set up for a number of situations. For example, there is the case of the Ambulance Strike Team from Chapter 2. The same sort of strategy described next for the storm chasers can be implemented to satisfy some of the crisis communications needs that were identified by that group.

Case: Storm Chasers

A storm chasing team asked if social media could be used as an alternative means of communication versus their traditional radios. The problem was that communication channels get congested by different groups trying to communicate simultaneously. This causes confusion, interjects ambiguity, and delays the dialog as one person waits for another group to finish their interaction. The storm chasers wanted to know if there was some other alternative means of communicating using new technology. A real-world series of verbal exchanges were provided where the dialog exchanged was analyzed to model the patterns and sequences of their interactions. A model based on this network emerged indicating that Twitter could be used to support very complex situations in a very easy manner as long as it was intentionally set up to direct the information flow a particular way.

Let's step back for a second and briefly discuss relationships as they relate to people and information flow. There are three basic ways information can be disseminated: (1) one-to-one, (2) one-to-many, and (3) many-to-one. Twitter supports all three types in a variety of ways. If I Follow you and you Follow me, then we have a one-to-one relationship. When you tweet something out, I will receive it and, when I tweet something, you will receive it. By being Followed by others and Following people and organizations, we now have a one-to-many and many-to-one relationship. For example, if I have 50 people Following me and I tweet something, those 50 (people or organizations) will receive that information. Also, whenever someone I'm Following tweets something, I receive it. When I tweet, it goes to many people and when many people tweet, I receive it.

The next two figures demonstrate how information travels through two different relationships: one-to-many and many-to-one. Figure 5.4 demonstrates a single account in Twitter and how the information flows to those who are Following that account. Figure 5.5 demonstrates the information flow from those who the person Follows to that one account.

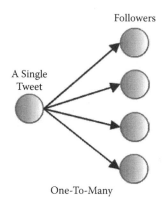

FIGURE 5.4   Followers on Twitter.

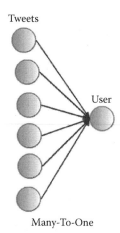

FIGURE 5.5   Following on Twitter.

ONE-TO-MANY; MANY-TO-ONE

When one person tweets, many Followers receive it. As for the following others, when they tweet, the user receives all of the information. Based on these models, I will demonstrate how going "viral" has the potential to spread information quickly through ReTweets. Figure 5.6 models what a single tweet, when ReTweeted, can do when spreading virally.

This exercise demonstrates how these relationships work together by providing you with directional diagrams indicating the flow of

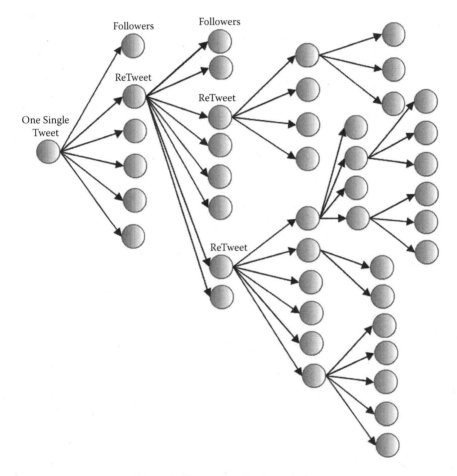

FIGURE 5.6 A tweet being ReTweeted and going viral.

information. A tweet consists of 140 characters or less. Don't let this short limit fool you, tweets can contain some powerful information if used strategically. Some extra things that can be beneficial for this case is that pictures or videos could be added, Twitter applications are available for smartphones making it easy to read and send out tweets, and links to other information can be added and can be short-ened automatically for efficiency purposes using applicaitons such as Tweetdeck. Information can be directed for gathering purposes by using hashtags, and geo-location devices are common in laptops as well as smartphones.

CASE: TWITTER FOR STORM CHASING

This case provides an example of how using an alternative means of com-munication, Twitter, can be used to coordinate efforts between members of a team chasing a storm. A transcript from a 'real world' event is used to demonstrate how 'strategically' subscribing to group members using a predetermined relationship can be highly efficient and effective for send-ing and receiving information.

Although this exercise is based on a storm chasing scenario, it could be used for many emergency groups requiring the same sort of communi-cation needs, e.g., in search and rescue (SAR) efforts, for riot control, and severe weather tracking, to name a few. This particular example comes from a storm chasing event where a local television station is monitoring potential tornadic activity for its viewing audience.

Scenario: A weather channel WKRP is aware of potential tornadic activity and requests storm chasers to be on standby. Storm chas-ers are ready. The following series of communications are from the original transcript that occurred. After the transcript is pre-sented in full and in its original state, each message communi-cated translated into tweets. Characteristics will be identified to indicate the flow in which the information needs to go and the direction of flow of communications identified as needed between the members.

Problem: Normal radio is used, but they are confronted with the noise that comes with multiple users outside of this event sharing the frequency with other emergency agencies.

Case Study: The communications between a weather station and its storm chasers. Below are the communications that occurred during an event.
Key Words: wx = weather, svr = severe, wrn = warning, tor = tornado, tvs = tornado vortex signature, meso = mesocyclone
Users: ke5ejq = skot, kd5gsp = fred, kd5mxv = susie, kd5omi = alan, kd5dcv = jason

Original Log of Transactions of Team:

KFSM WX: All chasers are activated and requested to go mobile.
KE5EJQ: Command, this is skot, will be en route to HWY 23N/HWY 64W to get a view on cell moving into Western Franklin County.
KFSM WX: 10-4, use caution as you approach, you will punch a hail core with Doppler estimated hail in excess of 1.0 inches in diameter.
KE5EJQ: Copy message.
KD5GSP: Command, this is Rick, I am available for assignment.
KFSM WX: 10-4, I'm currently watching a cell that is showing a meso with low-level shear in Sebastion County. Let me know when you cross the county line and I'll have you a target location.
KD5GSP: 10-4.
KFSM WX: In reference to the Sebastian county storm, nws tulsa has issued a TOR wrn until 11:30 PM, use caution KD5GSP ... KE5EJQ, be on guard, same cell will be in your area within the next 30min.
KD5GSP: Roger.
KE5EJQ: Roger.
KFSM WX: KD5GSP, are you in a position for me to patch you thru to go live on air?
KD5GSP: Yes and have impressive view of rotating wall cloud.
KFSM WX: Okay, that information is being relayed to NWS Tulsa, the production room will be calling you and you will be live.
KD5MXV: Command, I'm now available. Awaiting assignment.
KFSM WX: kd5gsp and ke5ejq are one storm moving from Sebastion to Franklin ... however, you are closer to a storm that will soon be entering into Washington County from Deleware County ... start traveling that direction and await further instruction.
KD5MXV: Copy, en route.
KE5EJQ: URGENT, visual on rotating wall cloud, appears to be lowering into a funnel. nothing on ground at this time

KFSM WX: 10-4, please update frequently.

KE5EJQ: Still strong rotation, I am now entering into the precipitation and am losing sight.

KFSM WX: 10-4, travel north to a safer location where you can have a better visual.

How Can the Original Prior Transcript Be Implemented by Using Twitter?

First, the Twitter accounts must be made to represent the stakeholders. The group names will be changed. These accounts could be private or public, further restrictions can be made where only those identified as team members are allowed to be Followers to an account. The players include:

1. The Weather Channel's Command and Control/Headquarters—Logistics Decision Maker
2. Storm Chaser Groups (many groups each with single identity), five Groups for this case

Six Twitter Accounts Are Required

CandC
SC_Skot
SC_Fred
SC_Susie
SC_Allan
SC_Jason

Note: These people are on the move so the names do not reflect an area, but a traveling vehicle. However, these groups could be anything, areas (counties, neighborhoods, Sebastian County volunteer firemen, etc.), domain specific groups (Red Cross, CERT, International Association of Emergency Management, Firemen of America, etc.), so remember that a group is a group by its definition, which should fit the need of the task/goal. Groups, who are on the move, as in situational awareness, should be named appropriately such that they are uniquely identified and not logically tied to any specific geographic location. Geotagging will identify where the tweet originated, which is an added benefit.

Following

If a group wants to receive information from CandC, they go to that page and click "follow." Now, every time CandC tweets a message, the followers will receive it. If CandC wants to receive information from a storm chaser, they will follow that storm chaser's account. The following *following* should be in place:

> **Action**: CandC *follows*: SC_Skot, SC_Fred, SC_Susie, SC_Allan, SC_Jason

And then, in order to receive the tweets from CandC, the groups will follow CandC.

> **Action**: SC_Skot, SC_Fred, SC_Susie, SC_Allan, SC_Jason *follows* CandC

How Tweeting Would Be Implemented for the Case

Communication 1: [Weather Station: CandC tweets:] *All chasers are requested to go mobile [Send] (See Figure 5.7)*
This can be received through a cell phone, laptop, desktop, BlackBerry, Droid or iPhone (smartphones); all communications through Twitter can be conducted through any of these technologies.

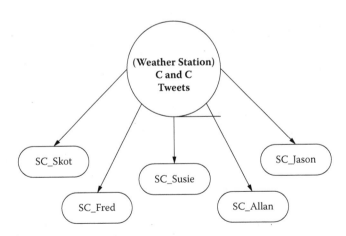

FIGURE 5.7 Model of information flow of communication 1: TV station sends out tweet to storm chasing team.

137

Communication 2: Original information: KE5EJQ: command, this is skot, will be enroute to HWY 23N/HWY 64W to get a view on cell moving into Western Franklin County

This information is tweeted a bit differently as added information in the tweet makes it such that less text is required so the transaction is shorter. To Tweet to any Followers:

[SC_Skot tweets:] enroute to HWY23N/HWY 64W to get a view on cell moving into Western Franklin County [Send]
To direct tweet to Weather Station:

[SC_Skot tweets:] **@CandC** enroute to HWY23N/HWY 64W to get a view on cell moving into Western Franklin County [Send]

Whereas on a radio, a user needs to provide a verbal identity, there is no need for Skot to identify himself as this is accomplished by default as each tweet is identified automatically by the user who made it. If the user wants to confirm that the tweet went to another person, he/she can go to that person's site and see it. However, a private message also can be sent with the Direct Message. Further useful information is passed along through the ability to allow geo-tagging or some other means of location identification to send along with the tweet so that this information can be instantaneously placed on a map providing a visual interpretation of the data that is quicker for the decision makers to interpret. This is covered in Chapter 7. A visual (a pic) could be taken with the smartphone and sent automatically along with the text reported tweet.

Figure 5.8 shows the information directed from the prior tweet.

SC_Skot also could tweet this to another storm chaser by simply adding the @ tag in front of the account name, @SC_Fred, and now this information will be directed to that user, but will also show up to any users following that account.

Communication 2 with @ tag: [SC_Skot tweets:] will be enroute to HWY23N/HWY 64W to get a view on cell moving into Western Franklin County @SC_Susie

Figure 5.9 provides a diagram of how the @ can be used before another person's account name to direct information directly to that person.

Communication 3: [Weather Station CandC Tweets:] 10-4, use caution as you approach, you will punch a hail core with Doppler estimated hail in excess of 1.0 diameter

138

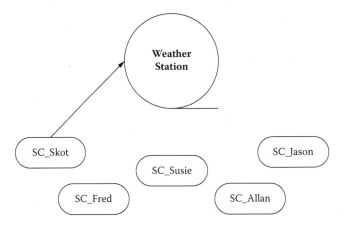

FIGURE 5.8 Model of information flow of communication 2: A single user tweets directly to headquarters.

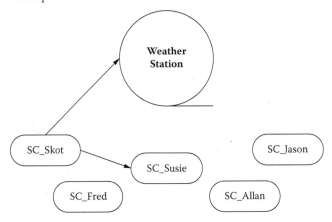

FIGURE 5.9 Model of information flow using @ tag to direct to other Twitter accounts.

This tweet, although sent to all followers, would be better to have the @SC_Skot in it since it was directed to Skot. The way to send the tweet would be up to the group leader who is really the director of a fusion center headquartered at the TV weather station. It would be beneficial to all of the team members to be aware of such information so, although it should be directed to Skot, the other team members chasing the storm also should

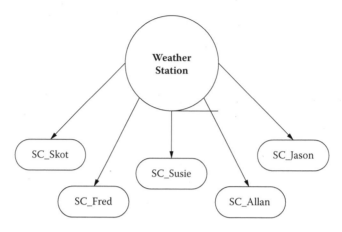

FIGURE 5.10   Model of information flow of communication 3.

be allowed to have the information. Otherwise, a private message could have been sent to Skot. Figure 5.10 presents a model of this communication.

Communication 4: [SC_Skot tweets:] D CandC *Copy that*

A quick tweet and the information is confirmed as demonstrated in Figure 5.11. By using a Direct message, only the CandC gets it and they are also sent an e-mail backing up the tweet as an additional way to notify CandC.

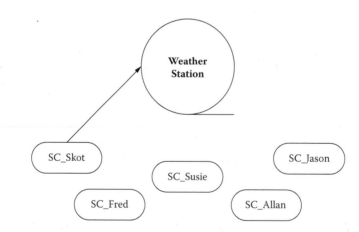

FIGURE 5.11   Model of information flow of communication 4: A single user directing information.

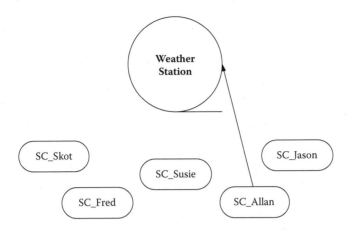

FIGURE 5.12   Model of information flow of communication 5.

Again, the information someone tweets is an individual choice, but in order to reduce information overload, it may be beneficial for a user to send a private message or a directed message in order to gain the attention of someone in a group in particular. The fewer words, the better, and given the level of dangerousness, a short confirmation is a good tweet.

Communication 5: [Allan tweets:] *I am available for assignment*

Figure 5.12 provides a model of this communication.

Communication 6: *Original Message from TV Weather Station: 10-4, I'm currently watching a cell that is showing a meso with low level shear in Sebastian County. Let me know when you cross the county line and I'll have you a target location*

This is a problem because, with spaces (and spaces do count), the message has 179 characters and is only allowed 140. First, direct the message given this is the response:

[Weather Station CandC tweets:] @SC_Allen watching a meso w/ low level shear in Sebastian Cty, will have u target when u reach county line.

It takes a little playing around sometimes, but you will find that most messages can be cut down a lot. Otherwise, if you must, tweet twice, back-to-back, to get in more information. However, when seconds are critical, Twitlonger should be used as spotter safety is paramount. Also,

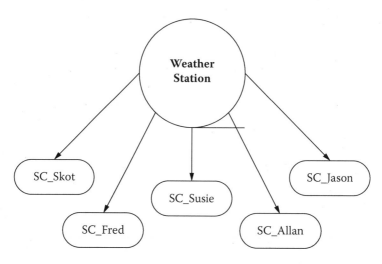

FIGURE 5.13   Model of information flow of communication 6.

if you cannot give Lat-Long, give major identifiers, e.g., passed the weigh scale on I-35, passed the water tower just NE of HH & 69 hwy. Figure 5.13 provides a diagram of the direction of the flow of information from the communication.

Go through more of these communications and draw your own directional diagrams to help you understand the information flow.

Added Benefits to This Particular Case

Neighboring community emergency management officials also can follow the Weather Station and know specifically what potential threats are coming their way by the knowledge shared from the chasers.

Text is clearer than audio, which lessens ambiguity of the information being sent. Both communication systems should be available in case one or the other goes down. For storm chasing in particular, both modes have their challenges. Storms are loud, making audio incomprehensible at times. Smartphones are vulnerable to the elements, so texting in the rain is not an option.

ONSITE WITH MICHAEL AMBERSON

UTILIZING CITIZENS IN EMERGENCIES VIA SOCIAL MEDIA

The initial hours of response can be quite confusing. You don't have all the information you need because you can't be everywhere. This is where utilizing citizens can be beneficial. They can be your eyes and ears. This is something that I did not consider when I initially set up my agency's Twitter account. I viewed it as a place solely where we post information.

A flash flood event on October 12, 2010, caused some dangerous travel conditions for many people on their way to work. That morning, I was tweeting flooding updates, which enabled me to monitor Twitter accounts that we were following. Someone posted a photo of an often traveled, flooded road in Glencoe, Alabama, shown in Figure 5.14. Once I confirmed the location through direct contact with the person who took the photo, we were able to get Glencoe to temporarily close the road until it cleared.

The catch is having someone available to monitor. It's not always that easy. Not every agency has a public information officer (PIO). Even for the ones that do, the PIO may be busy with interviews or on scene. That's why, in my opinion, it wouldn't be a bad idea to get a volunteer to monitor social media sites. This person wouldn't even have to be at the Emergency Operations Center (EOC). They could report any findings via phone, e-mail, or social media. Having a volunteer, especially if you don't have a full-time person dedicated to social media, can be a solution for continuous monitoring and to prevent information overload.

FIGURE 5.14 Photo tweeted from local's car to the emergency management agency (EMA).

CREATING A FLOW DIAGRAM FOR CRISIS COMMUNICATIONS

This prior case took apart the transactions that occurred during a real event, then mapped the required flows of direction and identified the accounts that would need to be created. Each message was translated into a tweet and the proper "directional" techniques were added to help direct information to the right people by using @ mentioning, and by members subscribing to one another in a particular manner. All of these methods were used to force the information to flow in an optimal manner for each decision maker identified in each step. The roles of the group members were used to help identify who is where in the hierarchy, which further identified who needed to be Following whom for the most efficient method of providing timely information.

This is a tedious process, but it is a process that identifies the dynamics behind the group members and matches them with the objectives of the group implemented through the various methods allowed by the social site. This same method should be used when you are analyzing your group's needs. The members of the group need to be identified along with their roles and permissions. This helps build the hierarchy for information flow that lets the designer of the Twitter Team understand which way the information needs to be directed. What all does the system allow or support? What are the restraints? These sorts of questions need to be answered during this analysis when building a flow diagram to support communications for a group tweeting or using whatever social site that has been selected.

Another important document to use in this design is a transcript of a real event that has occurred between the group members, if one is available. It doesn't necessarily have to be the exact group members, but it does need to mimic the interactions that will be going on between the group members in the real-world situation. A line-by-line analysis of the transcript should be made where information flow between members is mapped and further implemented into the design. A pattern should evolve that will indicate the characteristics that will be necessary to implement on each level. Also, the group should implement a design and test it before using it in a real world case. Once a group uses the design in a real world case, the interactions should be saved and a transcript should be used to further evaluate if the design worked as indicated or if further tweaking is desired.

> **Scenario Update:** A tornado has been spotted. How can the endangered population be notified? How can this be accomplished with Twitter and/or other forms of social media at this point?

COMPLEX GROUP SUPPORT

Groups can use Twitter much more effectively if there is a more organized approach. If we were to take on the prior diagrams showing how Twitter can be used for one-to-one and then one-to-many (and many-to-one) relationships and create a larger network, then information can be passed more quickly and accurately than before. A diagram in Figure 5.15 is presented in which each line in the network can send or receive a tweet from

145

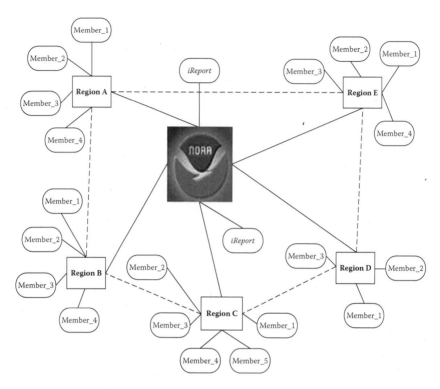

FIGURE 5.15   Twitter for a subteam diagram.

any other person in the network. If permissions were set up such that the local teams worked efficiently together, and then the same instances of permissions were set up for the next higher levels or alternative efficient paths of followers were set up strategically, the design could be leveraged because it would be scalable at that point. In the design, only particular paths have been designated. This is to create an efficient reporting path of information that will not create information overload but rather will direct information to those who need it.

TWITTER IS OVER CAPACITY

Just be aware, when traffic flow is high on the Internet highway, if the past is an indicator of the future, Twitter will not send your tweet because it

FIGURE 5.16   Twitter overloaded.

will be Over Capacity. If the event is large enough and like any disastrous or high-trafficking event, such as a large sporting event, so many people will be sending tweets with photos, etc. that the information will bottle-neck (Figure 5.16).

During the World Soccer Cup in 2010, Twitter stayed over capacity for a large amount of time. Many scenarios can be played when analyzing how social media will react during a terrorist attack, for example. Traffic flow is high before, during, and after some catastrophic events when the warning period is long enough. Tornadoes don't cause as much congestion, with the exception of large events, such as the Super Outbreak of Tornadoes in 1974 (Plotnick, Turoff, and White, 2010). On the other hand, as Hurricane Katrina approached New Orleans, many people called to check on friends and relatives. Local phone traffic was heavy due to the extra communications required during preparations. For example, dispatchers had high volumes of phone traffic during landfall and then after the storm passed, phone traffic was high due to the need for information related to damage assessment.

People were checking on those locally and nationwide, coordination efforts between first responders and practitioners in rescue efforts, etc.

SUMMARY

This chapter was meant to explore ways of putting forth a design effort to help manage the enormous amount of information in the Twitterverse as well as with other social medias and Web 2.0 technologies for information aggregation and crisis communication. When these technologies are integrated with a unified design, information will be better structured for the decision maker and better, more expedient decisions will be made. The time gap between an event occurring and the time it presently takes to gather information for disaster assessment can be greatly reduced. Optimal decisions must be made and are challenged during time-critical events. If the this gap can be reduced with information that is disseminated in an organized fashion and aggregated with a deliberate design in place, better decisions are likely to be made (White and Turoff, 2010). The chapter ends with a very serious word of caution to not be too reliant on these systems. Depending on the disaster type, the systems will either not be affected or could be greatly affected, pandemics versus hurricanes, for example. However, terrorists could cripple a group by attacking the public in some manner while also conducting a cyber attack. All forms of communication are vulnerable. Always maintain the more dependable forms of communications while leveraging the cutting edge technologies. Hope for the best, but prepare for the worst.

The next chapter helps agencies solve many of the problems that occur with managing documentation—online and off. Collaboration is key to planning and Web-based tools are available to support these needs in a transformative way. We are less bound to a geographic region due to "what's on our computer at the office." This level of collaboration offers us new ways to work and think.

EXERCISES

1. From the sequence of interactions, select a subsequence from the script and create a directional communication flow diagram.
2. Create a Twitter group system to model your agency and how it can be networked together to strategically direct information.

3. Get a transcript of a team interacting in a time-critical situation and graph out the design to optimize information flow and communication between the members of the team. Make sure to:
   a. Identify the roles of the users.
   b. Identify who should be Following whom.
   c. Are there different levels in the hierarchy that prioritize the information such that a directional flow can accommodate the need?
   d. Is the diagram scalable to be used by others in the organization but for larger events? Why or why not?

6

Collaboration and Document Management

INTRODUCTION

Communication holds a host of problem areas, such as the ability for information to be reflected in a real-time environment, so that those who have it can post it quickly and those who need it can get it quickly. Another problem of communication relates to the way in which policies and other text-based documents are created. At present, documentation that is a required group effort is passed around as an attachment from one member to the next, resulting in documentation that is created in isolation from one another with multiple copies. Formats differ from one software application to the next, making it difficult for groups to exchange and integrate information. When an emergency occurs, people need information, but static methods of information dissemination impede the ability for groups to provide accurate, up-to-date information for other group members within the same agency or working on the same task.

Emergency management agencies can be overwhelmed where busy personnel are overloaded by answering the phone and directing people to much-needed information. This much-needed documentation or information could be better disseminated utilizing collaborative technologies. Providing information in a more manageable and organized way can help reduce the work load on agencies and organizations. This is one way social media can help the disaster community in the fulfillment of basic requirements. However, documentation can help fill the information gaps that occur in time-critical situations. Further, policies, guidelines, emergency response plans, and other needed materials can be collaboratively created using free documentation software that can host the applications and files of a group either on or off computer hard drives and for free.

Many solutions can be used in a number of ways in order to satisfy the needs and demands of an agency. Documentation production takes up a significant amount of time as people call and request particular papers, forms, and reports for a variety of needs given the phase of emergency management in which one is working. Basic communications of e-mail can be better organized such that it's not a burden to interact while multitasking. Collaboration and sharing access is key to creating plans, policies, and reports. We will cover how to manage, disseminate, aggregate, and collaborate using a number of open-source systems that will help teach you to work together as a group, from anywhere there is an Internet connection and a Web browser.

The objective of this chapter is to introduce you to free sets of tools created to help easily satisfy your e-mailing needs, providing collaborative ways to work together on documents, Websites, wikis, forms, reports, and such. Google provides an entire suite of free tools that promote a different way of thinking when it comes to co-authoring, collaboration, and collective intelligence. Many different systems will be covered because it is best to keep multiple ways to communicate available, should one or multiple other systems be rendered nonfunctional. Also, different ways of communicating are provided to best fit the needs of the users, groups, and the system. Numerous ways of hosting your documentation will be covered so that your documents can be easily retrieved and located by search engines and the target population.

Wiki's are introduced and discussed. Wikipedia is the most famous example of the potential power of a wiki (or maybe now it is WikiLeaks). These applications are slowly coming around and still remain to be embraced. They lack structure, but templates are being offered as a remedy to this problem.

A Community Resilience 2.0 philosophy will be introduced. Ways of using social media to build a resilient community will be provided to further inspire more ideas of integrating the public into a comprehensive emergency management plan.

ONSITE WITH MURRAY TUROFF

COLLABORATION AS A NECESSITY

Disaster and crisis situations do not recognize any manmade boundaries: organizational; corporate; local, state, and federal governmental; property boundaries; etc. As the situation crosses more and more of the boundaries, the problems encountered grow out of the difficulties of coordination and collaboration among those artificial, separated entities.

When the problems faced require more than one-way notification, or even prior predictions of coordination actions, it becomes necessary to solve problems on a collaborative basis. There is too much emphasis on being able to predict the problems being solved rather than providing the flexibility to adapt to unpredicted situations and improve the resiliency of anticipation and response.

We are clearly entering an "age of participation" (Linstone and Turoff, 2010) where everyone who should be involved can be involved. It does not matter where the needed person or organization is and whether their participation was planned for. A citizen at a critical location with a smartphone may be asked to provide useful

FIGURE 6.1 Murray Turoff, professor emeritus, New Jersey Institute of Technology.

153

information or photos on an ongoing basis and serve a dynamic role as an observer. The press, the community, local organizations, such as church groups, can all be members of a response team if, in fact, this sort of participation is planned for and is a part of the planning and the training. The old concept of separate liaison individuals representing separate functional areas like fire, police, shelters, food and water, public works, garages, medical facilities, and contractors, does not provide a flexible structure that lets the decision makers interact and address common problems that must be solved in a highly dynamic nature by those most familiar with what is happening.

A simple decision, like which of a few hundred facilities most need the limited number of portable generators currently available, requires that everyone representing each of those facilities supply the best current information to allow the final action taker to make the best allocation possible at the given moment. This applies to every resource that is critical at a given time in the particular response process. Some common planning fallacies include (Van de Walle, Turoff, and Hiltz, 2010):

- Assuming a single administrator for a given county in the United States will resubmit requests for resources to the appropriate people in that county during a multicounty snowstorm.
- Assuming that everyone needed will be able to travel to a primary command and control facility.
- That limited resources can be allocated without direct input from the sources that need them.
- Not allowing or facilitating the help of citizens with skills and resources who have been trained and are available to help.
- Treating the press as an enemy to be denied dynamic situation reports, rather than turning them into sources of dynamic input.
- Treating the public as a potential mob rather than as local sources of help to less fortunate neighbors and potential observers.

- Upper management creating plans that ignore the potential contribution by those that are going to have to execute the plan.
- Ignoring the contributions possible by commercial food and water sources, garages, clinics, religious groups, contractors, local professionals, etc.

We need wide-scale community collaboration in planning, threat development, detection, training, mitigation, and preparedness as well as response. We need wide-area collaboration cutting across all the manmade boundaries. The fact that, in many cases, the professionals in local emergency organizations cannot work together directly and dynamically is the paradox we still face.

Designing support tools integrated into real-time, computer-mediated communication, and administrative tools to involve dynamically whatever organizations and individuals are needed to deal with an ongoing situation should be the primary collaborative objectives of a new generation of technology.

COLLABORATION

Collaboration is a key component to fit the needs of our ever-changing work environment. People need to be able to work together and have access to the same materials in order to effectively co-author and participate virtually. This can be accomplished at present by using a variety of tools available. Google will be covered first along with some basic functions that prove most powerful. In order to use the tools available through Google, one must first get a Gmail account (G = Google). Google hosts a suite of tools making documents, presentations, spreadsheets, wikis, photos, Websites, calendars, and many other useful applications capable of being co-authored by anybody anywhere there is a browser and the Internet. These sorts of applications, with the exception of wikis, are traditionally worked on by individuals in isolation from one another. If people are working on a site or document with others, it is usually where one person has "access" or permission to work on the document while others wait. Now, Google is supporting Web-based collaboration. This makes working together much easier. Now any member can access and work on any document anytime. Many people can work on a *Document* in real time simultaneously while seeing what others are doing. In *Documents,* in particular, if many people are working on a document from many different places, but at the same time, then a user will see the words or changes as another co-author types them. The person making the edits is identified as they work on the document. This is an incredibly user friendly interface. Now, this and other applications, at present, have limited functionality. For example, Microsoft® Word 2007 has many more features. A useful characteristic that is built into most open source software is compatibility. You will find that whatever document, or presentation, etc., you create, you will have the ability to save it in a large variety of formats. This allows the document to be used freely with other applications like Word 2007 or Open Word. Most of the applications that are discussed have video tutorials that show you how to get started and then *Help* features to aid you when you can't figure out how to do something.

SOCIAL MEDIA REDUCES INFORMATION OVERLOAD

Social media can actually filter information and reduce information overload due to the recommendations people and organizations make to one another. The Internet, Web applications, and social sites are Knowledge Exchange Centers supporting an enormous amount of information shared between individuals and organizations (Turoff, White, and Plotnick, 2009; Turoff and Hiltz, 2008). Because information flows through people who post information on their Walls and on the Walls of others in Facebook, and who ReTweet other tweets deemed important/informative (valued useful by human judgment to be passed along to others), information is filtered by human intelligence. Humans act as an information recommendation system to one another with which they share a common set of interests (Starbid and Palen, 2010). Another important component that supports this "collective intelligence" through collaboration is that we, as individuals with accounts, autonomously select who we *Follow*. If we *Follow* an individual or an organization, then we have made the conscious effort to pull information from that source. How the group manages their Twitter account will prove its worthiness over time, but, nonetheless, information is being filtered on many levels through networking using social media.

With social media, information is presented in a brief, concise, and direct manner. Most of the time there is an additional link to more information if one wants to know more. This makes it such that information can be processed quickly. Tweets have 140 characters or less and posts

FIGURE 6.2   Example of a tweet integrating links for more information.

have a small text box that allows others to attach other media like videos, links, photos, etc. It is that so much information is tightly coupled together and presented in such a user friendly interface that makes social media a good fit for crisis communications and emergency management. In Figure 6.2, you can see instantly who the tweet is from (pic recognition), then there is the 140 character limit that provides plenty of space to let someone quickly evaluate if the information is relevant to their needs or not. When using the application TweetDeck on your computer, new tweets are notified with a "ping" sort of submarine sound and a flash of the tweet appears in the upper right corner of your screen, just long enough for you to gaze up and read it quickly. These applications are made for efficiency and have a set of tools that allow you to ReTweet, Reply to the message in public view, or send a Direct Message to the person who sent the tweet in private. The messages are automatically stamped with useful information like the user account name, time, date, and the application used. Figure 6.2 provides a visual demonstrating this in TweetDeck. A message is written along with a link to the article and more useful information that is promotional to a business.

Figure 6.3 shows where the original information was posted on a Friends Wall in Facebook. The link to information was captured, the title was put in, and then tweeted along with more information provided by another link. This is the power of being able to use the two different sites together to reach a larger population.

Again, this information is direct and descriptive; quick to identify if it is important enough to share or not quickly.

The Venn diagram in Figure 6.4 presents a visual demonstration representing how information is filtered by humans simply using themselves and their own unwritten criteria to pass information along to others. It is the selectivity that occurs as information is passed along from one person to another. The Venn diagram provides an example to show how information is filtered through ReTweets in Twitter and with

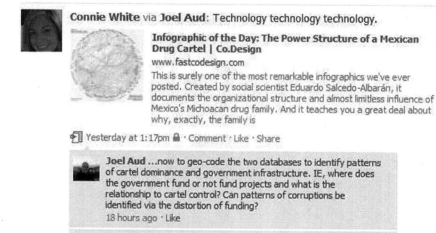

Connie White via **Joel Aud**: Technology technology technology.

Infographic of the Day: The Power Structure of a Mexican Drug Cartel | Co.Design
www.fastcodesign.com
This is surely one of the most remarkable infographics we've ever posted. Created by social scientist Eduardo Salcedo-Albarán, it documents the organizational structure and almost limitless influence of Mexico's Michoacan drug family. And it teaches you a great deal about why, exactly, the family is

Yesterday at 1:17pm · Comment · Like · Share

Joel Aud ...now to geo-code the two databases to identify patterns of cartel dominance and government infrastructure. IE, where does the government fund or not fund projects and what is the relationship to cartel control? Can patterns of corruptions be identified via the distortion of funding?
18 hours ago · Like

Write a comment...

FIGURE 6.3 Information posted on Facebook then tweeted.

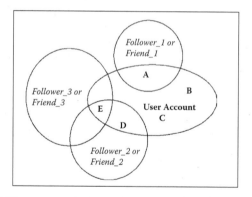

FIGURE 6.4 Humans as recommendation systems.

Friends and Sharing in Facebook. Let's use the example that you have for the User Account. This User Account, say my Twitter Account, represents the information that I am interested in by using the letters A, B, C, D, and E. These letters could represent a variety of information like A = social media, B = emergency management, C = open source software systems, D = education, and E = severe weather. There are three people subscribed to my account: Follower_1 or Friend_1, Follower_2 or Friend_2, and Follower_3 or Friend_3. This means that those three subscribers will receive any information that I pass on. However, everyone who Follows me or who is Friends with me will not have *everything* in common with me, they will not share all of my interests, but a select few. If I tweet about social media (A), then only Follower_1 or Friend_1 will be interested and more likely to pass the information on. If I tweet something about severe weather (E), then only Follower_2 and Follower_3 will be interested and Follower_1 will ignore it.

So, for every tweet that I make, my Followers are either interested in the information provided or they are not. If they are interested in the tweet, then I have provided them with some possibly interesting information. Otherwise, they can choose to ignore the tweet or post if it is not of value. On Facebook, this sort of "common interest" can trigger some more relevant information by providing space for a forum discussion. On Twitter, it makes it convenient for others to ReTweet the information and pass it on to others with one click that takes about one second. This creates a network of human recommendation systems that direct the flow of information to manage a large amount of information, filter and focus, then channel it in the right direction and to the right people.

GROUPS OF EXPERTS SHARING INFORMATION

Groups are easy to create in Facebook and on LinkedIn and other group social sites. Facebook, in particular, has groups that can be either Open to the public, Closed to the public (although searchable), or Secret, which are Closed but not searchable. There are pros and cons to the information flow of all group types, but the decision to have a group with one status or the other is up to the group so that they feel they have the best fit for their needs. A Closed group of people affiliated to some particular "domain" or "problem" for a specific purpose can aggregate resources, build a reservoir of data, and provide valuable information to one another. This can be conducted by members posting links to information as demonstrated earlier in Figure 6.2 and Figure 6.3. Photos can be collected and aggregated for group members to view. During time-critical situations, posting such videos and photos for the group to evaluate and comment on can prove to be a most valuable tool given it is both real time, online, and available from any smartphone. Figure 6.5 demonstrates the useful functions

FIGURE 6.5 Some of the options available when posting photos on social media.

provided for photos in Facebook (and in a number of applications, such as Picasso and Flickr) where information can be quickly shared with others.

Not only can people comment on the photo, but then it can be rotated, Shared with others, Tagged with identifiable information, etc. All of these photo open source sites provide a host of functions where photos and such can be viewed by a collective group of people. Facebook is just one way to leverage this ability into a way to use images and videos as educational tools, demonstrations, or for something where time is of the essence concerning damage assessment and the safety of a population.

Therefore, initially, one will argue that the Internet and social media just add to the overabundance of information that must be weighed and evaluated in making decisions during crisis, but, actually, if networked strategically, this can be a tool in which information is culled; where the most valuable information, from the available information and knowledge being exchanged online, will be funneled and directed to those who need it most, in a timely and more orderly fashion.

E-MAIL

You may be wondering how one e-mail system can make a difference. Google has provided a system that is free and has a number of features built into it to provide the user with a very user friendly and motivating environment. People also can chat with one another and call each other over the system. What's unique about the e-mail system is in the way the user interface is laid out along with the functions. It's very intuitive and laid out well (Figure 6.6). G-mail also has some features to help you manage your e-mail:

1. G-mail combines all the interactions between one sequence of mails into one folder. This means that every time you get a reply from someone you mailed, and they e-mail you back, and then you reply, and so on and so forth, the mail for that entire e-mail thread is all in one folder. This means that, instead of having four separate mails, you have one folder that includes the mails, so you get all of those responses kept together.
2. Every user in the e-mail gets a different color for their name. When many people are interacting in one e-mail, you can expand the e-mail and will see that each user has a unique color to identify them in the group of e-mails. This helps you quickly identify a person that you are looking for.
3. If you want to respond to someone's e-mail and do it intermittently, each response from you will be indented and will have another color. This goes for each new response to a particular

161

FIGURE 6.6 An example of a G-mail layout.

part of the e-mail discussion. For every new indent, a new color is provided. This helps, in addition to the indentations, to thread logical sequences together and helps you stay on track with the right discussion.

4. There is a great automatic history of users that the system remembers. Thus, when you go to type in someone's e-mail address, the system remembers and aggregates all possible users. It searches the names as you type, thus reducing the pool until you see a match and then just click it.

5. The Google search engine is part of the e-mail and can find any match you need in a convenient manner. There are also filters that can help you when finding information is most difficult. Of course, new features are being created and implemented to help you better manage your information. There are Labels and other functions provided that can help you better organize your e-mails as well.

Just as Facebook provides a list of Friends that are presently online and on Facebook, so, too, does G-mail. G-mail has the added ability for you to put a very short status comment by your name and also allows you the ability to show others if you are available ("green") or not ("red") by providing a little bullet by your name colored to indicate your availability. If you are in another application or nonactive, your bullet will turn "yellow" indicating this to others who can see you. You can only see other G-mail users with whom you interact. You also can click a name in the list to activate the chat function. More than one person can chat at a time, too. Video is offered in addition to this so there are many media alternatives provided in this one communication system.

TASKS

Task lists, both large and small, can get lost and, during time-critical situations, can be a challenge to maintain. Stick'ems provide a solution, but things can get messy quickly. Another way to utilize your system is to use the Task application that is included in the G-mail application. Your G-mail account provides you with a Task list. This is a convenient way to keep up with what you need to do, especially during time-critical situations when a piece of paper is not around or likely to be found again.

E-mail is just the beginning when using tools from the Google Suite for your emergency management needs. There is also a Calendar in the upper left menu where you can click and trigger your personal calendar. You simply click the date of an event and enter information. Details can be placed in a form and reminders can be provided to you by e-mail and "pop up" windows at time intervals provided by you. Everything is intuitive and very simple to use. One of the most powerful tools featured with the Google suite is the Documents functionality. Look up Calendar and you will see Documents (Figure 6.7).

Documents is a collaborative tool where you can work with others on a document that is stored online in your Google account. Anyone with a G-mail account can access a document that is Shared with them. Any

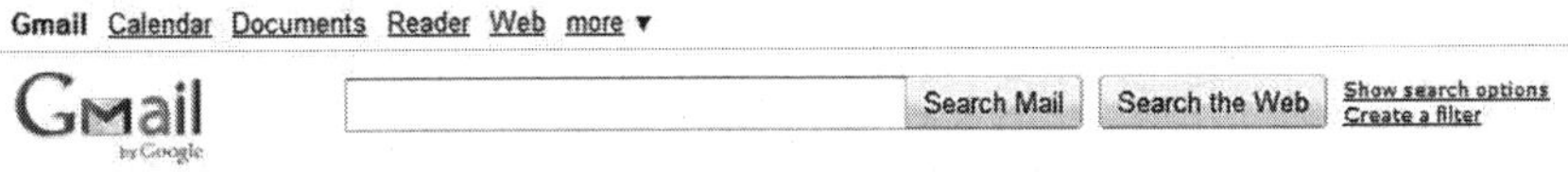

Gmail Calendar Documents Reader Web more ▼

Gmail
by Google

Search Mail   Search the Web   Show search options
Create a filter

FIGURE 6.7 Shown are Google Suite options.

document you create, you have control over as was discussed in Chapter 2. This is because you created the document and are considered the administrator of it. You can add other G-mail users to View or Edit the document through a Share function. This document also can be shared with others you want or with the world by providing a link where others can access the document through that link. The document can be embedded into another site as well. One real-time feature is that, as the document is worked on and modified, it's automatically updated, so those accessing it though the link always get the latest version.

Now that you have access to the Google Suite of tools, you also can collaborate on budgets in the Spreadsheet and on presentations through the Presentation tool. To use these features, when creating a document, simply make that selection. You also can upload any of these formats from Microsoft and they will convert over. This is a good format to use because anybody anywhere in the world can work with you after a single click of a button. Links to documents, presentations, and spreadsheets can be included in tweets or posted on your Facebook Wall, or anywhere you want someone to have access.

Permissions are provided to all of these pieces of information. You have the ability to let others see the information or restrict the viewing audience. This makes this tool especially beneficial when providing materials to one target group over another.

The Google Suite has so much to offer any agency; all anybody needs to do is to click the dropdown box labeled "more" in the menu. A host of tools satisfying a number of needs is provided. We cover a couple more of the features later, but want to make sure organizations and individuals know there is a lot out there for you to use for free.

WORD FILES, PRESENTATIONS, AND SPREADSHEETS

Open Office

Open Office is a suite of open-source software that rivals Microsoft® Office. This suite of software applications is commonly used by the international community. Open Office is "the leading open-source office software suite for word processing, spreadsheets, presentations, graphics, databases, and more. It is available in many languages and works on all common computers. It stores all of your data in an international open standard format and also can read and write files from other common office software packages.

It can be downloaded and used completely free of charge for any purpose" (www.OpenOffice.org, accessed January 5, 2011). In the United States, we are mostly influenced to use Microsoft Office. It's taught in the core curriculum of most degrees providing the user a basis for computer literacy. The same skill set can easily be transferred over to the Open Office environment providing a free alternative to agencies helping reduce the cost that accompanies proprietary software.

Google Documents, Presentations, and Spreadsheets

Google Documents is an easy to use, yet very powerful tool for co-authoring. This is different from Open Office in that the files are hosted free online. Anybody can access his/her documents from anywhere there is the Internet and a browser. This not only provides a department with an alternative to proprietary software, but also provides storage and a space for people to work. You don't need the space on your hard drive anymore or can use it as an alternative for storing documents, a backup. Other people can be invited to collaborate and edit the document for group needs while others can be allowed Viewing privileges. Spreadsheets can be used to reflect real-time resources available as many people can access the same spreadsheet and enter data and other information as needed. This supports ad hoc document needs where a group may need to quickly bring together information on a spreadsheet indicating whose got what and who needs what. Normally, someone is in charge of aggregating this information, but when anyone can access a document online, anytime, this provides groups with a powerful way to quickly access the needs against resources available and provides the group somewhere they can enter the information. This could reduce errors, and also, the person with the information is directly accessing the document to enter it thereby eliminating the need for others to receive and enter the data that can cause human error especially in time-critical situations. The document can be sent as a link to others so that the document can be sent with a tweet or posted on the Wall of a Facebook account. The document also can be downloaded so that it can be sent as an attachment. This provides the user a number of ways to work with the document and disseminate it. This is a secure environment as well. Google has many security features built into its system on a number of levels providing a department with an extra layer of security.

Another desirable feature of these applications (documents, applications, presentations) is that when a person clicks the link that takes them to the document to view, as the document is updated by the group, this is automatically reflected. However, at present this is a feature; you can select for the document to remain static at the point you save it and provide it as a link. Further, the document can be embedded into another site, such as a homepage. Thus, the document is available in a window and can be scrolled through, providing complete access to the document as well as the ability for it to be printed. One last useful feature I'll mention is that the document is automatically saved every few seconds. Personally, this was a difficult concept for me as I was trained to Save my document at the end of each edit. However, if you just can't wait even a few seconds, like I often experience, you do have the ability to Save now.

FORMS AND SPREADSHEETS

Forms and spreadsheets can be the most valuable applications to use during any phase of emergency management, but, this can be especially useful when unexpected events have occurred and ad hoc information, resources, experts, and such must be aggregated quickly and accurately. Instead of forms being sent to all of the potential users, the users now are directed to the Form that is available in the "cloud" for anyone to use when online. Cloud computing just means that the software (and, in many cases, the documents and other such deliverables you may generate) is not on your hard drive, but is now available to you from "somewhere" else by a group hosting it online for you. This makes it such that the Form isn't going to the people, but the people are coming to the Form. Forms can be created using themes that help them conform more to the look and feel of any organization so that everything doesn't look standard. Logos and such can be uploaded to indicate an "official" form. These forms are a great way to collect information, just like using a survey. Forms can be e-mailed to a user group where the user population just clicks the link in the mail, fills out the Form, then submits the information. The information aggregated can be viewed in real time through the various ways that Google Shares documents, through publishing as links, embedding in other sites, by Sharing with other editors, viewers, and administrators, etc.

The Form is a great fit for a dynamic, volatile, wicked problem like what we often see in disastrous events (Turoff, White, and Plotnick, 2010; White and Turoff, 2010). You have structured problems that occur every day and have a procedure implemented that solves the problem. On the other end of the spectrum, there are wicked problems. These are

166

situations that don't have a right or wrong answer, but a better or worse decision implemented because there is no way to know what was right or wrong given all of the contingencies involved. There is no real stopping point in the problem and the event has not occurred before exactly as on this present occasion, therefore, there is no way to know what is right or wrong. Since the Form can be created and modified anytime (which really reflects information in a database being created), it can be used to fit the need of the wicked problem as it unfolds. The Form can be modified anytime as needed and it's easy to do for anyone who has permission to change these sorts of features. This sort of real-time collaboration can help crisis officials better manage the unexpected. These tools are equally valuable in day-to-day routines and should be used as such, not only for the services they provide, but so that members will remember how to use the system (Turoff, Chumer, Van de Walle, and Yao, 2004). This is a critical component to the successful use of any system for disaster management. People should be familiar with the system during nonemergent times so that when the stress of an emergency occurs and people need to use a system quickly and effectively, they will remember how because they have been using the system on a day-to-day basis.

Take into consideration that documents and other valuable files should be stored and backed up during vulnerable system situations. Google has great security in hosting information, but, under certain circumstances, the network may be vulnerable to outage, and, on these occasions, although the information on the site will remain in place, it may be more valuable to print out a copy of necessary documentation to keep on standby to fulfill the needs of the present situation, assuming the worst case scenario occurs and the system goes down. The system may not be accessible to those in the affected zones where the communications infrastructure may be compromised, but many external experts and decision makers may be located anywhere geographically and remain able to contribute to the ongoing problem at hand using these collaborative systems. This way, when the people who lost connectivity get successfully back online, decisions will have continued as well as possible because other people could continue to work, information will continue to be updated, and this will be reflected to the users when they can get back online. All of these sites are accessible through smartphone technology as well. This supports a great deal of potential communications using social media where users can be located anywhere and on the go. This is critical when resources are low and people are overworked during a crisis. People can contribute more from the field and not have to worry about making it to

167

specific geographical locations wasting both time and gas. Valuable data can be gathered from the field just by using the applications (photo, video, uploading, tweeting, posting) provided by smartphone technology.

AN EXAMPLE FORM FOR RESOURCE AGGREGATION

Below is a demonstration showing how Forms work, which exposes the powerful capabilities this sort of collaborative application holds. I have created a simple form where organizations can provide a list of resources they have available. Figure 6.8 shows what Resource List Form looks like when being created; a variety of question types can be utilized. It's important to ask questions in a way that best aggregates the information. This is with all software available as such. For example, QuestionPro, Survey Monkey, and polling gadgets and applications all offer a variety of ways for someone to gather information. This is important so that decisions can be made quickly from the visual interpretations of data provided by the Reports produced by the application. Figure 6.8 is an example Form created using Google Docs.

Figure 6.9 shows the Form as a live site. It is modifiable by anyone who has permission, anytime they choose, while others will be able to access and fill out the form to enter data into a spreadsheet, which can be used further in databases to help manage information. This information could be further displayed on a crisis map indicating the information on populations at risk, resources that are available for immediate distribution, and any other such requirements that may be needed before, during, or after any emergency, disaster, or catastrophic event.

So many of these open source systems are created for people to use online and to learn, for the most part, on their own. Make sure to understand how to use the Help function. It is very good and provides multiple sources of avenues for education to conquer any questions that may arise. For example, Figure 6.10 shows how easy and intuitive "notification rules" are to utilize.

Anytime anyone wants to learn more or needs help understanding a feature, simply click the Help link. This is now often seen as a little question mark in a circle with some background color by the side of a feature, so that it's easily accessible. Moodle uses this feature, for example. In Google, there are many ways that are offered to help any user. They offer other documents that provide more information, video tutorials, and demonstrations linked to YouTube and brief sets of steps providing

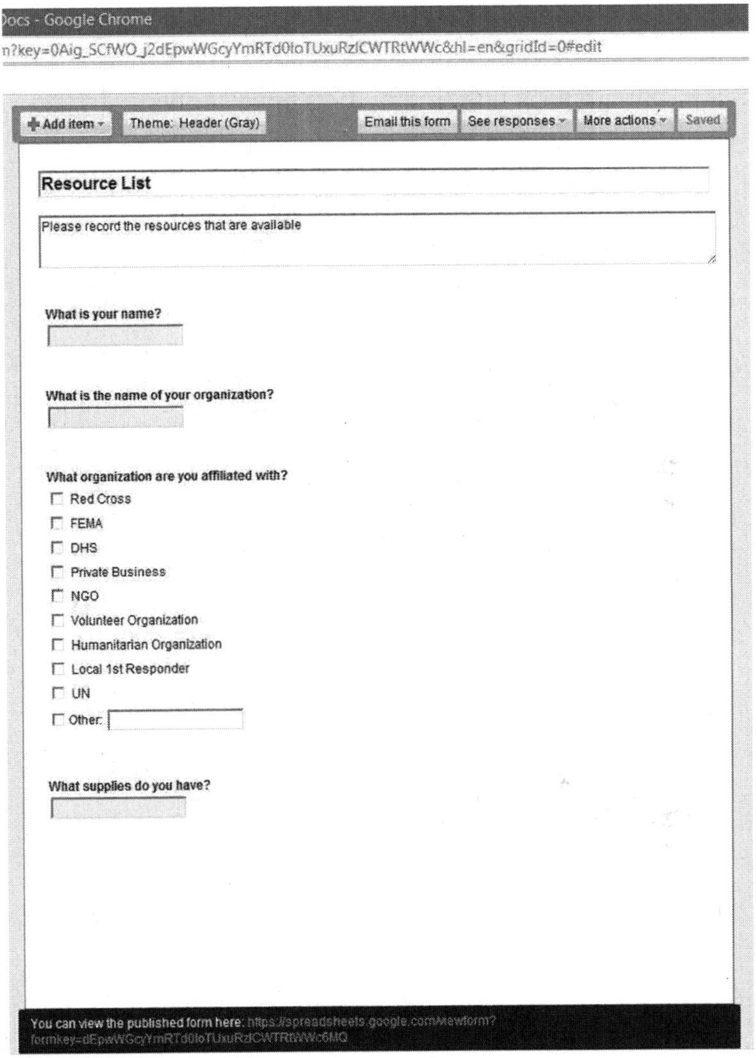

FIGURE 6.8 Google suite of tools: The Form.

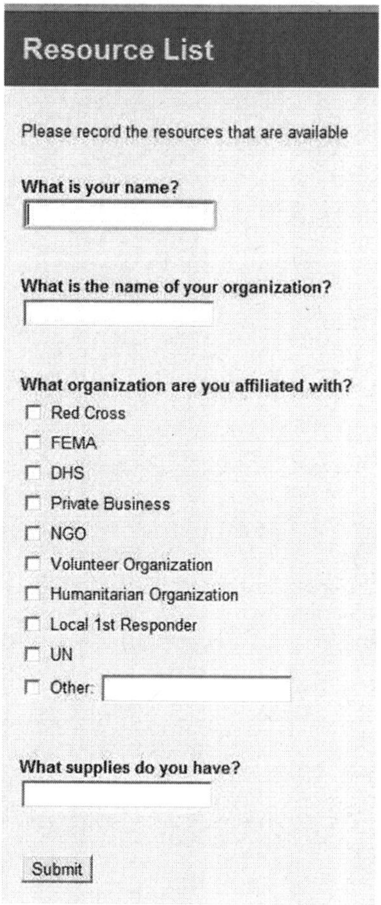

Resource List

Please record the resources that are available

What is your name?

What is the name of your organization?

What organization are you affiliated with?
- ☐ Red Cross
- ☐ FEMA
- ☐ DHS
- ☐ Private Business
- ☐ NGO
- ☐ Volunteer Organization
- ☐ Humanitarian Organization
- ☐ Local 1st Responder
- ☐ UN
- ☐ Other:

What supplies do you have?

Submit

FIGURE 6.9 Shown are data reflected in real time.

a quick answer to any given problem. Figure 6.11 shows the various ways in which Help is offered for the aforementioned Set Notification Rules window screenshot.

The integration of these and other components is a very important secondary benefit. One site, system, or file is easily linked to another site, system, or file, and this includes, as well, a lot of these social sites. For example, it's easy to tweet something and have it automatically posted to your Facebook page Wall. Or, you can take a photo with your Droid,

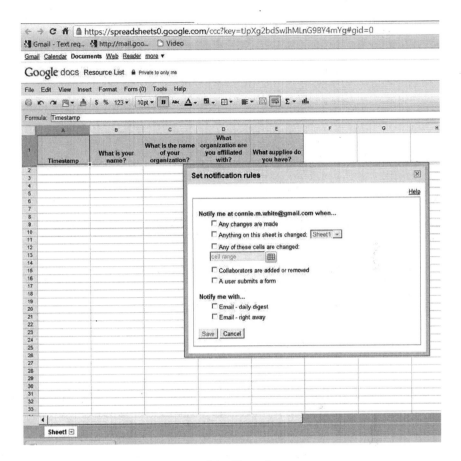

FIGURE 6.10 Google Suite is user friendly and easy to use.

then Share it and post it on Facebook. Another example is when Twitter or Facebook sends a notification of a Direct or personal message to you by sending an e-mail to your primary e-mail account, like Google Mail. This is also a useful tool when working collaboratively on Web-based systems. Continuing with the Form example from Figure 6.12, once the Form has been created and disseminated, an e-mail is sent providing you with information that summarizes the information you need to access and modify data quickly. It allows others to do the same as well, where control can be strict or loose depending on the settings selected by the creator of the doc.

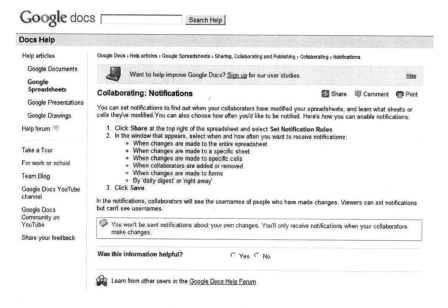

FIGURE 6.11 Help provided on Notification Rules.

Finally, this not only provides another valuable tool for the toolbox, but it is an example of real-time collaboration that your organization could be using right now. Utilizing such applications can be beneficial in that information is aggregated and organized in real time and with flexible, dynamic capabilities so that the information needs can be modified "on the fly" for any situation unexpected or otherwise. Tutorials are available, text-based videos, and other modes of materials that provide quick learning through effective online educational materials. You need to learn how to utilize this free online learning environment that accompanies most of this technology.

SLIDESHARE

Sometimes information in the form of files needs to be shared. Depending on the sensitivity of the information, and the intended audience, an information and communication system can be designed and developed. You identify the information (i.e., files) you want to share with others and then must consider how the others, the target population, will be able to

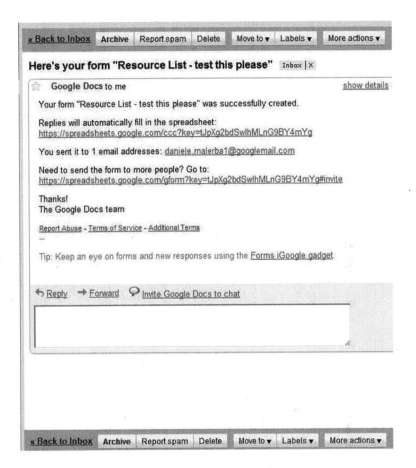

FIGURE 6.12 Confirmation e-mail from Form Notification.

access and download this information. When you know who your target population is and have identifying information for them, then dissemination is not such a challenge. However, when you want the people to come to the document, then challenges arise. Documentation for the public, for other open educational groups, for any broad audience where exposure based on titles, keywords, and descriptions is desired can use sites that are created to host a variety of documents and other file types. For example, Picasso and Flickr host photos that can be opened to the public or private. For documents, we will cover the site Slideshare.com. This is a free site where you can upload your presentations and document files. If you use the right title, keywords, and description (along with other ways to categorize your work), people who are looking for this information online should be able to easily find and view it. Using the right "words" in these descriptive areas increases the chance of retrievability given all the information that is available and searched on the Internet.

Slideshare.com provides a great way to let others in the world easily access information like this. Like most of the systems described in this book, information can be restricted to a few or be open to the public.

How do you know if people are viewing your documents? This sort of feedback would let you know if your document was being reached or not. This is important because this sort of feedback lets you know if you are successful or not with the objective of dissemination. If no one is viewing the document, you may need to consider changing some of the descriptive information. One major problem can exist when the title does not reflect the content of the file. Metaphors and other such nondescriptions can be counterproductive when using search engines. SlideShare and other sites, social media, and Web technologies offer ways to help you analyze the activity on your site or concerning your interests. A book could be written on "How to Analyze Social Media." SlideShare offers some simple statistics. It also allows user feedback and is, like every application online, changing constantly to fit the needs of the users. An example is provided next in Figure 6.13.

Slideshare maintains a frequency count of the number of views, recommendations, favorites, tweets, and posts to Facebook, and allows for readers to Like the information and comment on it. This is the common set of ways people can express their opinions on any material. You have the ability to allow documents and presentations to be viewable by everyone or by only a select group. This is a very useful feature when working on group projects or when only a select group needs to have access to information. Slideshare allows others the ability to print the information that you placed online. As so many sites offer, one can tweet or post the information straight from Slideshare to Facebook and other social sites interconnecting and further disseminating the information. Of course, always use caution and common sense in the information you put on the Internet. Although Slideshare, as well as other sites, have security features built in, sensitive information should be disseminated in very selective and secure manners when transmitted on or over the Internet.

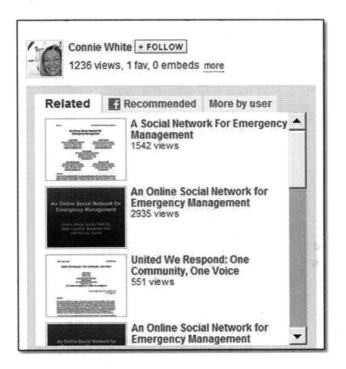

FIGURE 6.13 Slideshare information.

SKYPE

There are many ways to communicate using the technology available to us online. Audio is no different. We can leave video/audio comments on Facebook and on uStream, but this is not real time. Chatting allows real-time interaction, but sometimes people need to talk to each other for one reason or another and only real-time audio will fit the need at that moment. Google provides a Call Phone feature. However, Skype is the popular mode of choice. Using something like Skype or Google simply further leverages your computing ability, i.e., all you can do through your computer. Skype is user friendly and provides not only audio, but live video of the people communicating with one another.

Skype serves as a free phone and even a video phone by sending communications through Internet services rather than phone services. A number of celebrities use Skype, and, yet, it's still not utilized in the emergency management domain. This is one of the common problems with a lot of social media and Web 2.0 technologies: practitioners and other stakeholders don't consider it a seriously useful tool because of the way it is utilized in other settings.

Skype.com allows users to speak to one another and add video for viewing one another. Although, I must admit, some seem to have a better reception than what I ordinarily experience, Skype still provides emergency managers a way to interact when face-to-face interactions are required. As with most of these online services, a basic free account is offered with additional features acquired for a modest fee. Many people can interact on Skype simultaneously and you have the ability to chat or send a user a message through the same function. They have it such that if I need to communicate with someone who also has a Skype account, I can click their profile from my available contact list, and then leave them a message in a text box that is always available at the bottom of the communication window. Figure 6.14 shows a screenshot of Skype.

Skype is integrated into other systems. Smartphones have applications to add Skype as a service. Skype gives you the ability to speak to anybody in the world who also has Skype. When colleagues are overseas, Skype is a free way to communicate and see each other. Skype is part of the Moodle open source system that can be used for group support.

Skype provides practitioners and other responders the ability to stay connected with family members and loved ones when they are away helping others. Providing this basic need can provide comfort to those away helping others, assuring and providing confirmation to the responders that their family member and loved ones are okay. There is no replacement for this to help someone maintain focus on their job.

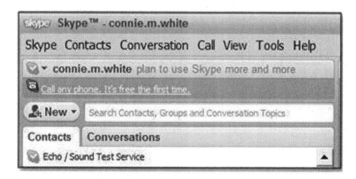

FIGURE 6.14   Skype menu screenshot.

Skype also offers subgroups of officials the ability to meet quickly and make critical decisions best communicated face-to-face. This could be used further as a way for someone to stream an ongoing scene to another person for damage assessment purposes and the like. Skype may be a better tool when information is more sensitive and need only be viewed by one or a few. These conversations are not recorded, not by Skype, anyway. This is what makes it different from live streaming of content, something like uStream, which will be covered in the next chapter.

WIKIS

Wikis are sites where anybody can change the contents of the site at any time. This has incredible potential for the emergency domain if we can just figure out how to use it properly. Wikis are used by a lot of people and Wikipedia is the most successful example of what a wiki can become and do. MediaWiki.com is the free and open source system that Wikipedia and many other successful wikis are built on. Moodle has a wiki function and Google has a wiki with templates. However, Google has collaboration ability where many individuals can collectively work on the same document through their online account space; Sharing is a feature that is part of the Google philosophy. So, really, their Websites are wikis as they allow collaborative editor ability. The great power behind a wiki is the ability to have a real-time site reflect the needs of the situation (or any other information) where anyone can contribute to the content of the information. As soon as you do something to a wiki, it's done. That is what everyone or anyone who is allowed to see the wiki can do. This can be both a very useful or very problematic feature. Wikis still need further development to be embraced and used by practitioners and emergency officials.

A single user could be designated to manage and keep information consistent. However, this remains, for the most part, unexplored. I want to present some work on wikis from some earlier research we conducted in two areas: (1) how wikis would be beneficial for emergency management, and (2) could wikis be used efficiently as an integral part of the decision-making process where the wiki was used as the space where practitioners interacted (White, Plotnick, Turoff, and Hiltz, 2007; White, Plotnick, Aadams-Moring, Turoff, and Hiltz, 2008)? I really thought wikis would be used more by now, but they are only used by a handful of more tech-savvy groups, and not generally used by emergency management agencies or first responders.

Type	Access	User Restrictions
I	Fully Open	No restrictions
II	Lockable	All pages public, but editing restricted in various ways
III	Gate	Some pages public, others restricted to registered users
IV	Members only	All users must be registered; may involve further group restrictions
V	Fire walled	All users must be on specific network
VI	Personal	Notebook usage on one system or private web site directory

FIGURE 6.15 Types of wikis.

In general, there are six categories of wikis that have security restrictions based on user access (Leuf and Cunningham, 2001; White et al., 2008). The accessibility varies greatly from one extreme to another and can be managed in a few ways in order to optimize and fill the needs of the organization. Figure 6.15 provides a list of the types, their access, and any user restrictions that may exist with that particular type of wiki.

Wikis offer a host of security levels. Of course, WikiLeaks may put this into question, but that was the setting allowed and information that was disseminated intentionally by its users. Wikis can have greater security levels if set up properly. Some problems that arise with wikis are that anybody can write anything on them. The last person to access and update a wiki changes the information on the wiki permanently, until subsequently modified, and this can create problems. Wikipedia has many techniques in place to maintain credibility in the information contributed to the site. However, for the common wiki set up for free, standards and rules may need to be put in place.

Wikis simply aren't used much yet by emergency management professionals. Once the proper templates are created and managed correctly, · greater real-time collective intelligence will be generated to handle time-critical situations.

DOODLE AND SCHEDULING

Scheduling meetings for people in the same organization can be a difficult task to fulfill. Now, add the challenges of scheduling a meeting for people with different schedules, from different organizations, across multiple time zones and in other countries, and a monumental time-consuming task has been created. This isn't good anytime, but during time-critical situations, this can be one more tool for management in expediting the decision-making process. There are many ways that meetings can be scheduled. Facebook has an Events feature where people can be invited. Google has a function like this that integrates the meeting details into the Google Calendar where, like so many collaborative files, details can be added to your personal calendar or distributed as public to everyone in the group, adding the event to the group members' calendars. However, these are invitations with specified times and don't allow a variety of time slots that will be more apt to better fit the group, providing the group members' different time slots increase the number of people who will attend the meeting. This is good for any phase of comprehensive management.

One application that provides this flexibility is Doodle. Doodle.com is a great, free, online scheduling and polling tool. This tool is great when trying to schedule a meeting between people who are on different schedules, are not commonly available to one another, and/or live in different time zones. The system is such that you can create a set of available dates and times for a meeting. Each group member is sent an e-mail with the link and they respond indicating when they are available. By process of elimination, through the visual that is provided, a group can quickly deduce which time slot is a best fit for all. Figure 6.16 provides an example of the user interface. Normally, scheduling would be in some text-based format. By creating a visual interpretation of data, faster decisions can be made. Throughout this book, you will note that I mention many different ways to support fast decision making. When adding many of these techniques from a variety of systems to fit numerous objectives, a lot of time can be saved. This is good for at least two reasons: (1) the less time you spend on tedious tasks, the more time you can dedicate to more important things like serious work; (2) during time-critical situations, time may not be a luxury and decisions must be made or the decision will be made for you. Having the ability to bring together experts quickly and manage information in real time can support crisis communications and decision support of crisis managers—and the public.

To select certain dates, one only needs to click the block of that day; any days from any month can be selected. Figure 6.16 shows the next step in selecting what time slots you want to make available.

Next, you select to whom you want to send this invitation (Figure 6.18).

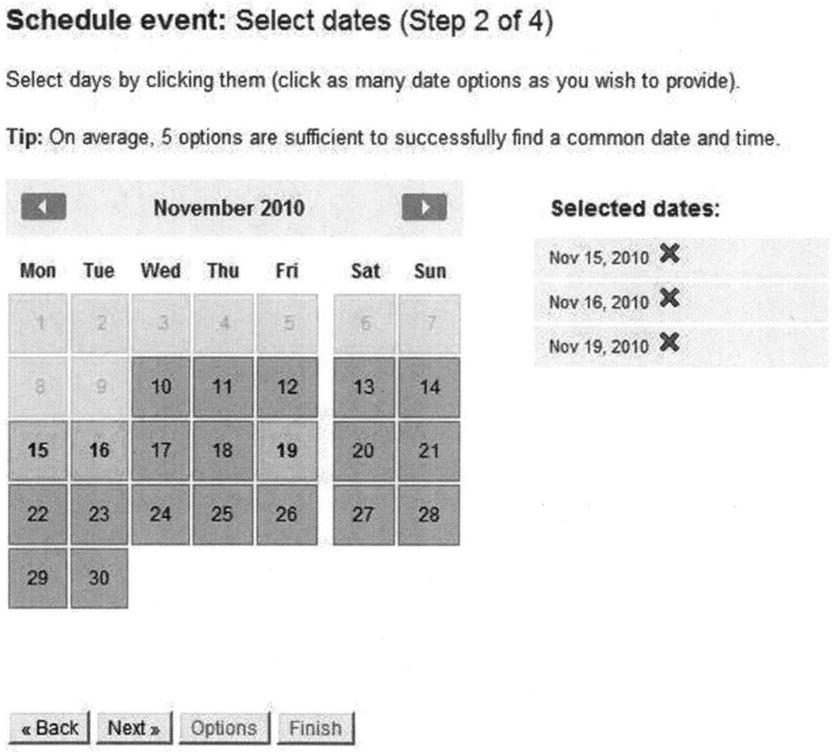

Schedule event: Select dates (Step 2 of 4)

Select days by clicking them (click as many date options as you wish to provide).

Tip: On average, 5 options are sufficient to successfully find a common date and time.

		November 2010						Selected dates:
Mon	Tue	Wed	Thu	Fri	Sat	Sun		Nov 15, 2010 ✖
1	2	3	4	5	6	7		Nov 16, 2010 ✖
8	9	10	11	12	13	14		Nov 19, 2010 ✖
15	16	17	18	19	20	21		
22	23	24	25	26	27	28		
29	30							

« Back   Next »   Options   Finish

FIGURE 6.16 A screenshot of time blocks available to members.

This makes it convenient and complete. You can simply get the URL that is created along with the invitation and put it in a tweet (shorten URL, too) or as a post on a Wall in a Facebook group or mailed to a group. The resulting schedule is presented in Figure 6.16.

Next, Figure 6.17 provides a screenshot to demonstrate how easy it s to set up alternative dates for others to select from.

Later, you can see from Figure 6.18, Friday, November 19, 2010, is the day that everyone can meet. It takes about half a second to see this result. Of course, it may not always be so clear cut, but there will be obvious times that will be better for the group to meet demonstrated by the visual interpretation of the data received.

This is real time and provides immediate feedback on when a group can meet. Details can accompany the schedule providing group members

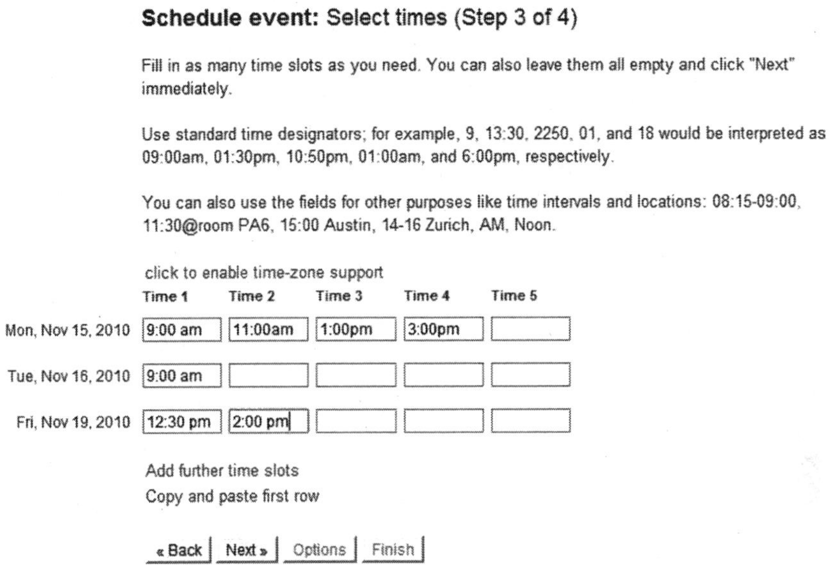

Schedule event: Select times (Step 3 of 4)

Fill in as many time slots as you need. You can also leave them all empty and click "Next" immediately.

Use standard time designators; for example, 9, 13:30, 2250, 01, and 18 would be interpreted as 09:00am, 01:30pm, 10:50pm, 01:00am, and 6:00pm, respectively.

You can also use the fields for other purposes like time intervals and locations: 08:15-09:00, 11:30@room PA6, 15:00 Austin, 14-16 Zurich, AM, Noon.

click to enable time-zone support

	Time 1	Time 2	Time 3	Time 4	Time 5
Mon, Nov 15, 2010	9:00 am	11:00am	1:00pm	3:00pm	
Tue, Nov 16, 2010	9:00 am				
Fri, Nov 19, 2010	12:30 pm	2:00 pm			

Add further time slots
Copy and paste first row

« Back   Next »   Options   Finish

FIGURE 6.17   Time blocks available to a user.

the information they need most. Doodle also conducts Polls so that you can quickly assess a situation if need be. Of course, polls are a good way to get community feedback or group opinions when needed. We will cover other ways and systems that do polling, applications for sites in particular, but for a quick way to set up a poll and provide a group a link, Doodle is an excellent system. I'm sure there are other systems that do polling on a deeper level. What is important to gain here is to develop a mindset to think collaboratively and search for free online systems to fit your needs.

QUESTIONPRO

Surveys are useful to help gather data in order to help support decisions that must be made. Gathering opinions can be quite useful, too, as perception is as important as reality in the long run. For example, AlabamaBeaches used twitter as a tool to let people know what was going on with the oil spill and to try to combat the perception the public had made from images on the large news networks. Tourism in 2010 in Florida was greatly impacted by public perception. Before AlabamaBeaches started their campaign

181

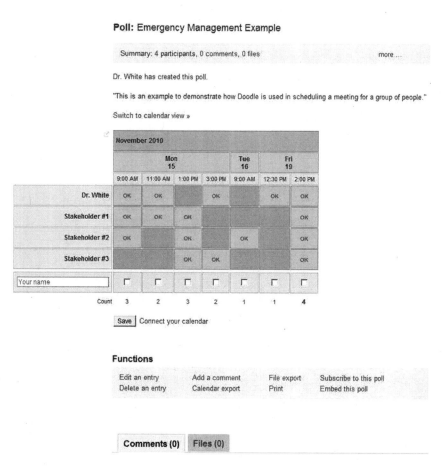

Poll: Emergency Management Example

Summary: 4 participants, 0 comments, 0 files   more...

Dr. White has created this poll.

"This is an example to demonstrate how Doodle is used in scheduling a meeting for a group of people."

Switch to calendar view »

November 2010							
	Mon 15				Tue 16	Fri 19	
	9:00 AM	11:00 AM	1:00 PM	3:00 PM	9:00 AM	12:30 PM	2:00 PM
Dr. White	OK	OK		OK		OK	OK
Stakeholder #1	OK	OK	OK				OK
Stakeholder #2	OK		OK		OK		OK
Stakeholder #3			OK	OK			OK
Your name	☐	☐	☐	☐	☐	☐	☐
Count	3	2	3	2	1	1	4

Save | Connect your calendar

Functions

| Edit an entry | Add a comment | File export | Subscribe to this poll |
| Delete an entry | Calendar export | Print | Embed this poll |

Comments (0)   Files (0)

FIGURE 6.18 Visual interpretation of available dates.

using Twitter, they could have measured public perception using a survey although this was a situation measured in dollars already from the lack of tourists visiting. Surveys normally take a lot of time alone simply in distributing them, hoping people fill them out, then getting the surveys back to calculate the end results. This is no longer required given there are multiple survey systems provided online. Although there are a number of survey applications available, we will feature QuestionPro. QuestionPro.com is a free survey software system. Polls were just covered, but a survey provides an agency a better way to gather information and interpret data into meaningful results that can be used in decision making. Figure 6.19 provides an

182

> 1. Which emergency management functions seem to hold the most promise for the use of online social networks? Please put a 1 for the most important application to which such a system might be used. A 2 for the next most important and continue until you don't feel any remaining potential application is suitable for this technology.

Average Rank		1	2	3	4	5	6	7	8	9	10
Damage assessment an..	3.57										
Collaborative proble..	4.67										
Consultation for rea..	5.42										
Planning or exchange ...	5.92										
Training or exchange..	5.00										
Collaborative exerci ...	4.46										
Citizen engagement o ..	4.29										
Peer exchanges among ..	6.69										
Best Practice exchan...	6.59										
New document evaluat ..	7.06										

Data Table	1		2		3		4		5		6		7		8		9		10	
Damage assessment an ..	5	35.71%	3	21.43%	0	0.00%	2	14.29%	1	7.14%	0	0.00%	1	7.69%	0	0.00%	1	9.09%	1	9.09%
Collaborative proble ...	1	7.14%	4	28.57%	0	0.00%	1	7.14%	0	0.00%	2	15.38%	3	23.08%	0	0.00%	0	0.00%	1	9.09%
Consultation for rea ..	3	21.43%	0	0.00%	1	7.14%	0	0.00%	3	21.43%	0	0.00%	1	7.69%	0	0.00%	3	27.27%	1	9.09%
Planning or exchange ...	0	0.00%	1	7.14%	2	14.29%	3	21.43%	0	0.00%	2	15.38%	0	0.00%	2	16.67%	1	9.09%	2	18.18%
Training or exchange ...	0	0.00%	2	14.29%	3	21.43%	1	7.14%	3	21.43%	0	0.00%	2	15.38%	0	0.00%	1	9.09%	1	9.09%
Collaborative exerci ...	0	0.00%	1	7.14%	6	42.86%	0	0.00%	2	14.29%	2	15.38%	0	0.00%	2	16.67%	0	0.00%	0	0.00%
Citizen engagement o ...	3	21.43%	2	14.29%	1	7.14%	3	21.43%	0	0.00%	1	7.69%	1	7.69%	2	16.67%	1	9.09%	0	0.00%
Peer exchanges among ..	0	0.00%	0	0.00%	1	7.14%	1	7.14%	2	14.29%	1	15.38%	1	7.69%	4	33.33%	1	9.09%	0	0.00%
Best Practice exchan ..	1	7.14%	1	7.14%	0	0.00%	1	7.14%	2	14.29%	2	15.38%	4	30.77%	1	8.33%	1	9.09%	0	0.00%
New document evaluat ..	1	7.14%	0	0.00%	0	0.00%	2	14.29%	1	7.14%	2	15.38%	0	0.00%	1	8.33%	2	18.18%	4	36.36%

FIGURE 6.19   Simple statistics provided on QuestionPro.

example of data that was gathered both as a visual representation in the form of a bar chart, but also with simple statistics provided. This makes distributing surveys a quick and easy way to gather data and information.

This software, like the others mentioned previously, is easy to use. There is a tutorial that demonstrates how to do most everything and the design is very user friendly. As with most of the free versions of software applications available, there is a limited amount of functionality with an improved, more feature-rich version offered for a nominal fee. At present, it offers up to three surveys allowing 10 questions each. For a modest monthly fee, more features can be added. Other features include being able to have more questions on your survey. Another worthy feature is the ability to have an infinite number of surveys.

COLLABORATIVE TOOLS AND
COMMUNITY RESILIENCE 2.0

Communication is a key component for a community resilience program. The Internet supports individual and group needs to serve social aspects. Social media and other Web 2.0 technologies like Facebook and

Twitter can be used to serve a number of purposes for various stakeholders during various phases of emergency management. Recently, the aftermath of the Iran election demonstrated the power behind social media, such as Twitter, using technology already in people's possession, such as cell phones with camera capability, iPhones, Blackberries, and such. Moreover, people know these technologies or can easily learn to use them. Groups can create accounts in Facebook and Twitter. These can be used for a variety of purposes (e.g., for the distribution of information, event announcements, individual expert identification, mass emailing, situational awareness) where each can be tailored to meet the needs of the individual, business, government entity, education facility, hospital, and ad hoc group formations. Such uses include:

- **Expediting recovery efforts through quicker communication restoration.**
  There are so many ways that people can send and receive information, post information, or tweet important bits of information for others to retrieve using social media. The more quickly communications are restored, the better. Given the multiple ways people can interact, using social media will expedite recovery efforts. However, because the media use the Web, areas may be disrupted, but the Internet is distributed and can be used by those in the peripheral areas who can bring information closer to those without information and who need it most.
- **Building, maintaining, and strengthening relationships between partners prior to an emergency.**
  On a business level, social media provides a better means for networking and connecting on a deeper information-wise level, which is consistent and more searchable than any rolodex. This can help strengthen relationships prior to any disaster or maintain records after the event, given the records will still be intact and available.
- **Keeping responders, rescue personnel, and emergency management professionals connected to their loved ones.**
  Social media can help loved ones keep in touch with one another. It can allow people to let others know that they are okay. Social media also can be used to help first responders and others working in the field deal with the stress of not being with family. Using video, pics, e-mails, and other media-rich technologies can help

184

relieve the worry and stress about family and so help people focus on their work.

- **Organizing grassroots efforts that use community members as resources.**
  The first responders to any scene are often the local public. After checking on family, people check on neighbors. Given the overwhelming need for information reporting and the state of the 911 intake capability, social media provide other means to upload information to the appropriate people. Citizens can be used to monitor, filter, and distribute information during these times as well as during noncrisis times. Databases of information on community members can help neighbors and volunteers network to provide aid to those in need and increase the community's ability to be self sustained in the event of a disaster.
- **Helping to identify resources using maps and other GIS capabilities.**
  Social media provides a mapping ability where users can click on a location and enter information, pics, and videos and such to augment disaster relief information. The social geographic information system (GIS) ability can help in recovery efforts and also in reporting damage so that emergency management can quickly get the information required for funding. More accurate information can be obtained more quickly, potentially expediting funding efforts.
- **Broadcasting public announcements and other group messages.**
  Social media provide many ways for government officials or anyone to post videos on official or nonofficial sites to private or public groups. This saves time and money as it can be done at little cost with great rapidity. This makes it such that those who need to be focusing on bigger problems can more quickly return to their duties and also post information to the press, the public, and/or others who need it.

HOW TO ENGAGE WITH THE PUBLIC

Although Twitter is a powerful tool, it must be used in a strategic manner in order to be effective. Tweets should be engaging and not simply a one-way method of an agency to disseminate information. It helps to add a "human" component to the information and lets your target population know that you are there to help them. This next set of useful tips came from an article informing bloggers how they could build their community with Twitter. These guidelines also can be used by emergency managers to help them maintain their target market, i.e., their community using social media (Brkan, 2009).

- **Interact with your followers, fans, group members, and friends by asking questions**.

  Ask your community and Followers questions that will trigger them to think about things like readiness. For example, is your community resilient? Learn how from www.someWebSite.com. It will be good to provide them with links to more information. There are many occasions when such a tweet will prompt users to take some sort of action. Links to preparedness videos, educational resources, and ongoing events can be promoted in this manner.

- **When someone tweets or posts a question to your organization, provide them with an answer**.

  These answers, like all tweets and posts, must be brief, but links can be added to provide the user with more information. A set of predesignated links should be aggregated to help the person managing the Twitter account so that this information can be sent back to the person wanting information as quickly as possible. It is important to respond to people as quickly as possible so that the information is timely and relevant.

- **Be an expert and offer other useful information to users**.

  It's important to not hoard information. This can happen for a number of reasons; competitiveness may make a group not want to ReTweet someone else's information or *Share* it by posting it on their *Wall*. It's important to provide expert information to your user population or community. By Following important groups yourself, or having access to information through Facebook *Groups* and *Friends* who are experts, you have the ability to filter information and promote culled tweets and posts and YouTube videos, etc., to others who Follow you due to your expertise in an area. Over time, your community will associate your account with important information that is not only from you, but also from other expert resources.

- **Seek out new partnerships and information in the Twittersphere or Internet.**
  New groups are embracing social media and creating accounts. It is important to know when relevant groups surface on Twitter or Facebook, for example. Also, the emergency domain is a dynamic and volatile environment. Stay on top of the information floating around by looking for or paying attention to others' hashtags and keywords. For example, #Paula emerged as the hashtag identifying a newly formed Hurricane. Before the event, who knows what it meant. Later, it will take on a new meaning or lose its meaning altogether because it's not an active hashtag anymore. Collaborative documents, such as what was discussed using Google docs, will actually send you an e-mail and notify you that a new collaborative document or spreadsheet has been created and *Shared*.

It's important to understand that social media can be used in a variety of ways to help communities to be more resilient. If a community were to embrace the technology for its power, once there is an effective saturation level, the community would be stronger because communications are stronger, information is passed along more freely, and other media rich technologies leverage the stakeholder's ability to work collaboratively so that there is a more efficient and resilient community. Fugate recently stated, "The public, including the private sector and nonprofits, must be included in the mitigation process and that means emergency managers, even at the federal level, will have to begin to trust 'the public and their devices,' including Twitter."

SUMMARY

This chapter was meant to expose you to many different alternative applications that can be used, and to also try to teach a new way of thinking through collaboration. When many people can access the same document anytime, add a calendar event, work on a proposal, or make forms available for reimbursement purposes, collaboration cannot only expedite the process, but also can decrease uncertainty and lessen ambiguity (White, Hiltz, and Turoff, 2008). The community is and remains the greatest untapped resource for emergency management. Community resilience should include a grassroots effort where social media is utilized in a number of ways to support the safety of the community. However, it's not enough to just provide the community with information. The community should be used as participants supporting local efforts (Palen and Hiltz, 2009). Citizens should be engaged with and not directed so that they take on more responsibility for themselves. The community members already know a lot of information where it concerns their own safety. Engage the public, make them more responsible for their own safety, and a greater resilience will network and emerge.

ON BOOK WEBSITE: SMEMBOOK.COM

Managing Documentation for Emergency Management Purposes

authorStream Video Lecture
http://www.authorstream.com/Presentation/conniemwhite-438714-managing-documentation-for-emergency-management-purposes/

Five-Minute Tutorials
Capturing screenshot to use in PPTs
http://www.screencast.com/users/connie.m.white/folders/Jing/media/5822c029-1217-4a38-ba22-0dc4d826b74e

Upload and Share Documentation/PPTs on SlideShare
http://www.screencast.com/users/connie.m.white/folders/Jing/media/55f18e29-4a48-4b3e-bb33-a255a0c05586

Google Docs
http://www.screencast.com/users/connie.m.white/folders/Jing/media/dd6f86fa-692f-4c75-99f0-60f2a5f24a67

Google Wiki
http://www.screencast.com/users/connie.m.white/folders/Jing/media/0aba1bc0-5a86-4f71-822a-0e29f1173649

Dragon Naturally Speaking
http://www.screencast.com/users/connie.m.white/folders/Jing/media/d568b295-adf7-48f4-80db-596e29c5af96

EXERCISES

1. Create a single Document and invite other group members to collaborate. Provide the group members with *Editing* ability. All group members should get online at the same time and work on the document simultaneously to experience the real-time interaction and how it's directly reflected.
2. Create a disaster scenario by creating a Document and inviting group members. Have the scenario such that each member interjects ideas in between other ideas creating a more complete and thorough scenario. Make sure each member of the group adds and interjects at least five ideas.
3. Include ways social media will be used during the scenario, providing specific examples.
4. How can an organization solicit and maintain a group of followers?
5. Can and should citizens be used in emergency efforts? During which phase? Please provide a list of specific examples per phase (response, recovery, preparedness, mitigation).

7

Visuals, Mapping, and Disaster Management Systems

INTRODUCTION

Visuals can be very powerful sources of information for first responders and emergency management, especially during the immediate aftermath of a disaster. An overwhelming number of individuals in the population carry a cell phone or smartphone or camera that has the ability to take a photo or video and then upload the contents to the Internet in a matter of minutes, if not seconds. Social media, Web applications, and smart technology have integrated many capabilities that help add more descriptive information to the visual through text, audio, and geoLocation devices, increasing its value. Add this to potential held within the power of the masses where information could be uploaded and exploited a number of ways. This holds great potential for decision makers where data can be aggregated for damage assessment, reporting severe weather, increasing border security, identifying pandemics, evaluating routes/logistics, or any other information that can be derived from images and leveraged using social media.

This chapter begins explaining some of the basics of Web-based photography and videos. What will be covered are ways you can add information to these visuals, aggregate and disseminate. A number of

191

useful mapping applications are presented introducing collaborative mapping tools that you can use and edit any way you want. Citizens and community members have voluntarily rushed to the aid of efforts where mapping was greatly needed. A case study based from the Haiti response is used as an example. Disaster management software systems are created by tech-savvy groups of humanitarians that work together from all over the globe in an ongoing and enduring effort providing a variety of technical assistance for disaster relief organizations. Just as many responders deploy to a geographical site, disaster management software teams deploy as well, but to an online site where around the clock efforts are volunteered as a system is rapidly set up and populated with data. These systems help manage the information that will be needed by individuals and organizations on the ground who will aid in response and relief efforts. For the larger part, all of the available free systems are built, supported, and launched through groups of volunteers. The Haiti earthquake is used as a case exemplifying the humanitarian response where many open-source software systems were leveraged together by a variety of volunteers to capture data providing help to the Haitians, the military effort, and to each other as they worked together to eliminate redundancy and harness their abilities to make a common operating picture. The chapter closes providing an idea-based case. A new concept based on gaming and crowdsourcing is presented. This highlights some of the difficulties present in harnessing the collective intelligence of the online community for tasks only humans can perform for the rapid response feeds needed for data management in response efforts.

The information in this chapter is important because it demonstrates that social media can be further leveraged with open source systems and community of volunteers. People collaborate freely all over the world in order to build these complex systems to help those who cannot help themselves and to help better organize response efforts. Disasters have the same general needs after an event has struck an area. These needs are defined in requirements and specifications guiding software components that are created to satisfy these needs. Because every disaster is different, many of these components can be selected and used as needed, which further supports an efficient and effective response effort providing customization.

ONSITE WITH BRANDI SIMPSON

Dispatch is a critical piece of the emergency services puzzle. In many situations, dispatchers, or communications officers, are the first emergency services personnel to know that an incident has occurred. Dispatchers are the first step in the response effort to all emergency situations. Without skilled and trained dispatchers, responding emergency services agencies' functions would come to a halt. Dispatchers are tasked with notifying the proper agencies when an emergency situation occurs. And, regardless of the situation these call-takers keep control of the information coming in on the phone from an emergency.

Communication during a crisis situation is key to protecting citizens and responding emergency services personnel. Details of the incident are of utmost importance when responding to an emergency situation. Dispatchers answer initial calls from citizens within the emergency area. The main objective of dispatch is to gather as many details as possible regarding the emergency. Dispatchers then

FIGURE 7.1 Brandi Simpson, Police Communications Officer II, Alabama Department of Public Safety—Highway Patrol Division.

pass along these details to responding units. Emergency services entering the area will know what type of emergency incident they are responding to. By knowing as many details as possible about the situation, dispatchers can provide responding units with information so that these units know what type of equipment will be needed, what type of injuries to expect, and what type of obstacles they may encounter while responding.

Information will be more readily available once emergency personnel arrive on the scene and assess the situation. However, the very basic information received during the immediate aftermath will be the basis for the response effort. Where, what, and who are the main components necessary when gathering information? Where did the incident take place? What happened? Who was involved?

Advancements in information technology, whether it be equipment, programs, Websites, or training, can be an aid to dispatch when relaying information. Social media can be utilized in dispatch by allowing call-takers to pass along information to responding personnel. Social media also can be used by dispatch to alert the general public of areas to avoid in the event of an emergency. For instance, Twitter and Facebook are growing tools that can be utilized for many emergency services agencies. Dispatch can use Twitter and Facebook simply by creating an account specifically for the agency. Dispatchers taking calls can tweet or post the information gathered. By specifically addressing it to certain people or groups, all responding units can receive the information at the same time.

Using Websites, such as Twitter and Facebook, can link agencies together without tying up emergency phone lines as well. Each emergency services agency can Friend or Follow the other as long as they have an account. Agencies, such as police, fire, and ambulance, can communicate through Twitter and Facebook with as much ease as talking on the phone or radio. Agencies can link their Twitter and Facebook accounts together. Information added on one site will be added to the other site at the same time for Followers or Friends to view.

An excellent example of Twitter and Facebook aiding dispatch is following the occurrence of a highway emergency. In the event of an accident on a major and/or heavily traveled roadway, a State Highway Patrol communications officer could access their State

Highway Patrol account and add information regarding the accident. Only relevant information, such as the roadway name or number, estimated length of road closure, and alternate routes, should be posted to the site. Followers or Friends can view the information to avoid the area by using the alternate routes posted. This would reduce traffic congestion in the area. Also, this will reduce the number of calls to the dispatch office from motorists wanting to know why they have been stuck in traffic for an extended period of time. Using these additional tools would keep emergency lines open and clear of irrelevant calls. Many communications centers are understaffed. By taking away some of the calls, communications officers can focus more on radio traffic coming in from responding units. The main priority of a communications officer is the safety of the responding personnel.

Many times in the event of a highway emergency or traffic hazard, State Highway Patrol offices depend on the general public to let dispatch know what they encounter on the roadways and where these issues are located. With so many Department of Transportation offices not keeping accurate and up-to-date information available, motorists could access the State Highway Patrol site to view all reported highway problems in the event of inclement weather or accidents. When motorists are stopped and can safely post or tweet information to the State Highway Patrol site, dispatch should receive notification. A unit can be dispatched to the location to check the hazard. This information also will be readily available for other motorists who are or will be traveling through the area. By accessing one site, motorists could be aware of traffic problems throughout an entire state. This would work well with travel problems such as icy, flooded, or blocked roadways as well as accidents.

For instance, an Interstate bridge crossing the Tennessee River is prone to icing in cold temperatures. Following a cold and foggy or rainy night, hundreds of phone calls come in to local 911 centers, sheriffs' offices, and State Highway Patrol posts requesting information on the condition of the bridge from motorists who regularly travel that section of highway. A large number of the calls could be taken off the dispatch centers with linked Twitter and Facebook accounts. Local news stations could give out Website information for the motoring public to check prior to leaving home. On numerous occasions, bridge icing causes multiple accidents to occur before Department of Transportation and State Highway Patrol personnel can get to the scene. These accidents typically block both north- and southbound lanes during prime rush hour traffic. Traffic delays of over two hours can be expected. With Twitter and Facebook accounts, State Highway Patrol offices could post information regarding these accidents. Motorists could use alternate routes of travel to avoid causing further traffic congestion in the area. It also would help these motorists to get where they are going with much less delay.

In order for Twitter and Facebook to be useful for agencies, such as the State Highway Patrol, guidelines and procedures policies should be set in writing by the department heads. These guidelines should include what can be posted to the site as well as how the information is to be posted. Policies should include reprimands as well for abuse and misuse to avoid problems. Employees failing to follow the set guidelines for use of the sites would be punished by means set forth by the department.

As more and more phone companies and individuals switch to smartphones, these Website services will continue to become more of the norm for accessing information. Many people use their smart-phones to access much of the information they find necessary to their daily lives. Once sites are created, information on these sites should be submitted to all local news and radio stations for dissemination. By advertising Twitter and Facebook as a hassle-free way to check roadway information, a large number of calls to dispatch centers could be averted. Also, this information would be available to all emergency services that are Friends or Followers for them to disseminate to their personnel.

PHOTOGRAPHY

Digital image capability (i.e., photography) is built into many devices, cell phones, smartphones, and, of course, the digital camera. Cameras are now built with the capability to upload the images to a variety of sites, such as Picasa, Flickr, Facebook, and Twitter. Photos can be uploaded in a variety of ways and with only a few touches to a screen, in some cases. This makes them very easy to "move" during emergent times. Further, images can be tagged in particular places where others want the eye directed to inform the viewer with more information. Descriptions can be added along with each of these pictures providing the details needed for further clarification. Where Facebook and Twitter can have images posted to them, Picasa and Flickr provide editing and mass storage capability. Facebook does allow for albums, but it is one component of a larger system where Picasa and Flickr have the primary function of photo management. During the creation of this book, I have strived to use open source to meet the needs of the diagrams, charts, and images. I have a good bit of background using PhotoShop and other photo software, but was challenged with satisfying the requirements of the editors. Although I knew of Picasa (it seems to appear sometimes when you are working with images), I felt it too cumbersome because it did not fit the structure and logic I was used to. After coming up empty handed searching for an open source photo image software that could crop, turn images to black and white, and further manipulate the images by contrasting light and dark, sharpening, saving in the right formats, and other much needed tools, I looked again at Picasa. Picasa is available through the Google Suite or stand alone. It had everything I needed and simply was so intuitive that the logic slipped by me. All I had to do was look and it was incredible, not only what was available, but how the software worked with me and on my computer to make editing photos easier than I've ever witnessed. Just like on Flickr, images can be uploaded and stored where they can be accessed by others or referenced as a link. The next screenshot provides an example where a screenshot was being manipulated. One can easily see in Figure 7.2 the Menu items when working with an image and what's more impressive is how the Basic Fixes, Tuning, and Effects seamlessly appear. Again, as with most of the software covered in this book, the photos and Picasa can be accessed and worked with from anywhere the user has an Internet connection and a Web browser. This is a very powerful and free photo software.

VIDEO

Video is used in many ways to aid in emergency management goals. Videos are used to provide tutorials for responders; they are used on all levels of government and provide a resourceful way to get out a message. On the other hand, video, photos, and other streaming visuals can provide much useful information for response and recovery efforts. Although officials can leverage video, so, too, can the community. Community members

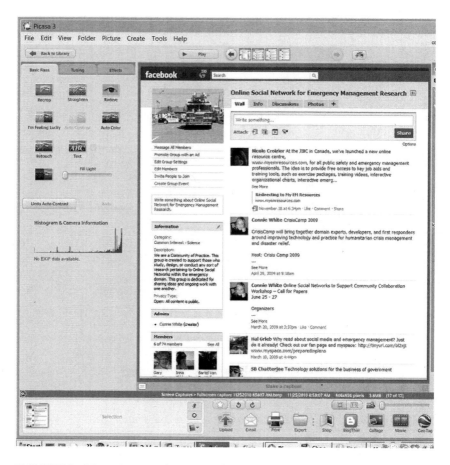

FIGURE 7.2 Menu items and options of Picasa.

are the first responders to any emergency as they are the ones directly affected by the event. Family members check on family and then, in turn, look for their neighbors, etc. In Victim Assistance software programs (Locate/Report Missing Persons), pics can provide a good visual especially when children are involved. The community and their technology can be used to upload pics, video, and such for damage assessment much quicker than officials can. The gaps between what officials are able to do are where the community can play a crucial role. iReports are already an accepted method of delivery to official management groups, organizations, and news groups. Video can be created on or uploaded to Facebook, is used to record a visual post as feedback as an additional mode of communication for sites such as uStream, and is used in a variety of other ways.

EQUIPMENT

Videos, pics, movies, and the like can be made with relative ease. Cell phones, Blackberries, iPhones, Droids, and other smart technology with uploading capabilities can be used for such purposes. Laptops have built-in cameras in their screens, along with the input and output devices for sound (i.e., microphone and speakers). Other traditional technology can be used where the information is then passed through to the Internet via other software or hardware, simple things like a digital camera that then is plugged into the computer where the visuals are now uploaded and disseminated. A laptop can be leveraged using the right equipment for higher quality videos where time is not critical, such as in educational videos.

The sound settings and such should be tested prior to use. For example, one common problem is when a presentation or video is recorded, but the sound on the laptop is at its highest setting. The sound, however, will not be as loud as needed. Also, speakers can make a huge difference in sound quality—laptop speakers versus Bose 5.1 Surround Sound with a USB plug. It's important to make sure that the equipment is set to serve the need and no more. If a higher sound quality is not required, then using Bose may be overkill. Equally important is the quality of input. A quality device is the Snowball microphone where sound input can be from an individual to a group in a crowded noisy area or to a group in a subdued area. This is a good microphone to use when recording lectures or speeches or to use when making high quality announcements. If sound quality is poor, people may not be able to clearly understand the message or may find the noise unbearable. However, there is a trade-off for quality and quantity. The best images and sound require a lot of space. This could be cumbersome or even counterproductive in that the information cannot be uploaded or downloaded efficiently and, therefore, may not be received successfully by anyone.

WEBSITES

Google provides an easy way to build and host any agency's Website or any site for any occasion. A site can be created for a temporary or permanent purpose. Sometimes, it is beneficial to put an event on a site all by itself and then provide a link to the site.

For example, a homepage can help groups to "put a face" on their organization or agency providing useful information and links to other useful information. This can help reduce the load on any agency where common questions for information may be easily provided by creating a Website. If a user group wants a particular URL, they also can go to any domain name group (search on Google) like GoDaddy or MyDomain.com and create some Web page URL for under $10 per year. This name can then be forwarded to the Google site where the information can be found by the people or person in need. Google has a special feature where people can collaborate on this creative effort. Just like the Documents, Calendars, etc., can be Shared, so too can the ability to collaboratively participate in the creation and upkeep of the designated site.

SHARING

Sharing is a way to pass along information that was provided by another source. Most news articles, Wall posts, videos, and other media have this as a built-in function. The Sharing option is found on smartphones and is the term to look for when you are trying to move information from one medium to another. For example, once a photo is made by a smartphone, the user can Share this picture to Facebook, Twitter, and other e-mail accounts just to name a few media. Google Documents are Shared with other people where the Share option provides the editing versus viewing option for others with whom you Share the document. Survey software allows the user to Share the survey with Facebook; shopping sites allow the user to Share the information from that source. Sharing is the fastest way to upload time-critical information when in the field and using a smartphone. Sharing is a very fast way to pass along information.

PUBLISHING

There are many times in which a document needs to be sent or viewed by a group, but there exists no efficient way to accomplish this task. For example, you cannot put a document on Twitter or Facebook. Normally, we attach documents either in an e-mail or in a forum. One way to get around this is to Publish your document (presentation, form, etc.) to the Web. This can be accomplished by using the Google Suite application Documents. In the window in the upper right is the Sharing option. This allows the user to Share the document with other collaborators, but also has the option to Publish the document to the Web so that it can be Shared with the world. This function provides both a link and the ability to embed the code into another Website allowing the user to view the document instantly. This is a bit tricky and will be covered here. Embedding code is a bit tricky, too, as one has to bring up unfamiliar code. A demonstration is provided next. We begin with Figure 7.3, which shows the window that comes up once the user has clicked the Share option.

To allow anyone access to the document, you simply highlight the *Document link*, copy it (Ctrl-C), then paste it (Ctrl-V) into any e-mail, Website, tweet, post, or discussion. If you make any updates to the document, they will be reflected immediately and the next time the document

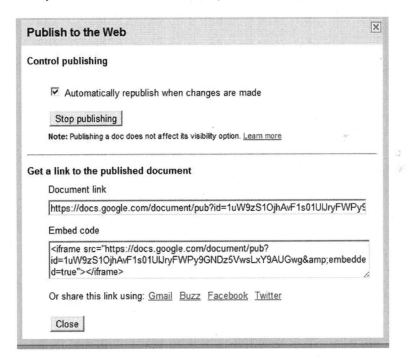

FIGURE 7.3 Sharing a link or embedding code.

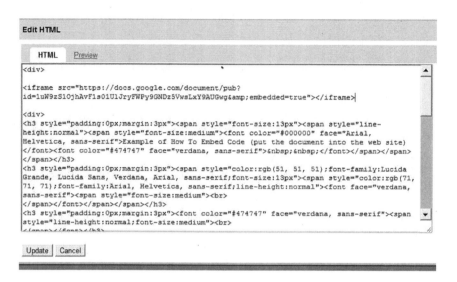

FIGURE 7.4 Embedding code into a site.

is "clicked" and retrieved, the updates will be viewable, or not, if you set the document to Not Update.

The Document can be embedded into another Website, for example, like Google. Embedding the code into a document provides a viewer with instant access to the document within a Web page (i.e., nothing is clicked and brought up). For example, in Figure 7.4, an example is provided demonstrating how to embed code into a Google site. First, the code must be copied (highlight and click Ctrl-C) from the **Publish to the Web** window. Next, paste the code (Ctrl-V) directly into your Google site. This is done by opening an existing Website, clicking Edit Page, and then clicking the HTML editor option in the menu. This is where things may look a bit foreign. However, find the tag word <div> and Paste the code directly after that. You can play around later and learn enough HTML code to place it elsewhere on the Website.

Next, save the site and then you should see this next screen shot (Figure 7.5). This is what the site will look like after you have saved the site but before you view the site while not editing it—which is different.

Now the document is inside the site as an object where it can be scrolled through and such. Figure 7.6 is a screenshot of the end result. Notice how the document isn't that large. This is a feature that can be modified and is available for a lot of Gadgets.

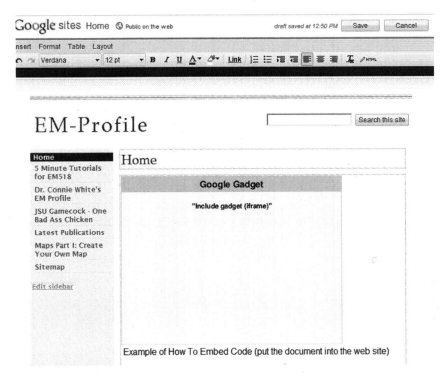

FIGURE 7.5   Google site view after adding embedded code.

To increase, decrease, or modify the Properties of the Box holding the content (viewable document in this case), Edit Page, then click the Google Gadget box. At the bottom will appear a selection of functions that can be selected, from where to place the box (Left, Center, Right) of page, Wrap ON or OFF; this allows the text in the document to go around the text box or be above it or below it (click and play around, nothing will explode) and then there is a Properties box. Click Properties. Figure 7.7 is a screenshot of what should be seen (to a certain degree, anyway) because things are always changing.

It is in the Properties box that you can manipulate the size and will have other alternative functionalities to select. It is best to play around and see what looks best. By increasing both the width and height to 700 × 800, a larger document is displayed within the site (Figure 7.8).

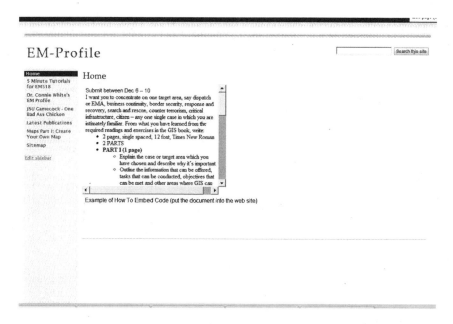

FIGURE 7.6 Embedded code in site: Small window.

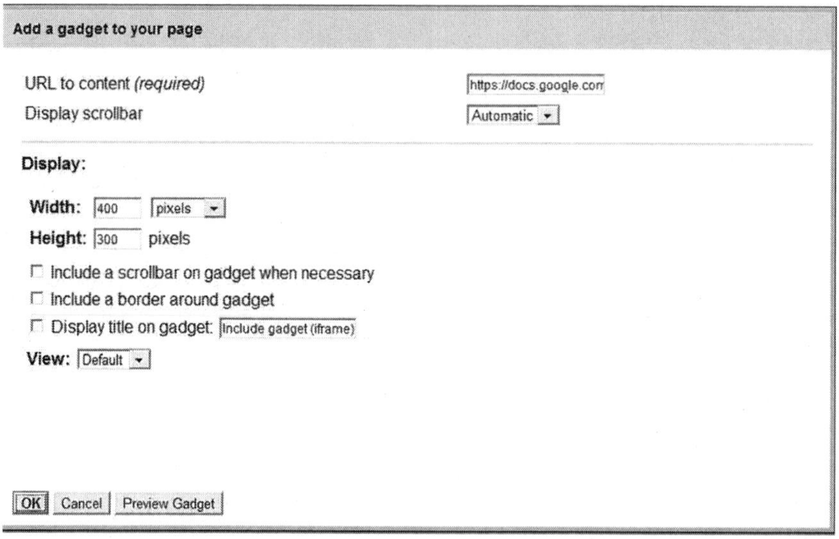

FIGURE 7.7 Changing window for embedded code on site.

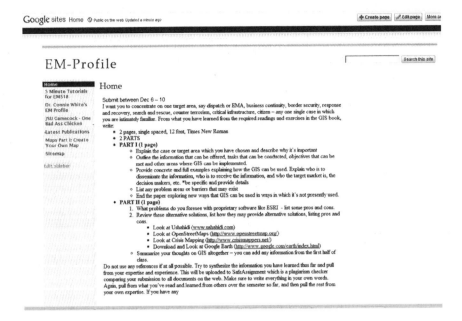

FIGURE 7.8 Embedded code with large window.

Having the ability to modify the size of boxes, photos, etc., is commonplace with site development. This is how a visually pleasing Web design is accomplished through design.

POWERPOINT WITH NARRATION

PowerPoint presentations are very common; however, audio voiceover can be accomplished by using the Narrating option in Microsoft™ Word 2007. This is very useful when the audience desires or requires more than all the text crammed onto a PowerPoint frame. This can be used as an additional way to reach those handicapped where the blind can hear the audio portion and the deaf can read the information on the slides where more useful links providing more information can be inserted. In order to make this accessible to those on the Internet, authorStream (www.authorStream.com) will upload and turn it into a movie presentation and provide a link hosting the video; this is free. Most of the free software obviously has limits, but for a small fee, these limits can be greatly increased. It would not be surprising for the Google Presentation software to have this capability in the near future. The last thing a presenter wants is to bore the audience to death by PowerPoint where the words are written verbatim on the slides. Voice-over can add the detail and explanation that should accompany a presentation providing useful insight and information.

JING

Sometimes an agency may need to create a tutorial on how to use something on the computer. For tasks such as this, a screen-capturing software is needed. Jing (www.jing.com) offers a solution. Many of the Five-Minute Tutorials were created using Jing. For this particular software, the "limited free" version allows only five-minute videos to be created. The user is then provided the option to have the video uploaded where a link is then provided to the user so that the video can be accessed and shared with others. This is a low budget solution for some of the more complicated explanations for those needing to know how to use a system. Now, this is the obvious reason to use Jing, but what about other useful solutions? If a group is reviewing a set of photos where a verbal explanation with a pointer is needed due to the situation having dynamic needs, then Jing would be a very good solution. Plans can be pulled up and explained, and quickly developed "best practices" can be shared. As with so many of the technologies available, it's up to the practitioner to see through the transparent uses to the more strategic uses that are not so obvious that aid in effectively managing disaster situations. So, although something is created for an intended use, other beneficial ways of utilizing the same *application* or *technology* can be limited only by one's imagination.

YOUTUBE

YouTube is the most popular site to place videos. These accounts are free and a range of formats can be uploaded and viewed. YouTube is used for a variety of purposes and all of these media provide the user a link and also the code such that the video can be embedded into a Web page or other social networking site. Here is an amateur video provided by the author: http://www.youtube.com/watch?v=wdyqffr8fO8.

206

YouTube or some other provider could be leveraged by emergency management if resources were deliberately located or identified so that all other emergency management agencies (EMAs) or crisis communications personnel could find them. Reservoirs of videos could be created where each group could use them for its own purposes. So, really good videos showing responders how to conduct a task, for example, could be shared with one another, providing expertise to one another and the world. People could vote on which of these videos they found most useful and automatically help retrieve the most useful. This could be similar to the American Idol of emergency management videos and presentations.

STREAMING LIVE VIDEO

uStream (www.uStream.com) is a professional site where a lot of government and other reputable organizations Live stream events free. Once the event is over, the video is visible to an audience. All of these social media have it so that anyone can view the content or it is available only to a private group. This helps create more uses as more sensitive videos can be private and where educational ones can be public and viewable by the masses. www.bambuser.com is another streaming site offering such services, but uStream seems to have captured the more business-oriented professionals whereas Bambuser is used more by the public for fun and appears less sophisticated. uStream is covered more in Chapter 9 as a method to help aggregate data provided it brings in a multiple of social media and ways to interact into one site.

STATISTICS

Statistics are provided by all of these sites offering useful information for emergency management (EM) to help determine effectiveness. Some videos may be more popular for viewing. With educational videos, this is an important bit of information that can help EM focus on best practices with its viewing target audience.

There are ways to track who is Following you or who has Unfollowed you, how many people Like your Fan Page, who looked at your Website or watched your video. Many of these systems have their own unique ways of informing the creator of useful information that shows the traffic on the site. Facebook provides profile stats now that are mailed to the

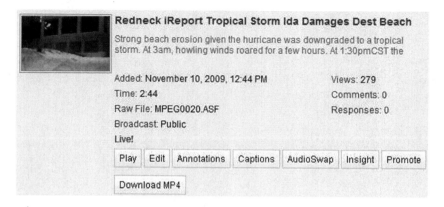

Redneck iReport Tropical Storm Ida Damages Dest Beach

Strong beach erosion given the hurricane was downgraded to a tropical storm. At 3am, howling winds roared for a few hours. At 1:30pmCST the

Added: November 10, 2009, 12:44 PM   Views: 279

Time: 2:44   Comments: 0

Raw File: MPEG0020.ASF   Responses: 0

Broadcast: Public

Live!

| Play | Edit | Annotations | Captions | AudioSwap | Insight | Promote |

| Download MP4 |

FIGURE 7.9   Number of views as an indicator.

user and also provide stats on Fan pages. However, these stats need to be analyzed carefully and viewed with a critical eye. Many of the Members or Followers may not be part of the target population, but may be merely others interested in Emergency Management Facebook Sites. Marketers and other groups may be included in stats. Although there are many confounding factors to consider in these numbers, they do provide some feedback on the use of a site and should be monitored. The agency may find that people are not finding their information. This could be an indicator that the proper keywords are not being used or that their attempt to be known on the online environment may not have the number base desired. These sorts of objectives should be listed in the initial design. This helps provide the agency with useful information. Figure 7.9 provides a simple example of how one can analyze if a video is being seen or not by tracking the number of views.

KEYWORDS

When uploading videos, if the public is to view the video, then proper keywords should be used. Single words clearly describing the video should be used and none repeated. Repeating keywords does not add to a successful search.

Groups should get together and create a common set of syntax for specific needs. For example, if groups were going to deliberately try to build up a video bank of useful online educational lessons, at present, there would need to be some structured way of identifying and, thus, retrieving these materials so that people can find what they want.

MAPPING, COLLABORATION, AND COLLECTIVE INTELLIGENCE

Mapping applications provide a useful tool for crisis communications. The Web-based tools are very easy to use, can be accessed with any Web browser, and are accessible through mobile applications. It is having the power to add so much media-rich data to a map in a collaborative real-time fashion that makes these tools so powerful. Right after a disaster has occurred is when information is needed the most, but is lacking the greatest. Providing people at the scene the ability to upload comments, photos, videos, news links, locations, and other such information creates a way to create situational awareness in an expedited time frame. This reduces the time that it takes for responders and others to discover and report incidents. This also provides the decision makers the ability to see what is going on while not on location, but from anywhere there is an Internet connection and a browser.

This segment is not about teaching you how to use these maps, but is presented to expose you to some of the mapping applications available.

Google Maps

Google Maps is an application provided through the Google Suite of free tools that we have already covered. There are numerous applications that should be explored and this one is no exception. Google Maps provide the everyday citizen or organization a way to customize a map to fit their needs. Any information can be added by anybody, making collaborative efforts most fruitful when quick data entry is needed. Options are provided in Figure 7.10. You can create your own map in a matter of seconds.

Detailed information can be added by you and anyone you allow, or it can be open to everyone. Directions can be provided, bridges that are out can be distinguished by "pinning" a balloon or icon that represents information that can include details, or a photo or video. Many of the systems and smartphones have geoLocation devices inherent to the hardware that provide much more useful information when needed. These maps are accessible and modifiable through the Android mobile smartphone. The

209

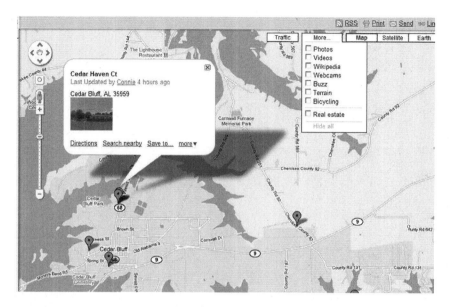

FIGURE 7.10 Google Map options.

smart technology provided in these mobile devices is very powerful as directions can be navigated by voice and directions are available for driving or walking. Simply having the ability to have the My Location feature that maps wherever you may be and displays it on your phone is phenomenal. This is obviously a powerful tool when things are in disarray.

Google Earth

Google Earth is an incredible application downloadable from earth. google.com where any address can be put into the search space and the corresponding location will come into view. Many layers of data are offered to help maximize the visual needed for a purpose. Google Earth has 3D imagery and can "fly" you anywhere on the globe. Figure 7.11 shows the initial view before zooming into a location. Google Earth has a host of features. It's up to the user to determine which of these systems will best fit the needs of the agency in order to help reach the objectives. Also, each of these systems has different functionalities to offer. One may be helpful in one situation where another may be used for another.

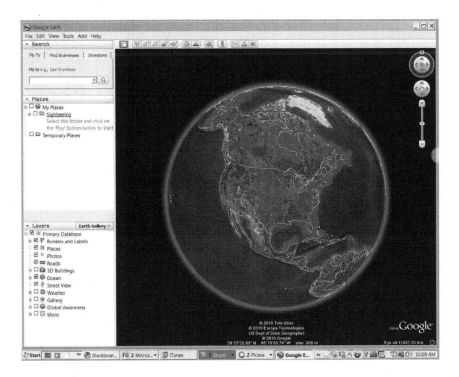

FIGURE 7.11 Screenshot of Google Earth interface.

Collaborative Mapping

There is a huge ongoing effort to provide maps and the ability to create maps for anyone anywhere. Maps are offered for free, some of which are greatly detailed and others not. A community can build information on top of present information that is offered in "layers." Each layer of existing geographical data provides more detailed information, such as state and local boundaries, streets, and businesses. The uses of these maps are limitless for emergency management. Others around the world are providing us with examples of just how useful something like this can be during the aftermath of a disaster. Katrina devastated the citizens of New Orleans, isolating them from one another throughout the city and surrounding areas. The same proprietary software exists now that existed then and yet the results and lack of information just demonstrates how useless this sort of information can be when it's not in the right hands. Many are leaving the "gaps" in data to be filled by civilians and

211

others who know the terrain better than anyone else. Knowing who is in trouble and where they are can prove to be a more daunting task than previously thought, especially when it's in one of our most famous cities in the front yard of America.

OPEN SOURCE AND COMMUNITIES OF PRACTICE

Communities of groups aiding in emergency response consist of international groups that comprise many of the segments needed for response efforts. This is also true for the computer application development discussed in this chapter. Groups are coming together in an effort to push this idea into end products that can be used for a variety of purposes. Some of the groups are discussed below as an example of the growing movement.

RHoK

Another technological humanitarian movement is demonstrated through Random Hacks of Kindness: "A community of developers, geeks, and tech-savvy do-gooders around the world, working to develop software solutions that respond to the challenges facing humanity today" (www. rhok.org). By collaborating on a global level, the future holds enormous potential in the development of software that will not only be free and available to all, but will be superior to any proprietary product available. It's just a matter of time.

Crisis Mappers

An excellent description explaining the power of collaboration comes from the homepage of The International Network of Crisis Mappers: "Leveraging mobile platforms, computational linguistics, geospatial technologies, and visual analytics to power effective early warning for rapid response to complex humanitarian emergencies" (http://www.crisismappers.net/). It's the ability to have software support from anywhere in the world that can support an ongoing crisis situation for those needing it on the ground.

OpenStreetMaps

OpenStreetMaps is a combination of mapping applications and communities working together to populate the information onto a map. This collaborative mapping tool is very easy to use, which makes it available to a number of people. Sometimes, only the locals know how to describe where something may be found, providing descriptive details that are only locally known. It's by having a community contribute information to the map that will provide the details that may be needed in time-critical situations. OpenStreetMaps is a favorite used by many organizations (Figure 7.12).

Wikimapia

Another useful tool worth exploring is Wikimapia. It is "an online editable map—you can describe any place on Earth, or just surf the map discovering tons of already marked places" (www.wikimapia.com).

These systems, for the most part, are best utilized for response and recovery purposes. Given this, the maps also can be created ahead of time where multiple maps are on reserve to launch when a certain event has occurred. For example, evacuation routes should be created ahead of time so that they are ready to be used at any moment. However, other critical components need to be created to further help the emergency managers and planners best analyze the scenarios that could happen, given the threats of an area. Questions such as: How will flooding affect area A given x amount of rain has occurred over y amount of time? Given the tremendous efforts going on in the humanitarian open source software system community, these additional functionalities may be created and available sooner than we think.

FREE WEB-BASED DISASTER MANAGEMENT SYSTEMS

Humanitarian free and open source software (hFOSS) is built specifically for humanitarian needs. This software is used not so much in the United States as it is in other countries. These systems are proving most beneficial and are developing to meet the needs of all emergency management agencies. The Haiti earthquake is used as the foundation in which to present a case where such hFOSS systems were successfully implemented and used. Communications, language barriers, and other challenges are met head on by these groups who are creating more sophisticated systems as we speak.

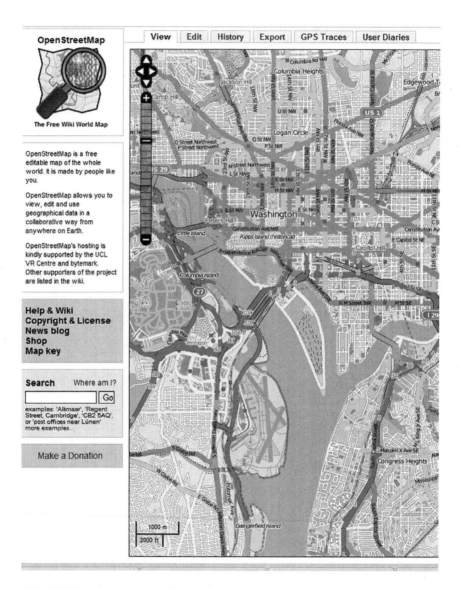

FIGURE 7.12 An example of OpenStreetMaps.

ONSITE WITH DANIELE MALERBA

THE HAITI EARTHQUAKE

On Tuesday, January 12, 2010, a 7.0 earthquake occurred 10 miles southwest of the heavily populated capital Port-au-Prince, Haiti. Over 230,000 people were killed and the country's infrastructure was severely damaged. The international response between different nongovernmental (NGO) and international organizations was swift and without delay, sending people and goods quickly in order to assist during the response and recovery efforts.

Although mobile phones were still able to send and receive information over the network, phone calls were impossible to make due to the congested phone stations. One of the most problematic issues after major disasters is that cellular phone base stations are unable to put through the massive amount of calls that are being made by worried friends and relatives of potential victims. It is, therefore, difficult for people to send and receive calls because the lines are overloaded beyond capacity. Texting provides an alternative and feasible way to communicate under such conditions. Short message service and mobile Internet connections do not need to be live; congested phone stations can sort these messages quickly and deliver them to those in need.

As it was initially impossible for Haitians to communicate with their relatives by using live calls, some of them turned to other forms of information-sharing, relying on text messages and tweets in order to be able to inform relatives about their families' welfare.

Social media was used to send help requests and news over the net, becoming a bastion for both news channels and relatives abroad. According to *The Guardian* (www.guardian.co.uk), "Twitterfeeds gave an impressive picture of the ongoing earthquake and the *Guardian's* live blog on the rescue mission used social media as well as information from other news organizations." CNN even opened a section on its Website called *What we're hearing via social media*, where a group of journalists was analyzing tweets on the Haitian catastrophe in order to filter messages of condolence from first-hand news. Further, social network use in news broadcasting after emergencies encouraged a greater engagement of people living outside the disaster area who felt sympathetic toward the affected population.

As reported by most news organizations, the Haiti earthquake brought about a massive response by both the island's residents and the world population. Because most people were cut off conventional media due to its unavailability in the aftermath of the quake, it became essential for the Haitian population to find alternative ways to communicate with relatives and rescuers.

Because the Internet connection was only working sporadically, Twitter, above all others, became a vital means with which to share thoughts, requests, and messages. The information from these tweets proved to be a vital part of crisis communications. As an example of such, the following table provides an analysis of the tweets tweeted immediately after the quake. These were categorized into three emergency functions: assessment, coordination, and response.

The assessment groups provided first responders with information of the problems resulting from the disaster. Coordination and response involved the actual research of injured people by inquiring about resources and, further, locating the injured.

Table 7.1 shows a selection of tweets published on Tuesday and Wednesday, the first two days after the earthquake. This is used as an example of how social networks are now starting to help the public share vital information amongst friends and loved ones in moments of major distress.

The use of social networks made by part of the Haitian population immediately after the quake showed that employing Twitter as an emergency platform is perhaps the clearest demonstration that new technology mixed with broadband connections and know-how can lead to better results than the adoption of conventional systems.

Because information posted on social networks entered into the public domain for the first time, those who were eager to help were able to do so by surfing the Internet. Twitter and social networks eventually helped create a rapid response team based in New York City mostly composed of Haitian immigrants living in the United States. As first responders were mostly English speaking and as Haiti's official languages are Haitian Creole and French, it became imperative to interpret the tweets, thereby providing its members with reliable information on people's location and needs.

216

Table 7.1 Tweets categorized

Assessment	Coordination	Response
"oh shiet heavy earth quake right now! in haiti"	"were ok at the oloffson.. internet is on !! no phones ! hope all are okay..alot of big building in PAP* are down!"	"If anyone in Haiti is reading this, please go out and help in the streets, it's very ugly out there if you haven't seen it #haiti @eq"
(5 p.m.)	(6 p.m.)	(8 p.m.)
"Earthquake 7 Richter in Haiti, just happening #Haiti"	"there is a tsunami alert ! everyone stay safe !! fires seem to also be burning in downtown PAP"*	"After Shock every 10 Mns! I can't stay where I am! I have to be in a safe place! I got All the Message! I will do my best To Call ur family"
(5 p.m.)	(6 p.m.)	(8 p.m.)
"Just about all the lights are out in Port au Prince.. people still screaming but the noise is dying as darkness sets"	"If U Need To get in Touch With Friends & Family in Haiti. Send me a Private Message with names and Phone Numbers. I'll get Back to U!"	"It's really ugly, just like in a bad dream. People need help, get out and help ! #haiti @eq"
(6 p.m.)	(7 p.m.)	(10 p.m.)
"Port au Prince is dark except for a few fires"	"Just came back from market. It looks like ground zero. People are trapped it's dark we need light and cell phone service"	"Phones are working somewhat in Haiti. Can't get a hold of my family though."
(7 p.m.)	(10 p.m.)	(8 a.m. – Wednesday)
"Phones are mostly down but sometimes you get lucky.. I hear that epi center of quake was near PauP @ asger_leth"	"all my guests slept in the driveway last night.. people came up from the streets thinking they were bodies.. neighbors helping neighbors"	"there are going to be shortages of food, water, medical supplies.. partially buried bodies will create health issues soon"
(10 p.m.)	(12 p.m.)	(12 p.m.)
"dead bodies are everywhere I havent seen one ambulance or any professionl med care anywhere in port-au-prince"	"The Rain is coming. Help! Coleman donate tents to Haiti we need shelter."	"The St Gerard Church has a school behind it that collapsed.I heard someone speaking from the rubble, feet were trapped he couldn't get out"
(12 p.m.)	(5 p.m. - Wednesday)	(6 p.m. – Wednesday)

Note: Twitter updates in Haiti.
* Port-au-Prince

Haitian volunteers living in North America started translating messages arriving to them from social networks as well as from local NGOs, sending them back to first responders within a matter of minutes (www.wired.com).

This particular cooperation between translators and responders was made possible because of the fulfillment of two important concepts of communication during emergency situations treated in this book: first, the use of existing social relations between individuals, that is, to encourage residents to help professional first responders during the first stages of the relief efforts; and second, the use of new technologies that bypass the well-known bottleneck created by the unavailability of conventional means of communication in the immediate aftermath of the emergency.

The high-tech response in Haiti mostly depended on personal connections shared on the Internet, which provoked an expansion of the borders within which first relief was possible.

Social networking and information and communication technologies (ICTs), in general, therefore, are becoming a viable solution for affected populations and emergency managers accordingly, since they are starting to be used and monitored in the many different phases of disaster relief effort.

Although many countries are now fully connected and their citizens are becoming Internet literate, many others do not have the same advantage. According to a report by *InternetWorldStats.com*, only 1,966,514,816 (29 percent) people were using the Internet in 2010, out of a world population of 6,845,609,960. Although penetration rates are high in North America, Europe, Asia, and Oceania, they are still poor in the rest of the world. The graph in Figure 7.13 shows differences of Internet availability in different areas of the world.

The contribution that new media can bring to emergency planning, response, and recovery depends on particular issues related to the availability of Internet connections, their stability after emergency situations, and the Internet literacy of those involved.

Note: Daniele Malerba is a consultant with the IT department at the World Food Program.

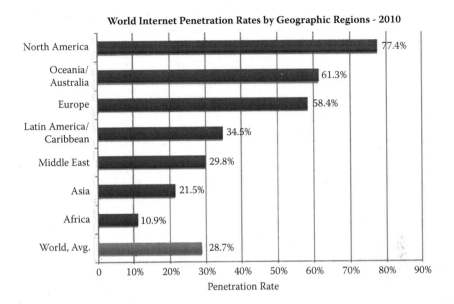

FIGURE 7.13 Internet availability in different areas of the world. (From Internet World Stats: www.internetworldststs.com/stats.htm)

Haiti Earthquake Case Study

The Haiti earthquake demonstrated an unprecedented international humanitarian response from the technology sector. A global community of civilians from different countries with a unified purpose came to the aid of the grief stricken country. This will be used as a case study showcasing two successful hFOSS disaster management systems, Ushahidi and Sahana. First, a description of the Haiti earthquake will be presented along with considerations of ongoing barriers that response and communications had to overcome. A variety of Free and Open Source Software for humanitarian response came to the aid of the Haitian people. Some of these systems will be described providing information on how they can be used by any emergency management agency anywhere, anytime. Actually, it is preferable that a system is used prior to the occurrence of a disastrous event. It's best to have organization information and resources available. Crowdsourcing and other nontraditional ways of gathering human resources for unexpected emergent response comes in the form of crowdsourcing, formal and informal. CrisisCamps are commonplace around the globe bringing a variety of groups together over a few days with one goal in mind: brainstorming and volunteering to help ongoing efforts that may be technology based. All of the groups interacting at a CrisisCamp have one thing in common, helping others (crisiscamp.com).

FREE AND OPEN SOURCE DISASTER MANAGEMENT SYSTEMS

Humanitarian free and open source systems (hFOSS) exist for disaster management. These systems are built specifically to meet the needs of response and recovery efforts. Such systems are built and maintained by a global team of volunteers for the most part. hFOSS is used around the world, but not so much in the United States. Our EMAs have proprietary software, which has great functionality if you can afford it and the hardware needed to support it. hFOSS has a community working together developing systems to meet the needs of those suffering from natural-, manmade-, and terrorist-related disasters. These systems are free for organizations to use and implement any way they want. Since these systems are licensed under the GNU (stands for: GNU's not Unix) (http://www.gnu.org), they can be customized and modified by any group to use in any capacity. These systems are very dynamic and are growing at a feverish rate. Software developers from around the world, at universities, and in volunteerism efforts, are congregating and organizing in efforts to increase the availability of disaster management systems to those in need. Sahana actually self deployed in response to Haiti's earthquake (Prutsalis et al., 2010), providing support to those on the ground and to those trying to organize efforts. They immediately began working on a module to support the needs of the hospitals. Many hospitals had been lost due to the damage, others were running in part, and newly erected hospitals surfaced. It was important that the people on the ground knew what was where, who had what supplies, and if there was room for victims, not to mention if the roads leading from point A to point B were open. Two very popular systems will be covered here: The Sahana Disaster Management System and Ushahidi. Others are sure to follow and it's the hFOSS, collaboration, volunteerism, and crowdsourcing that make such systems so powerful.

Ushahidi

Ushahidi was created originally to report acts of violence that occurred after the Kenya elections of 2008. A great number of people successfully

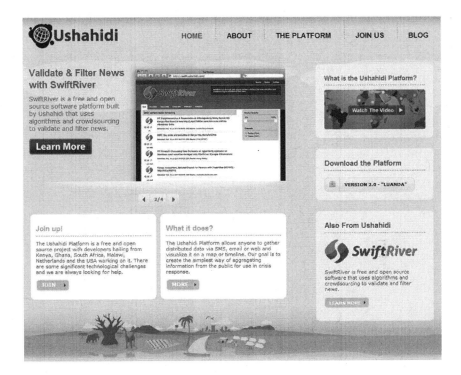

FIGURE 7.14 Ushahidi's home page.

used it. It was soon realized that this software could be used to aid in humanitarian efforts and was critical in the response efforts of Haiti (Figure 7.14).

From Ushahidi's Website:

> Our goal is to create a platform that any person or organization can use to set up their own way to collect and visualize information. The core platform will allow for plug-in and extensions so that it can be customized for different locales and needs. The beta version platform is now available as an open source application that others can download for free, implement and use to bring awareness to crisis situations or other events in their own locales, it is also continually being improved tested with various partners primarily in Kenya. Organizations can also use the tool for internal monitoring or visualization purposes http://www.ushahidi.com/ (accessed January 5, 2011).

ONSITE WITH PAT TRESSEL AND FRAN BOON

SAHANA EDEN AND THE HAITI RESPONSE

Sahana Eden (Emergency Development ENvironment)[1] *(numbers in brackets denote Links located at the end of the section)*, a project of the Sahana Software Foundation [2], is a Web services platform designed for rapid application development. It provides a number of applications and development tools out of the box (mapping; situation assessment; registries for persons, organizations, hospitals, and shelters; messaging; import and export in many data formats, etc.) with more on the way (logistics, volunteer, and task management). It is built on the web2py [3] Web services platform, which is designed to be simple to use, and which provides Web security, Web page templating, and interoperation with many database management systems. Eden adds a REST layer and convenience features for handling complex schemas. Adding and extending applications is easy—components from existing applications can often be adapted or used intact. Volunteer software engineers assist with development and deployment. Eden is used by several colleges in open-source development courses. Modules developed and ready to use are demonstrated in Figure 7.15.

Eden was deployed in response to the Haiti earthquake and Pakistan floods in 2010 [4,5]. Here, we describe briefly what was done, what was effective and what wasn't, and, when it was not effective, what the cause might be, and how to resolve it.

Mapping

Up-to-date street maps were not available for Port au Prince at the time of the Haiti earthquake, which hampered responder efforts. Following the earthquake, both government agencies and private organizations made high-resolution satellite imagery available [6].

This unprecedented public access to satellite data enabled the global OpenStreetMap community, in only 26 hours (working from their home locations outside the affected area and using their usual tools and processes) to trace Port au Prince streets, adding information on collapsed buildings and spontaneous settlements (both tents in the streets outside people's homes and larger

What is Sahana Eden?

Sahana Eden is a Family of Applications to Help You Help Others.

Solutions are available for Disaster Management, Emergency Management, Development, Humanitarian and Environmental sectors.

Free and Open Source means that it is easily Customisable and Extensible.

- ➪ Project Brief

The following modules are available:

- **Requests Management** - Tracks requests for aid and matches them against donors who have pledged aid.
- **Volunteer Management** - Manage volunteers by capturing their skills, availability and allocation.
- **Missing Persons Registry** - Report and Search for Missing Persons.
- **Disaster Victim Identification**.
- **Shelter Registry** - Tracks the location, distibution, capacity and breakdown of victims in Shelters.
- **Hospital Management System** - Hospitals can share information on resources & needs.
- **Organization Registry** - "Who is doing What & Where". Allows relief agencies to coordinate their activities.
- **Ticketing** - Master Message Log to process incoming reports & requests.
- **Delphi Decision Maker** - Supports the decision making of large groups of Experts.
- **Mapping** - Situation Awareness & Geospatial Analysis.
- **Messaging** - Sends & Receives Alerts via Email & SMS.
- **Document Library** - A library of digital resources, such as Photos & Office documents.

Sahana Eden is a project of the Sahana Software Foundation

- Want to Use Sahana Eden?
- Want to Contribute Sahana Eden?

FIGURE 7.15   Sahana disaster management modules.

encampments) [7]. The satellite images were of such high resolution that damage to buildings was clearly visible. Street names were added, based on old (1994) public-domain U.S. military topographic maps, which were scanned and georeferenced [8].

These newly constructed maps were converted for use on handheld GPS units, which first responders then used to navigate in Port au Prince.

They were also made available on the Web, on many sites. (The map is currently online at Telascience [9], though information drawn from other servers that have since been taken down, such as the Sahana Haiti server, is no longer available.)

Haitians outside the country, working through Crowdflower [10] and SamaSource [11] (two crowdsourcing businesses), used the maps along with their knowledge of the affected area and the language of local report, to extract and verify information from SMS messages sent from Port au Prince, and thus locate people trapped under the rubble.

These maps were also used as part of the Humanitarian Information Center (HIC) mapping products. The author made extensive use of the Google Earth Super-Overlay when planning the installation of wireless networks in Port au Prince for NetHope [12] (Figure 7.16).

FIGURE 7.16 Fran Boon, with NetHope at the time—a consortium of 32 of the leading international humanitarian organizations, providing long-distance wifi connections to member offices, medical teams, and local NGOs.

An attempt was made to generate maps for Pakistan following the floods, but with much less success largely due to a lack of either publicly available satellite imagery or street maps.

Organization Registry

Sahana was asked by responding agencies to provide a tool for entering and viewing a database of all the responding agencies. This database was populated both by professional representatives of the agencies and by volunteers collecting information from whatever sources they could find. Information for nearly 700 organizations was recorded. This effort was deemed successful, as the organization database was used to help coordination.

Hospital Registry

Sahana was asked by the Pan-American Health Organization (PAHO) to provide a tool for entering and displaying a database of medical facilities. A "GeoLocate the Hospitals Challenge" [13] was established that had a great response from the global community of volunteers, creatively using a number of sources to get details for all the hospitals. By the time the challenge was ended, 162 medical facilities were recorded. (This was just three short of the total eventually found.) The challenge succeeded because it was a simple, well-structured task. Figure 7.17 shows the interface of functions provided in the module.

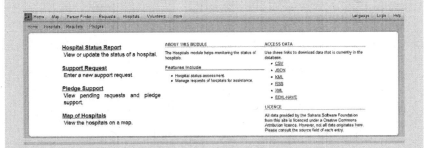

FIGURE 7.17 Interface of functions provided in the module of medical facilities.

The hospital data was then exported, using the open EDXL-HAVE standard [14], into PAHO's internal systems. PAHO then extended the database to include pharmacies (this information had to be gathered by personnel on the ground), and served as the master repository of medical facility data for responders.

A contrasting data collection method was used when Sahana supported Humanity Road [15] during the Exercise 24 [16] disaster simulation. Humanity Road (HR) was tasked with providing a database of medical facilities for several Southern California counties, and parts of Baja California. Hospital data was obtained from a Medicare database. A commercial database that permitted limited free access provided the number of beds in each hospital. Smaller clinics and Mexican hospitals were obtained from local online directories. For the more structured sources, text was extracted from Web pages, collected in spreadsheets, and reformatted into CSV files, then uploaded directly into the Sahana database, bypassing the user interface. HR volunteers then entered the remaining facilities from unstructured data, and geocoded the addresses. There were 275 facilities entered in this manner by half a dozen HR volunteers and one Sahana programmer communicating closely via Skype.

Short Code 4636

Before the quake, Haiti had been preparing for an election. Ushahidi [17] had acquired a short code to use with their election-monitoring tool. When the earthquake hit, InSTEDD [18] worked with the local Telcos to get this short code put into operation early and without charge.

Availability of the service was advertised in Port au Prince using loudspeakers on trucks (since radio service was down, and trapped people were more likely to have functioning mobile phones than any other means of communication). This announcement was further relayed by citizens via their mobile phones. Messages from trapped people, often to their relatives, were relayed to 4636.

InSTEDD repurposed their Emergency Information Service to process SMS messages received on 4636 for the Red Cross, U.S. military, and other first responders. Crowdflower and SamaSource volunteers translated the received messages from Kreyol, geolocated them, and called the senders back to verify incidents and get more information, since the original messages were often insufficiently detailed.

Request Management

After the initial effort of pulling survivors from the rubble, the messages became more focused on other needs: requests for water, food, and shelter. Sahana was asked to provide a Request Management tool to allow NGOs to match these requests with pledges for support (based on a model that had worked in previous emergencies for government agencies). The tool was built; however, this isn't a way that NGOs are used to operating, so the tool was not used for Haiti.

Issues

Two main issues determined whether a particular application was adopted and used. First was whether the assumptions about workflow and data built into the application matched the procedures commonly used by aid organizations. Second was the presence of an organization that actively wanted to use the application, especially, one that had requested the application. Other issues included language barriers, lack of support for ad hoc volunteers or NGOs from major aid agencies or governmental agencies, and simple exhaustion of workers on the ground.

Mismatch between software and user procedures is addressed by a fundamental principle of software engineering: customer-centered design. Users and domain experts should be deeply involved in application design to be sure the resulting product will fit the processes they have in place. As critics of humanitarian ICT have warned, responder agencies do not have the time or attention to devote to adapting their procedures to the software [19].

One example of this mismatch was mentioned above—a request management tool that merely allowed posting requests for aid and offers of aid. Another example may better illustrate the issue. An incident reporting tool was implemented that allowed a user to enter a report as unstructured text. But responder agencies couldn't easily make use of unstructured text [20]. It had to be reread and interpreted by another human, and could easily be missing important information just because there was nothing in the user interface to remind the user to provide the information. What agencies normally did was assessments using detailed forms. This highly structured data required no reinterpretation and could be collated into reports, and the user gathering the data did not need to think about what to include. The incident report tool was replaced by a rapid assessment tool using standards developed by multiple agencies [21].

Links

[1] http://eden.sahanafoundation.org
[2] http://www.sahanafoundation.org
[3] http://web2py.com/
[4] http://wiki.sahanafoundation.org/lib/exe/fetch.php/
      sahana-ictd-case-study-2.pdf, section 6 and following
[5] http://www.slideshare.net/SahanaFOSS/
      sahana-haiti-iscram050310narrated
[6] http://wiki.openstreetmap.org/wiki/WikiProject_Haiti/
      Imagery_and_data_sources
[7] http://wiki.openstreetmap.org/wiki/WikiProject_Haiti
[8] http://wiki.openstreetmap.org/wiki/WikiProject_Haiti/
      Street_names
[9] http://hypercube.telascience.org/haiti/
[10] http://crowdflower.com/
[11] http://www.samasource.org/
[12] http://www.nethope.org/
[13] http://wiki.sahanafoundation.org/phase2/doku.php/hai
      ti:geolocatehospitalchallenge
[14] http://docs.oasis-open.org/emergency/edxl-have/os/
      emergency_edxl_have-1.0-spec-os.pdf
[15] http://humanityroad.wordpress.com/
      virtual-emergency-operations-center/
[16] http://24.inrelief.org/
[17] http://www.ushahidi.com/
[18] http://www.instedd.org/
[19] Paul Currion, "What Technology Wants" http://www.
      humanitarian.info/2010/09/28/what-technology-wants/
[20] http://www.humanitarian.info/2010/07/30/
      on-crowdsourcing-with-a-big-sigh/
[21] http://www.ecbproject.org/page/48

ONSITE WITH PAT TRESSEL AND SEAN CONNOR

PLAYSOURCING: GAMES FOR GOOD

SMS message received during 2010 Haiti earthquake:

> *On a besoin d Aide en nourriture, eau, etc .c est Hector numero, nan 3*
> *avenue du travail #26 nou yon 50taine ,pa bliye nou svp 2 main.response*
>   *We need help with food, water, etc. Phone number is_ we are located at*
> *3 avenue du Travail room 26. We are about 50 people. Please do not forget*
> *us tomorrow. Please answer.*

Disaster strikes. Reports start appearing from the public—incomplete, unstructured reports, sent on various media with locations specified only via local landmarks, in the local language. These could contain valuable information, but … extracting it isn't something aid workers are trained to do, and it would pull them away from actually responding. What to do?

When Steve Fossett's plane disappeared over the Nevada desert, Amazon.com offered the use of their Mechanical Turk platform, where volunteers examined satellite images and identified those that showed signs of a crash.

During the 2010 Haiti earthquake, trapped people phoned relatives, who sent SMS messages to a dedicated short code. Later, survivors sent requests for aid. These were unstructured messages, with locations incompletely specified, in a language not known to most non-Haitian aid workers. Haitians living abroad, who spoke Kreyol and were familiar with the area, worked via Crowdflower and SamaSource (suppliers of personnel for short-term tasks) to interpret and geocode the messages, and fill in missing information by calling the senders.

One common criticism of crowdsourcing is that the data it yields are unstructured, partial, and unverified. The Haiti earthquake example suggests a solution—point more people at the problem, to do translation, data cleaning, image interpretation, classification, etc., of raw crowdsourced data. That is, for crowd(source) control, we want another crowd.

Tasks, like image interpretation, dealing with incomplete and unstructured text, researching missing information, and communicating with people are hard to automate, but people do quite well. As a play on "artificial intelligence," these types of work are called "human intelligence tasks" (HITs), or, as Amazon.com calls it, "artificial artificial intelligence."

How can we find people to work on HITs during emergencies? Relying on getting the word out and assembling an ad hoc set of volunteers after a crisis has occurred suffers from precisely the charge most often levied against crowdsourcing—one cannot guarantee that a crowd will show up. So let's consider ways of efficiently recruiting and marshaling a crowd in advance, and one that's trained, motivated, and available when needed.

Two currently available means for gathering workers are:

1. Use an existing HIT service, such as Mechanical Turk, Crowdflower, or SamaSource. These are commercial services, but have donated use of their systems to humanitarian efforts.
2. Find volunteers through agencies that maintain standing volunteer pools, or through registries or Web portals for matching volunteers to needs.

Both are viable sources of volunteers, but have some drawbacks.

- For commercial HIT platforms, even if the use of the platform is offered for free, we would still need people. The registered workers are there to earn money. We would be asking them to put that aside to volunteer, or we would need funding. If we want to recruit new volunteers for a current crisis, we are right back at the problem of getting a crowd to show up.
- Volunteer agencies may not happen to have people with the needed skills, especially language. Agencies may need to be identified or established in some regions. Getting people motivated to volunteer based on altruism alone may not draw large numbers of volunteers, especially not in advance of a crisis.

We would like to propose a way of generating and motivating a pool of volunteers: "playsourcing." Think of all the people who are, at this moment, playing sudoku online, or commenting on political blog sites, or posting on their Facebook page, or tending their FarmVille farm, or playing World of Warcraft. In particular, consider all the people who are doing those things intently and with dedication, all the while thinking, "I should really be doing something else." We believe we can get some of that motivation, and give participants something they can feel good about doing, by embedding humanitarian HITs in a social game.

Playsourcing was introduced at the International Conference on Crisis Mapping on October 1, 2010, by Brett Horvath and Sean Conner of Kila Ventures. A proof of concept was implemented three weeks later at the first Geeks without Bounds hackathon, where the game Play This Or People Die! was one of the winning entries. The task was to translate, geocode, and classify SMS messages and tweets. It had a custom Web UI to display the tasks in an appealing manner. Awarded badges could be displayed on the user's Facebook page. The UI requested tasks from, and sent users' solutions to, a back end implemented using Sahana Eden. The back end received messages, managed tasks and users' solutions, and stored player data: skills (e.g., languages known) and experience points awarded for completing tasks.

"Useful games" go back farther. These have been used to solve or make headway on difficult scientific or data analysis problems. Some examples:

1. Foldit: Protein folding, determining the 3D shape that a sequence of amino acids will assume, is very hard to solve automatically. So, it has been cast as a HIT game. Players help predict protein structure, and also design new proteins of desired shapes.
2. The ESP Game (now Google Image Labeler): Classifying images according to what objects are in them is a goal of machine learning. Unfortunately, training a classifier requires images that have already been labeled according to what they show—a chicken and egg problem. As you have no doubt guessed, this need is satisfied by a game in which people label images. There's a catch. The player's choice has to be checked. This is incorporated into the game by pairing up players— they view the same image, but pick labels independently. If both choose the same label, they get points.

What are the potential benefits of turning humanitarian HITs into a game?

1. It can tap into an expanded pool of volunteers.
   a. Can reach people who might not be in the loop for volunteer opportunities.
   b. Can reach technically proficient users, e.g., the (video) gaming community.
2. Adding social interaction can improve motivation and help develop a volunteer community.

  a. Give participants recognition awards that they can display on social networks.
  b. Provide a way for players to interact while they are participating.
  c. Allow players to find each other on social networks.
  d. Reward players for assisting other players.
3. Participants may continue working longer.
  a. Make participation fun through rewards and entertaining design.
  b. Pacing of reward delivery keeps people playing to earn the next reward. (This is true even when people know it's happening.)
4. Volunteers can gain experience in advance of need.
  a. Can invite participation at any time with nonemergency tasks.
  b. Participant skills can be catalogued and evaluated.
  c. Participants can practice on actual crowdsourced data collected in prior events or simulated data for anticipated needs.

What features would be useful or fun to include in the game? Pretty much anything that can go into a social game or puzzle game, and possibly more active types of computer games, so long as the player isn't distracted while they are actually working on the task.

- Rewards: Experience points, levels, badges, titles, decorations—these all convey status. Exporting badges or announcing rewards to social networks lets the user show off their good works. The player might even be rewarded with virtual items for a virtual domain they are building in another game.
- Kudos: There are also nonacquisitive rewards: fireworks, a cheering crowd, a fanfare can all deliver a virtual pat on the back for a job well done.
- Collaboration: Adding a way for players to communicate can build a sense of community and allow them to assist each other.
- Competition: Show ranking of players and teams. Arrange competitions to encourage practice.
- Entertainment: Players need breaks from the tasks, but if they leave the game, they might get caught up in something else. One can offer a short game of Pakman, or suggest doing desk exercises along with an animated instructor.

- Imaginative display: Graphics can help convey the purpose and importance of the player's mission.
- Framing story: Tasks can be made part of an adventure without altering the tasks. For instance, Nintendo's "Professor Layton" game series inserts standard logic puzzles into a mystery story.
- Related news and information: Providing a news feed related to humanitarian work or emergency management can introduce the player to the larger humanitarian community.

What common game features should be avoided? Distractions are sometimes introduced intentionally into games to make them harder and increase tension or excitement.

- Timer: Users should take whatever time they need. The timer itself can be distracting.
- Animation: Like a timer, anything moving in the UI during the task is a visual distraction.
- Music or other sound: Although music is commonly considered to be innocuous, it may decrease performance on mental tasks.
- Animation and sound can make fine rewards, just not while the user is concentrating. If music is offered, the game should provide an option to disable it during tasks. Some users may prefer a plain interface so they should be allowed to turn off decorative graphics and animations.

Let's look in more detail at what a playsourcing system might involve. A HIT might be combined with a game in two ways:

1. The tasks themselves are unmodified. The game aspect enters via UI design and rewards.
2. Tasks are embedded in a story-based or role-playing game. This is possibly more entertaining, but much harder to implement. Gameplay could obscure the task or direct player concentration to the story rather than the task, possibly leading to poorer solutions.

Because of the risk of incorrect solutions in the second case, it is safer to present the tasks without modification.

If the HITs are not altered to fit the game, then the game aspect can be separated from the HIT aspect. This has an additional advantage. A game front end could communicate with a HIT back end system through a standardized application programming interface (API), allowing multiple styles of games to be developed and used interchangeably with multiple HIT systems. This also splits software development work along a natural dividing line; game developers are unlikely to be experienced in areas that might be involved in a HIT system: volunteer management, verifying user solutions, or the specific tasks needed (mapping, translation, classification). Likewise, developers with appropriate experience for working on a HIT back end—Web services, personnel testing and training, data analysis—might have no other game experience than playing.

That's not the only point at which the system might benefit from a division of labor. Most game systems have a game engine, which is software that provides a toolkit of game elements and common operations. This allows creative designers to concentrate on gameplay and art, and not have to deal with programming. The game development community can be engaged to devise and implement an appropriate game engine as well as work on the creative side. Ideally, the game engine would be FOSS to allow collaboration between all interested groups and availability to EM agencies.

There are two main options for a HIT back end:

1. Use an existing commercial HIT platform, such as Mechanical Turk. Advantages are that the system already exists and can handle high volumes of activity. Disadvantages are that funding would be needed. Raw data for tasks might need to be adjusted to fit the system's format for tasks. Feeding in streams of SMS messages, tweets, or other asynchronous data might require staging.
2. Develop a system tailored to the specific tasks needed for EM. This could be implemented on top of an existing FOSS Web service, such as Ushahidi or Sahana Eden.

These are not mutually exclusive, and either type of back end might be useful. The actual means of communicating with these back ends might differ, so the recommended HIT API could be provided as a thin layer of software that the game engine calls, that in turn sends appropriate requests to a particular back end.

Although the HIT system isn't the focus of the playsource idea, it is important to obtaining reliable results and overcoming objections to crowdsourcing. The HIT system would handle:

- Task administration
  - Provide tools for EM managers to define tasks

- Receive crowdsourced data
- Assign tasks to users
- Store results and deliver them to EM agencies
- Volunteer management
  - Deliver training
  - Qualify volunteers as ready for specific tasks
  - Provide feedback to volunteers and statistics to agencies
  - Allow specifying trusted experts and promotion to expert status via training and testing
- Quality assurance
  - Support spot checking by experts
- Do automated cross-checking (e.g., dispatch the same task to multiple users and compare results)

Finally, we want to be sure the game interface adds value. How might it be evaluated?

- Compare a game interface (or several) to a plain one: How long do people continue? How well do they perform? Survey users.
- Examine how the above results differ across user populations and how people got involved: general public, gamers, humanitarian volunteers, students, EM professionals.
- It's not practical (and perhaps not possible) to simulate the psychological setting of a disaster for purposes of testing (or at least, the Human Subjects Board would frown on it). Instead, keep appropriate usage and performance statistics over time, and look at differences across real events.

How does all that address crowdsourcing issues? Recall this applies only when information is received from the public, not to tasks where trained volunteers are researching and generating the data. There are two areas of criticism, the first is the crowd itself:

- Can't count on the crowd to show up.
- If it does show up, it mills around wondering what to do.

We've already covered enticing the crowd to showing up, get trained, and be ready to act when needed; this is a central purpose of playsourcing.

The second area of criticism regards bad data:

- Low signal to noise ratio: redundant messages, messages with no useful information, noncritical messages

- Incomplete and unstructured data
- Spam, exaggeration, deliberate misinformation

Let's recast those as HITs:

- Identify messages that do not add to what is already known. Triage messages according to urgency.
- Fill in missing information, e.g., by aggregating information by location or by incident, by calling the sender, or by getting it from references, such as maps or business directories. Record data using standard forms.
- Discard obvious spam. Look for symptoms of exaggeration or lying.

It's important to remember that playsource tasks are not ad hoc. The HIT component of a game, including instructions to the players, is set up by domain experts. Some of the above tasks (recognizing spam, checking whether the information is already known, and filling in missing information) are reasonably straightforward, especially with good instructions and assistance from software. Consider the task of determining if a message is redundant or filling in missing information. If received messages are being aggregated by location or incident, one can look at the data already available to see if the new message adds or changes anything; it doesn't have to be treated in isolation. Messages that don't add information take time to process, but here, it's part of the game; it's the player's time, not that of an aid responder.

The difficult cases involve a decision to ignore or set aside a message that is not clearly bogus or redundant, i.e., suspected exaggeration or lying. Most examples of untrusted messages used in criticism of crowdsourcing deal with political unrest, oppression, and war, not with disasters. In a disaster, any exaggeration or lying is likely due to wanting to get help faster, not an attempt to draw aid workers or the public into danger. The domain expert may be able to set criteria for distrusting a message. If discarding untrusted messages would be a risk, they can be handed off to an expert for case-by-case determination.

Then one day Laura the Explorer and her crack crew of cartographers are passing the time posing puzzles for practice when the call comes in: Floods in the Philippines! Roads are out, bridges are down. Here are new satellite images. Grab your graphics tablets and maps -- find routes around the damage and mark them in. Meanwhile, a De La Salle University student team, current first-place holders for Filipino to English translation speed and accuracy, receive eyewitness reports, translate them, and send them off to Laura and crew, to supplement the satellites. The alternate routes are uploaded by aid workers who hurry to help. Whew and w00t!

Organizations cited:

Crowdflower, http://crowdflower.com/
Geeks Without Bounds, http://gwob.org/
International Conference on Crisis Mapping (ICCM) 2010 http://www.crisismappers.net/page/iccm-2010-haiti-and-beyond
Kila Ventures, http://www.kilaventures.com/
Sahana Software Foundation, http://www.sahanafoundation.org/
SamaSource, http://www.samasource.org/
Ushahidi, http://www.ushahidi.com/

Game and HIT references:

Addictive Game Mechanics, Erin Hoffman, http://www.gamasutra.com/blogs/ErinHoffman/20090916/3065/Life_Addictive_Game_Mechanics_And_The_Truth_Hiding_In_Bejeweled.php
Amazon.com Mechanical Turk, https://www.mturk.com/mturk/welcome
Foldit, http://fold.it/portal/
Google Image Labeler, http://images.google.com/imagelabeler/
Professor Layton, http://www.professorlaytonds.com/

Crowdsourcing criticism:

Correcting Crowdsourcing in a Crisis, Paul Currion, http://www.humanitarian.info/2009/03/30/correcting-crowdsourcing-in-a-crisis/
If All You have is a Hammer: How Useful is Humanitarian Crowdsourcing? Paul Currion, http://mobileactive.org/tagging/crowdsourcing
http://www.humanitarian.info/2010/08/04/the-sorcerors-apprentice/
http://mobileactive.org/how-useful-humanitarian-crowdsourcing
http://www.humanitarian.info/2010/07/30/on-crowdsourcing-with-a-big-sigh/

Ushahidi demonstrates how powerful groups of volunteers are when time-critical situations arise. The system continues to develop and be embraced by others around the world.

The Sahana case demonstrates the technical issues that often plague a response and show how these issues were resolved in a high tech online environment involving a dedicated network of people with a common goal, and demonstrated what they can accomplish. The next case covers some trending concepts that are being explored where very large groups of people, who normally enjoy and devote a lot of time and energy in game playing, are being explored for the integration and harnessing of their collective abilities; where tasks are tuned into challenging games and where the same enjoyment from gaming is incorporated into aiding emergency response efforts. This is due to the enormous amount of information that needs "human intelligence" in order to be processed further and used in other Web-based systems (like Ushahidi and Sahana) as information to decision makers.

SUMMARY

A lot has been covered in this chapter. Images create a powerful visual interpretation of data that can be beneficial on many levels and in many ways to a variety of stakeholders. Tagging images with text, creating narration while creating or analyzing a video, and mapping are all results of how image-based information is leveraged using Web applications. Continuing with and further integrating the concept of community, volunteers, and free systems, examples of trend-setting actions were demonstrated showing how such groups of volunteers can map data, computer savvy humanitarians can develop entire systems, and mass human intelligence in crowdsourcing efforts are looking at the future to the present game-playing patterns that engross millions of individuals per day in efforts to harness this into a productive and meaningful engagement. All of these Web-based technologies offer people ways to contribute and offer humanitarian assistance based on their abilities that are geographically independent of their location.

The next chapter takes the open source concept and volunteerism and demonstrates how large complex systems can be created and used by many agencies creating a common operating picture for different agencies that have the same information needs to solve a variety of problems. A real world, detailed case study is offered to demonstrate the feasibility of building such systems.

EXERCISES

Team Assignment

Part I: Paper Submission

1. Provide an analysis of groups using visuals as such for their emergency management needs. Identify official groups on all levels of government using images and video. Provide an example of each.
2. Explain how these groups are using video and critique if it is working, could be better, or if the group could do more.
3. Show how emergency management uses video and such in all phases of emergency management. Locate and analyze at least one per phase by a group. Analyze the pros and cons.

Part II: Video Submission

Come up with a presentation based on some emergency management scenario your team creates. This scenario can be for any phase of emergency management on any level. All video submissions will be posted for all class members to view. Your submission/assignment is such that all of the three aforementioned technologies should be used. Focus only on five-minute videos.

1. One member will do a presentation with voice over and have a link through authorStream, which will cover the scenario and the Part I submission.
2. Another member will live stream something through uStream and then make it viewable for all.
3. A video will be placed on YouTube.

Groups will be created on Moodle and all work will be submitted and posted there. So, along with your submission, we will need the scenario. Remember to test, view, and critique your own work and alter as needed before posting. Your post should look something like this:

Team 1 Submission

1. authorStream Link
2. uStream link
3. YouTube link

Try to isolate your entire submission into video. (i.e., do everything using video).

Problem

1. Conduct an analysis/critique on Sahana; look up other information and view the Sahana site for screenshots and such. If you are able to install and play around with it, that would be good, but is not required. You may want to cover issues with the user interface:
   a. Is this easy to use?
   b. Do you perceive the modules and system useful and needed?
   c. Are there situations where this would fit one disaster type better than another; where you could suggest improvements?
2. Start work on defining a new module that you think would be useful.
   a. Describe why this module is needed.
   b. Describe its importance in the overall goals of emergency management.
   c. Draw diagrams or insert other visuals.
   d. Future problems or considerations or developments that can be added later or other modules this could be integrated with.
3. Create significant enhancement to an existing module.
   a. Describe what is lacking or what the problem is with the module.
   b. Describe how these additional modifications will help improve emergency management.

8

Free and Open Source Software
The Building Blocks of Customization

INTRODUCTION

In Chapter 7, the Sahana Disaster Management System and Ushahidi Systems were presented. These systems are developed using free and open source systems (FOSS). This makes it such that any group can take the existing code and then can build on top of this code to fit the unique needs of the agency. Larger systems are built from smaller components, all of which are open source, from the database used to manage the information to the language used to code the program; everything is FOSS. This provides organizations a way to create systems that don't cost as much as proprietary systems because many of the components have already been built and are free for anyone to use and modify.

Many open source systems exist and are used every day unknowingly by the public. Wikipedia is built of MediaWiki, which is open source. More complex systems are created to support the combined needs of groups who work within common regions. Virtual Alabama is a system borne from the Alabama Department of Homeland Security that used open source systems in order to build a system to meet the needs of numerous stakeholders. They evaluated such a system by "exploring and identifying ways to leverage existing state asset imagery and infrastructure data into a visualization tool that is affordable, scalable, maintainable, and capable of employing the power of existing and evolving internet based applications" (Virtual Alabama Fact Sheet, 2010). State leadership had the foresight to envision the benefits from such a system given the number of limited resources they had along with the considerable demands from a variety of statewide stakeholders. The system was built, launched, and is successfully used by numerous people and agencies across the state every day.

Many agencies and organizations will benefit from the development of systems that share information across organizational boundaries. The functions provided can serve many different groups, each in their own way to provide a unique need as designated by the group. Much of the information is in real time providing decision makers the best available information in which to base a decision for time-critical situations.

When the Virtual Alabama project was considered, numerous stakeholders who would benefit from such a system were identified. They include:

- Homeland Security
- Emergency management and fire services
- Public safety
- City and county government
- Economic development/planning
- Natural resource management
- Environmental agencies
- Law enforcement and forensics
- Education
- Agriculture
- Transportation
- Military

Because multiple stakeholders are involved, a conglomerate of useful tasks can be provided by this one system. Many mutually beneficial activities were identified. Virtual Alabama (http://dhs.alabama.gov/virtual_alabama/pdf_files/viral_fact_sheet.pdf) would help by providing information that supported the following tasks:

- Common operational picture
- Emergency evacuation routing
- Situational awareness/understanding
- Vehicle and asset tracking
- Critical infrastructure mapping
- Student density
- Identification of assets and vulnerabilities

ONSITE WITH JOEL AUD

Social media is the largest exchange of information in the history of humanity. Touching one-third of the world's population, it functions within the complex hardware/software/societal matrix of Web 2.0 and has emerged as a dynamic, self-referencing organic phenomenon independent of the control of any single company, agency, government, philosophy, or frame of reference. It operates with layers of trust and paranoia, degrees of sophistication and simplicity, and is redefining the form and function of virtually every element of humanity. It is a conduit for commerce and charity, a medium for religion and hate crimes, a lifeline for the lonely, and a pulpit for the zealous. We do not know, and perhaps cannot know, how it is reshaping our society and our role in society. Leaders of social media argue for absolute personal and corporate transparency, while equally informed and influential leaders advocate layers of protection for information. Drug cartels post brutal execution videos via social media and grandmothers view children they have never held. Jihadists post their rhetoric and security agencies post notifications and threat levels. It does not blink, sleep, or tolerate exclusion. Women tweet their labor pains, and schools schedule parent–teacher conferences. There are more "FarmVille" farmers (57 million) than actual farmers (2.2 million) in America, and predictably more virtual crop failures than actual crop failures.

FIGURE 8.1 Joel Aud, Border Security Operations Center senior analyst.

As a massively complex system, it has both obvious and hidden rules/patterns of organization. In the support of border security/public safety through leveraging of social media, several unknown and unsuspected rules/patterns have been revealed. Those rules/patterns hint at other rules/patterns yet to be discovered, and, from the lessons learned in border security, the rules/patterns have been identified as potentially massive disruptors of the conventional paths to provide public safety. Through social media in the Web 2.0 environment, it may be possible to make every participant both an advocate and a participant in public safety, and in the process negate/mitigate the barrier between disaster/crime victims and responders.

The providers, users, abusers, hackers, and advocates of social media are continually discovering the new and unsuspected points of leverage inherent in the rules/patterns. Mal-ware artists and cyber security experts struggle for control alongside the virtual farmers and virtual gangsters, while entrepreneurs craft desktop and mobile applications to generate commerce from each side of the conflict. They have learned there is the potential for incredible empowerment within social media. That empowerment can be in the service of citizens in response to real and critical needs. For those seeking to protect and serve society, it is mandated that we trace our electronic fingers across this new Braille of reality, and having gained sight, share it with others.

- Visualization of risks
- Plume modeling and real-time sensors feeds
- Implementation of protective measures during events
- Damage assessment

The benefits of creating a system such as this reaches out to all sectors of emergency management. Once a system such as this has been built and tested, it creates a model, a template from which other states can benefit. Others can now implement this model gaining the same benefits. This provides a jurisdiction and its stakeholders with the same sets of applications and functions that were already created thus saving time and money. As regions adopt such techniques, more information will be shared among the groups to fit the needs of broader areas. New benefits will be discovered and more applications will be created from the collective intelligence

ONSITE WITH JOEL AUD

CASE STUDY: THE USE OF WEB 2.0 CONCEPTS/ TECHNIQUES/TECHNOLOGY IN BORDER SECURITY

The Environment/Changes to the Environment

Texas shares a 1,252-mile border with Mexico. It passes through metropolitan, suburban, ranch, and wilderness areas with almost all of the land privately held. Although defined by the Rio Grande River, the river offers only marginal aid to border security. In many cases the water from the river allows brush and cane to grow to the point that smuggling and human trafficking is hidden from surveillance. With the exception of two major impoundments of the Rio Grande, the physical environment of the border has not significantly changed in centuries, but cultural and criminal environment has shifted dramatically.

Subsequent to the impact of NAFTA on the agrarian economy of Mexico, the border environment underwent a radical change. As Mexican "subsistent plus" farmers found themselves in direct competition with the massive farms of the U.S. Midwest, they could not profitably sell the "plus" of their farm produce to purchase what they could not make. Aware of others in their communities and villages that either went north to the United States for work, or engaged in drug trade, many followed one of two paths to provide for their families. The impact on the Texan/Mexican border was sudden and significant. Ranch families and small town residents that had for generations used labor from south of the border, or had lent a helping hand to northbound migrants were suddenly overrun with northbound migrants. The migrants did not know America and were often under the direction or guidance of predatory human traffickers and/or drug smugglers who, in turn, answered to increasingly influential and violent cartels.

The federal border security forces of Immigration and Customs Enforcement (ICE), responsible for the border points of entry (POEs), and Customs and Border Protection (CBP), responsible for the border between the POEs, accustomed to historic human traffic and smuggling, were suddenly confronted with well-organized

245

and increasingly skilled criminal organizations. As with any large organization's response to a change in an operational environment, both ICE and CBP had to work against the momentum and cultural understanding of their own organization to deal with the new border realities. Even as the federal response progressed in 2005, border sheriffs, border ranchers, and others dealing with the shifting reality of the border requested help from the Texas governor's office to deal with the sudden increase in border-centric crime. In response to the request, the governor of Texas requested the Texas Department of Public Safety (TXDPS) to stand up the Border Security Operations Center (BSOC).

Border Security Operations Center

The BSOC was charged with four major functions:

- *Improve cooperation between federal, state, tribal, and local law enforcement.* Members of various agencies charged with law enforcement in the border environment often did not know and, in many cases, did not trust members of other agencies. Some had never worked to any extent with other agencies and had little if any understanding of the policies, practices, responsibilities, limitations, or culture of the other agencies. The improvement to cooperation between agencies continues as deliberate effort to sustain a unified command for border-centric law enforcement.

- *Improve communication between federal, state, tribal, and local law enforcement.* ICE POEs, individual CBP sectors, CBP air and marine, FBI, ATF, DEA, the U.S. Coast Guard, USDA-mounted quarantine officers (tick riders), Texas Rangers, Texas highway patrol, Texas air and marine, Texas Department of Parks and Wildlife county sheriffs, Texas Military Forces, border community police departments, railroad police, tribal police, and a host of other agencies are each charged with some element of border centric law enforcement and each has unique radio frequencies, equipment, towers, protocols, and procedures. In addition, significant portions of the border lack any communication coverage. In the words of a border county sheriff, "You have heard of 'push to talk,' we have 'push to nothing.'" The improvement to communications continues as an ongoing effort to improve both operability and interoperability.

- *Improve the sharing of information between federal, state, tribal, and local law enforcement.* Each of the law enforcement agencies dealing with border-centric crime has their own body of historic knowledge and flow of information unique to their efforts. USDA-mounted quarantine officers (tick riders) ride horseback along the border and see face-to-face elements of the border to which other agencies do not have access. Individual county sheriff offices know their county at a fundamental grassroots level, while both the TXHP and the CBP work from a border-length and/or statewide perspective. The improvement in information sharing continues as an active effort to identify, capture, normalize, geo-code, and then share, in a common format, border law enforcement information.
- *Provide technical support to federal, state, tribal and local law enforcement.* If combined into a single state, the border counties would comprise the poorest state in the union. The resources available for border-centric law enforcement are limited, and the resources of equipment and technically skilled personnel are even more limited. License plate readers, mobile fingerprint readers, long-range thermal imagers, autonomous surveillance platforms, and a host of other technologies with the potential to significantly amplify the effective manpower of border law enforcement require an understanding of the technology, the use of the technology, and use of the data from the technology. The technical support of federal, state, tribal, and local law enforcement remains an ongoing process leveraging the emerging tools of the long tail, Internet protocol granularity of data, commercial off-the-shelf equipment, nonproprietary software, an open source development environment, thin clients, and other emerging technology.

For the purpose of this discussion, the use of the Long tail, Internet protocol granularity of data, Commercial off-the-shelf

247

equipment, Nonproprietary software, an Open source development environment, and Thin clients (LICNOT) in the service of border-centric law enforcement will be examined in the context of the O'Reilly Web 2 concept. LICNOT was developed in general ignorance of the O'Reilly Radar concept of Web 2.0. Through the benefit of greater technical depth and the sheer brilliance that exemplifies their products, the O'Reilly group has identified, labeled, and delineated the nature of Web 2.0. The O'Reilly concept represents a more robust and tested context for the discussion of the Web 2.0/social media tool set, and the discussion of LICNOT is only provided to explain migration of thought and practice in attempting to meet the needs of border centric law enforcement.

Examples

The three examples examining LICNOT, Web 2.0, and social media were selected for what they revealed. In each case they literally exposed rules and behaviors that were neither suspected nor anticipated. A border camera project taught three suspected rules and one unsuspected rule. An open source-derived common operating picture pointed to the possibility of sharing and protecting data in the same system, and a pattern for growth of social media was revealed in the deployment of a flood notification architecture.

Trial Deployment of Border Cameras and the Birth of Long Tail Surveillance

In November of 2006, the BSOC deployed a test system of 20+ cameras along the border, fed the video from the cameras directly to the Internet, and invited the entire world to watch. Deployed for 28 days, the project garnered over a quarter million watchers, generated 27.5 million hits, and was briefly the no. 1 Google search (Figure 8.2).

The project generated the four rules of "long tail surveillance." The four rules are:

1. **If it is on the Internet, it will be viewed.** This is a function of the "Long Tail" phenomenon of the Internet as popularized by Chris Anderson in the book *The Long Tail: Why the Future of Business Is Selling Less of More* (Hyperion, 2006). Anderson discusses the concept that although 90 percent

248

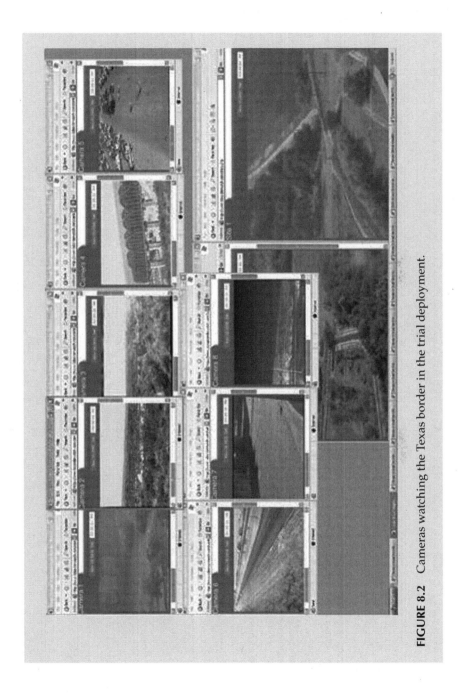

FIGURE 8.2 Cameras watching the Texas border in the trial deployment.

of Internet traffic transpires on 10 percent of the Internet's Websites, the remaining 10 percent of the Internet's transactions transpire on the remaining 90 percent of the sites, and those sites stretch out over a near infinite diminishing long tail of sites. Anderson's book deals with the commercial implications of the long tail and the concept that the Internet provides a near infinite consumer base for products. In simplest terms, regardless of your product, the consumer base of the Internet is so large that if they can find you, they will buy your product. Inherent with the near infinite market is also the reality of near infinite competition. In "long tail surveillance," the near infinite audience of the Internet is tapped and in the deployment of the test border camera system, the importance of the near infinite audience in the long tail became apparent. Regardless of the lack of activity, across the spectrum of the Internet, there was a reliable audience for the constant video feeds from the cameras.

2. **If it is on the Internet, it will be watched 24/7.** The world wide scope of the Internet audience and long tail phenomenon combined to ensure there was always an audience for the feeds from the cameras. The middle of night time of potential smuggling was prime early evening viewing time in Asia, Australia, and the subcontinent of India, and the early morning hours were prime viewing for Europe. A bar in Australia had each feed from the trial deployment displayed 24/7. It was surveillance monitoring system that never blinked and was ready to respond.

3. **If viewers are provided a means to respond, they will respond.** By providing watchers a means to click a button and generate an e-mail to report when they saw something on the video feeds, viewers were engaged in the process. When they saw something, they clicked and typed out an e-mail detailing what they saw, and in that process became engaged. Their engagement, combined with the power of the long tail and constant audience of the long tail, produced the fourth and most unexpected rule.

4. **The responses from the Internet will be self validating.** A spider crawled up on the lens of a camera and generated 65

e-mails in the first minute, and, at that point, the fourth rule became apparent. Because the responses from the viewers arrived from across the nation and planet at approximately the same time and contained essentially the same content, the responses were self validating. Although an individual could send a message claiming he or she saw Pancho Villa crossing the border, to generate a simultaneous series of e-mails with approximately the same content from around the planet is almost impossible. In simplest terms it was "spoof proof."

The four rules combine to outline the idea of long tail surveillance. If it is on the Internet, it will be viewed, it will be viewed 24/7, viewers will respond, and the responses will be self vetting.

Automation of Long Tail Surveillance

Because the responses will be closely aligned in content and time of arrival, and will be contained in a consistent media of e-mail, an automatic process for the analysis of the data was made possible. By moving the data into a "tag cloud" application, the flow of data could be displayed as a dynamic image with the most commonly used word being displayed in the largest font, and the most recently used word being displayed in the darkest font (Figure 8.3).

From the tag cloud in Figure 8.3, you can quickly deduce "Internet, long, and tail" are all important in the paragraphs. When e-mails say essentially the same thing, the picture becomes even clearer. This means the video feeds from the cameras do not need to be constantly monitored, but rather, the key words displayed in the tag cloud provide a display of the trends of responses to the video

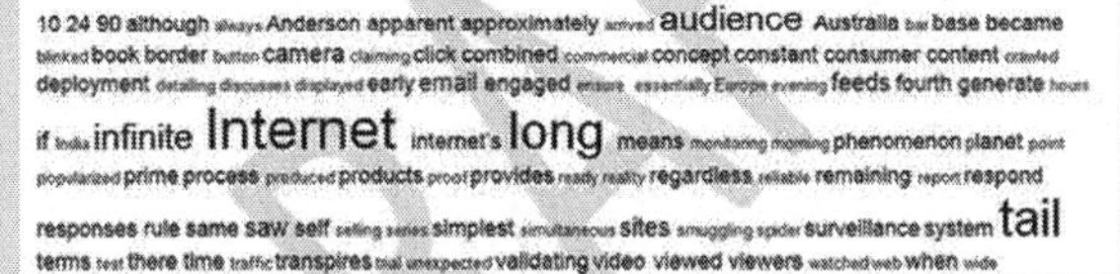

FIGURE 8.3 A tag cloud of the four rules of long tail surveillance paragraphs.

feeds. The Internet protocol (IP) level of data granularity allowed the information to be delivered as e-mail from any browser and then subjected to IP level analysis and inclusion in a tag cloud.

Transparent Surveillance

By the very public nature of the long tail surveillance architecture, surveillance shifts to a very transparent environment and out of the control of a single body or organization. If the world is empowered to watch, it is also empowered to know. The scope and nature of viewers ensures a level of vigilance not easily achieved by dedicated surveillance monitors. By way of example, the lowest census for viewers during the 28-day trial deployment was just under 1,000 viewers monitoring 21 cameras, or roughly 50 viewers per camera. This means that for many surveillance monitoring applications, a dedicated viewer mindlessly watching a set of monitors may be significantly less effective or efficient than allowing the world to watch, and by an inherent feature of the Internet, it may be more commercially feasible for the world to watch.

Taking It Commercial

Thomas L. Friedman in *The World is Flat* (Farrar, Straus, and Giroux, 2005) details how the combination of the Internet and the propagation of cheap connectivity now allow a more equitable access to the world and the outsourcing of information work. Extending the concept to long tail surveillance, the flat world has the potential to allow the world to watch and, through financial engines that power the new economy of a flat world, get paid to watch.

As an example, a firm can enroll cameras from any camera that can provide an IP video feed, feed the video to the Internet, and host it on a scalable virtual server farm in the Internet cloud, offer a reward for watchers that respond when they see something, with 50 percent of the reward going to the first responder and a sliding scale to subsequent responders, and then pay the responders using PayPal. This model allows the outsourcing of long tail surveillance to the rest of the planet, streamlines the reward for vigilance, and ensures the transparency of surveillance in the service of both private and public safety. Multiple firms and state agencies are now exploring the potential of long tail surveillance and the leveraging

flat world economic infrastructure of the Internet. They are building a social media/flat world/long tail surveillance architecture that
will radically change how surveillance is used and the transparency
of that surveillance.

Common Operating Picture

In the process of the BSOC coordinating the efforts of federal, state,
county, and local law enforcement, the need for a common operating picture became apparent. Federal law enforcement agencies each
have organization-specific terms and map coordinates as do state,
county, and local law enforcement agencies. In the coordination of
multiagency operations, it leads to confusion and misidentification
of events. Customs Border Patrol (CBP) use one set of map coordinates, Texas highway patrol uses mile markers, county law enforcement uses familiar ranch or road references, and border city police
law enforcement officers use addresses.

To add to the problem, conventional law enforcement record
management systems, written for the profitable large city markets,
use city addresses as the standard designation for locations. For
operations in the remote locations of the border, such address-based
record management systems are, at best, limited. Paralleling this limitation, border law enforcement agencies frequently lack the financial
or technical infrastructure to host or readily access law enforcement
record management systems.

To counter the geospatial notation limitation of existing law
enforcement record management systems and the overlapping and/
or conflicting geospatial information designations of different border-
centric law enforcement agencies, the BSOC developed a low-cost,
open source solution. Initially build as a mash-up of components to
be a simple geospatial record management system, it was designed
to meet the immediate needs of border-centric law enforcement. First
named the Joint Information Support System (JISS), then TexMap, and,
finally, TxMAP, the common operating picture allows the capture of
border-centric law enforcement events and the sharing of the common operating picture to law enforcement agencies across the border.

A combination of Drupal, Media Wiki, Google Earth, and
MySQL, the use of the open source components allowed rapid
assembly with significant additional benefits (Figure 8.4). The use

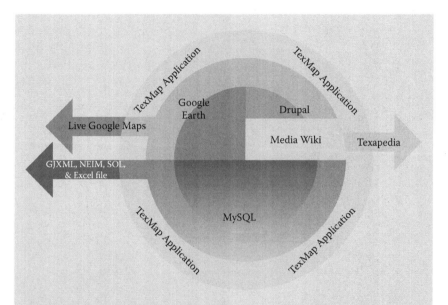

FIGURE 8.4 The components of TxMAP.

of Drupal in combination with Google Earth allowed the creation of incident data entry forms with an embedded Google Earth application that allows a user to click on a map, a satellite image, or a hybrid of both map and satellite image to tag the location of the incident. The use of Media Wiki allows the tracking of changes, and the use of MySQL assures cross compatibility with and the ability to export to other applications, such as Microsoft® Excel.

As the Google Earth-embedded application captures latitude and longitude with the data from the incident, the data can be extracted from the MySQL database and imported directly into Google Earth for display. The data display engine of Google Earth was termed the "blue marble," and the smaller, less-polished data-gathering, browser-based application was termed the "blue pebble." Although there are more robust geospatial tools available, Google Earth has the advantage of a strong user base and a strong open source development community. Most of the tools needed for the development of the solution existed in some form in the open source community.

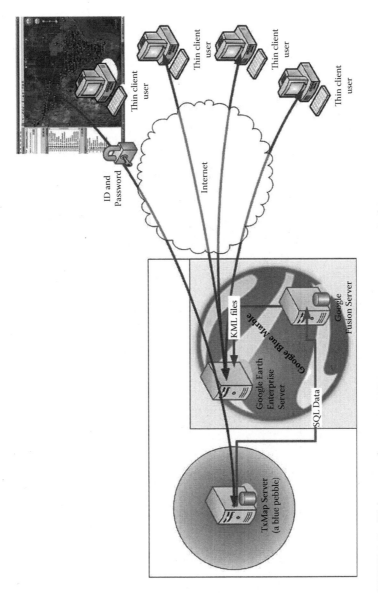

FIGURE 8.5 ID/password gateway.

Because TxMAP engages multiple federal, state, local, and tribal law enforcement agencies, a method for secure data sharing was borrowed from Virtual Alabama with the guidance of Chris Johnson of the U.S. Space and Rocket Center in Huntsville, Alabama. The method allows the sharing of public data with the embedding of links to private data. Data is displayed as a layer on Google Earth with embedded icons for individual records within the data. Clicking on an icon reveals the metadata from the record. The metadata is the public information the organization is willing to share with the community that can access the Google Earth layers. Within the metadata, a URL link can be imbedded linking the ID/password gateway (Figure 8.5) to the data the organization wants to share with only certain authorized individuals.

Through this architecture, an agency could publish to TxMAP the data they wanted to share complete with geospatial references, and embed a link to an ID- and password-protected gateway accessing their private data. The agency maintained the gateway to controlled data, which freed TxMAP of the responsibility of maintaining the validation and authorization burden for the data and allowed the agencies to share in a geospatial format, data critical to the decision process.

After two years, TxMAP has evolved to become the all hazard/all state, Texas Department of Public Safety common operating picture for the state, and continues to grow in capability and application. Other applications are now recognizing the importance of the geospatial display of data, and are deploying "drill-down-from-location" information architectures. Through the efforts of dedicated geospatial professionals, it now has multiple law enforcement layers and additional layers to support the critical decision process.

Flood Watch and Migration to Important and Urgent

Parallel to the law enforcement centric functions of the BSOC, as a member of the greater Texas Department of Public Safety community, there is responsibility to also provide support in the protection of the lives and the welfare of the citizens of Texas. In times of need, such as hurricanes or floods, the BSOC resources are often tasked to support the Texas Division of Emergency Management. In response to a need for situation awareness during the 2010

June and July floods on the lower Rio Grande River, the BSOC fielded a server-based application to provide accurate and timely data on flood conditions. The application scraped the National Oceanic and Atmospheric Administration's Hydrometeorological Prediction Center Web page,* composed an e-mail summarizing the data from multiple active river monitors reporting to the Web page, and transmitted the e-mail once an hour during critical flood conditions. Because the data were summarized into a hourly e-mail, it became a predictable touch point of important information. Shortly after the subsidence of the flood, the same email audience was provided an urgent notification on a nonflood topic. In the process of providing the hourly flood data, and the subsequent urgent notification, a pattern for furthering the reach of social media was developed.

Furthering the Reach of Social Media

Social media is built on a framework of trust and active participation. In the law enforcement and emergency response community, the historic perception of social media was that it was neither important nor urgent and, hence, was not suitable for law enforcement or emergency management use; however, the ubiquity of social media use and the role of social media as the first line of communications in multiple crisis events has changed that perception. Federal, state, and local agencies are participating in social media communities, but with mixed results. Some may be an exercise in simply "checking the box" that they have a social media program, while others are growing a user base. The patterns identified by the BSOC in the river level notification work may point to a more systematic procedure for the growth of a robust user base.

Toward more successful use of social media for law enforcement and first responders, content must be migrated from the "not important/not urgent" to at least the "important." This in turn requires a change in the importance of the content of social media to the use community (Figure 8.6).

By providing content that is of significant interest to the user community and delivered in a consistent format on a predictable

---

* http://www.noaawatch.gov/floods.php (accessed September 12, 2010)

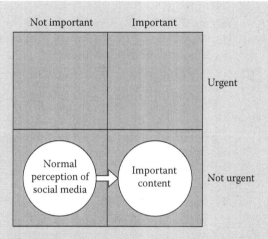

FIGURE 8.6 Migration of social media to position of importance.

schedule, the importance of social media can be elevated. As an example, in the lower Rio Grande River community, the hourly transmissions of the river stages became an important reference point for the users. The data was not exciting or entertaining, but it was useful and was delivered in a simple format on a consistent basis, and through the mobile device accessible media of e-mail. By providing the user community a reliable source of useful information, the value and relevance of the content was elevated. In short, the content becomes important (Figure 8.7).

Once a community of users trusts and relies on the source of the social media content and are engaged in the use and the recirculation of the content, the community becomes a key leverage point for the potential migration of social media to become both important and urgent. In the case of an incident or event that is of urgent importance to the user community, an urgent notification can be sent to the established user community. Through this process social media becomes both important and urgent.

It should be understood that this process cannot be treated like conventional broadcast media. If the information that is provided for the establishment of a user community is not of value or of interest to

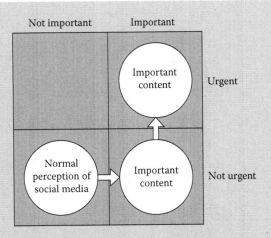

FIGURE 8.7 Migration of social media to important and urgent to the user community.

that community, a user community will not be established. In a world featuring the viral circulation of videos featuring a skateboarding dog, nonentertaining content can only survive if it is of importance to the user. If it is not important, it is at best background noise, and, like other clutter, will be ignored or, if possible, deleted. In equal measure, if the "urgent" message designation is used to push less than urgent information or information that does not relate to the user community and/or the normal flow of the normal "important" content to the user community, the abuse could potentially contaminate the foundational trust relationship between the sources and the users.

Leveraging Engagement

Parallel to the critical relationship of trust between the content provider and the user community is the force of engagement. It is the engagement of users in the social media that separates social media from RSS (real simple syndication) and other broadcast or push media. As social media facilitate the joining and interaction with the user community, they provide reasons for both receiving and contributing content. In the realm of law enforcement and/or emergency

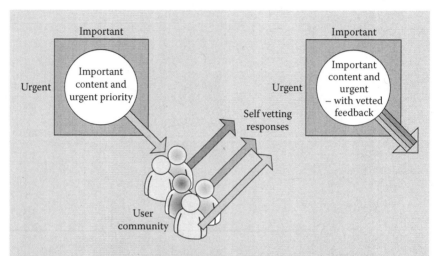

FIGURE 8.8 Important and urgent with self-vetting response.

management, this can provide a means to tap real-time grass roots data sources, solicit input, and deliver critical information (Figure 8.8).

As the user group is provided important content with an urgent priority, a response can be solicited. This can provide valuable eye-witness information, supplemental data, and early indications of rumors or misinformation. In a coastal community routinely provided with tide/time data, a radio or tweet report of a vessel in distress could trigger an urgent message to the user community that request any information or images from any other member of the user community. It literally becomes a force multiplier by leveraging the resources of the entire user community.

Tapping the fourth rule of long tail surveillance, as the responses will arrive at nearly the same time and contain nearly the same content, they become self vetting. Because they are in an IP level of granularity, the responses can be normalized, and vetted responses from the users can be pushed to other members of the user community. In a law enforcement or emergency response community, this can translate into both a more informed community and a powerful tool against misinformation.

LICNOT, Web 2.0, and Social Media

LICNOT evolved as a methodology for seeking solutions to border-centric law enforcement needs and can be thought of as a subset of the greater Web 2.0. In the same way, the various elements and functions of social media might be thought of as another subset of the greater Web 2.0 world.

The elements of LICNOT include:

- **Long Tail:** As mentioned in the discussion of the trial deployment of the border cameras, Chris Anderson popularized the concept of long tail and the nature of "meganiche" economics. Anderson described the near infinite body of consumers, and the border camera project discovered the near infinite audience. To put it in perspective, if you have one-tenth of 1 percent of the Internet watching, you have an audience of 1 million.

- **Internet Protocol** (IP) Level Granularity: When data is in IP level granularity, the barriers of incompatibility, translations, protocols, and other limits are reduced. A system with an IP camera can capture an image, transmit the image via a digital cell phone connection, store the image in a virtual server farm, and display the image on a browser agnostic Website because the IP packets are interchangeable at each stage of the process.

- **Commercial Off-the-Shelf:** Off-the-shelf products have the advantage of mass productions, proven robustness, and an established user base. In the case of TxMAP, Google Earth was selected because of the number of developers who knew the code environment of the product, but, more importantly, because it was a widely known and accepted geospatial tool in the law enforcement community and with the public in general.

- **Nonproprietary:** By using a vendor or manufacturer agnostic method or system, the pricing of the components remains competitive and no single supplier represents a possible point of catastrophic failure. The use of four separate software packages to create a law enforcement, common operating picture mash-up speaks to the power of not relying on a single best solution. As TxMAP has evolved, each major element has undergone a change in vendor or version without significant impact on any other single component.

- **Open Source:** The use of open source solutions taps the best of the Internet to ensure the robustness of solutions and the assurance of continual improvement. The LAMP (Linux, apache, MySQL, PHP) foundation of the Internet is open source, and it was the resources of the open source community that first made TxMAP possible.

- **Thin Client:** The drive for the minimum requirements in software and hardware is rooted in the scarcity of resources available to border law enforcement. Because almost any mobile smart device could receive e-mail, e-mail was the natural media for the river flood levels. Other methods could be used, but, by driving to the minimum, a broader user base was possible.

Web 2.0 was identified as an emerging trend and given the name "Web 2.0" by the O'Reilly Radar group. The Web 2.0 environment is defined by the attributes and patterns. The attributes supported by Web 2.0 include the following:*

- **Massively Connected:** In contrast to "one-to-many" publishing or broadcast patterns of conventional media, Web 2.0 is a peer-to-peer environment that constantly provides new ways of linking data and data users. The connectivity made the quarter million subscribers to the border camera trial deployment possible. It is not trivial that the most effective late night monitoring of the cameras came from the other side of the planet.

- **Decentralized:** No central authority drives or directs the Web 2.0 environment. Leadership and innovation can come from the edge as easily as the center. For broad spectrum of border law enforcement agencies, a decentralized philosophy of solutions was essential. The border is a dynamic law enforcement environment with criminal organizations constantly changing methods, approaches, and techniques.

---

* Web 2.0 Principles and Best Practices (O'Reilly Radar)

A centralized approach to information gathering, management, or distribution cannot meet the needs of border law enforcement.

- **User Focused:** Because Web 2.0 enables and often compels the user to participate and become engaged, the user is at the center. When the users were given the power to respond to what they saw on the border cameras (and they responded in mass), a new rule was revealed and the possibility of self vetting long tail surveillance became a reality.

- **Open:** At the foundation, Web 2.0 rests on the LAMP standard, which is composed of open source components. The ethos of that foundation supports open standards, APIs, and countless other shared resources. Had the code of initial components of TxMAP not been open, the mash-up would not have been possible. Had the protocol for e-mail not been shared, the river flood notification would have been massively more difficult. .

- **Lightweight:** In the same way the dynamic nature of the border demands a decentralized architecture, it also mandates a nimble means of response. Small agile software development that is frugal in both code and resources can provide a nimble function response, while more conventional development patterns are still collecting requirements. Time and again, victory is not to the biggest, but to the fastest and most nimble.

- **Emergent:** Web 2.0 is not a solution yet, nor will it be tomorrow or the next day, but it will continually be an approximation of a solution constantly evolving and changing to meet needs. There could be no better pattern for a solution set to meet the needs of border law enforcement or emergency management.

The patterns inherent in Web 2.0 include the following:*

- **Harnessing Collective Intelligence:** Because Web 2.0 compels participation and engagement, it becomes stronger with each participant. At the core of effective law enforcement or

---

* Web 2.0 Principles and Best Practices (O'Reilly Radar)

emergency management is citizen engagement and participation. The trial deployment of the border cameras had over
a quarter million watchers. Who could afford to pay for that
degree of vigilance?

- **Data Are the Next "Intel Inside:"** The strength of TxMAP
  is in the ability to gather data and allow the data to be both
  shared and protected. That is a uniquely Web 2.0 possibility.
- **Innovation in Assembly:** By the mash-up of Google, Drupal,
  Mediawiki, and MySQL, a remix of software and services
  created a new solution. Until the parts were linked no one
  knew the full capability, and we may not still.
- **Rich User Experiences:** By giving law enforcement the ability to tag a location by map or satellite image, it was free to
  provide better, more accurate data. Pushing forward, that
  capability will be extended to more and more devices.
- **Software above the Level of a Single Device:** Device centric applications have been supplanted by browser-based
  thin client tools. Because of Web 2.0, the hardware/soft-
  ware/user requirement standard for TxMAP was only for
  the machine and the user to be able to use a browser.
- **Perpetual Beta:** The rhythm and pattern of constant change
  on the border is not the environment for a conventional solution set. Only the nimble and quick will meet the needs.
- **Leveraging the Long Tail:** In a near infinite environment,
  there are infinite possibilities. The trial deployment of the
  border cameras garnered over 27.5 million hits.
- **Lightweight Models and Cost-Effective Scalability:** The
  limited resources of border law enforcement invite lightweight business models and software-development solutions that are cost-effective and can quickly harvest the low
  hanging fruit. The first version of TxMAP was built for less
  than $5,000 and 400 man-hours.

At no other time in history has any single medium linked so
many people in so many ways. Wikipedia lists over 190 social media
sites addressing issues of language, age, gender, health, profession,

interest, politics, religion, and countless other areas of focus.* In July of 2010, Facebook announced it had over 500 million members and the combined online time for Facebook members exceeded 700 billion minutes per month.

In the same way we did not know the fourth rule the trail deployment of border cameras revealed, and we did not intentionally set out to build a user community around the Rio Grande River flood notifications, we do not know what we don't know about social media and law enforcement or emergency management. At best we can engage with social media as it is supported and nourished in the Web 2.0 environment, and share what we discover. Societies are not crafted from observers, but from participants.

---

* http://en.wikipedia.org/wiki/List_of_social_networking_websites (accessed October 2, 2010)

---

that is certainly to be gained from such interoperable system development and sharing.

This leads us to the next case study. The building blocks of open source software can be constructed to build most any type of system. This next case provides a detailed example of how a group can leverage open source systems with a global community of volunteers. Some interesting patterns were detected as a result of this next system's implementation, further supporting that the community and civilians are a beneficial, and proving to be, invaluable resource. It is through the sharing of information and promotion of innovative ideas that new open source systems can be built to satisfy many homeland security and emergency management needs.

SUMMARY

This chapter provided a detailed case study that related how open source systems, technology, and civilians can be leveraged as one to help solve the larger problems with complex systems. It is important to understand how valuable open source can be to not only one organization, but to a conglomerate of related groups. Although the actual creation of such a system may be beyond our technical capacity, it is well worth the time to evaluate and collectively fund such systems that can be shared among groups.

This leads us to the final chapter of the book, which provides segments that focus on conclusive types of information. First and foremost, it's important to realize the vulnerabilities of social media and to always maintain the robust communications that have been tested over time. Many people reject social media and have justifiable reasons for this. Systems need to be tested based on their design to see if they will work as expected. Challenges are discussed and solutions are posed. A set of guidelines is provided to support a group's successful launching of a social media blitz.

9

Testing the System
Knowing When to Use or Not Use Social Media

INTRODUCTION

Systems fail, can be overloaded, and can crash when high numbers of people use them. It's best to discover these sorts of problems before an event occurs to reduce the possibility of the system failing. It is critical to conduct a risk assessment and identify, then plan for situations where social media will be useful and, more importantly, where it will not be useful. Social media is not the end-all answer to crisis communications and emergency management. There are times when social media will not be effective and will suffer many barriers, where other traditional methods are best suited.

Social media is not as trivial and predictable as some may think. It may not work as expected and may not be usable at all given critical infrastructure damage has occurred. Once a system has been designed and created, it should be tested. Just like any plan created, it's best to test the design with an exercise to help determine if the technology will work the way the agency intends for it to. Challenges arise in that scenarios need to be created in order to test the system. The stakeholders involved also should be included during both the scenario creation and exercise to test the system.

We have covered a number of ways to direct information in order to help reduce information overload; however, data need to be further aggregated especially during time-critical situations where previously described strategies may not suffice during high traffic times. A unified approach is discussed where a variety of types of media are interplayed in order to best leverage all information into a more concentrated view. The chapter ends by covering some guidelines providing help to get your agency off to a good start.

Next, a case study is provided that looks at a "doomsday" event and evaluates where social media may and may not be a good fit. Not all people have faith in social media nor do they all believe that it's a good idea to implement on such a grand level, or any level for that matter. The words of caution are verbalized by many. This case provides such an example.

AN ONLINE SOCIAL MEDIA EXERCISE
IN EMERGENCY RESPONSE

Exercises need to be conducted to test a system, but first a scenario needs to be created by the stakeholders. This provides a number of challenges. First, social media is new and it is difficult to predict what the users will be doing or how the stakeholders will use the system. Second, it may prove difficult to actually conduct an exercise given the scenario is ongoing. Since the scenario is online, it is difficult to keep a running clock and provide status updates to the user population in full. Collaborative efforts are best for scenario generation and until social media is more commonplace, there is no one best strategy to accomplish this task, but just like testing any plan, an exercise needs to be conducted to test the robustness of a system and to try to figure out what will be needed should such an event as what is laid out in the scenario occur. It may prove best to initially have scenarios that are basic and simple, then increase in complexity. Also, it will be a very important step to notify the community members and try to have them participate. One note of caution, make sure that the public is aware that a scenario is ongoing. One tweet could set off a series of events that could be spread virally and make it next to impossible to take back.

A list of goals and objectives should be available that the agency would like to see accomplished from an exercise. Further, the system should be evaluated to see if it meets the agencies, information needs and identifying other ways to better leverage these abilities. Just as in any exercise,

ONSITE WITH GREG CARTTAR

CASE STUDY: WILL SOCIAL NETWORKING SURVIVE THE BIG ONE?

When I was asked to contribute a segment on communications and social networking (SocNet) in disaster/emergency communications, I was in the middle of a period where I considered SocNet to be a toy and not worthy of consideration in emergency situations. I still consider it a toy, but I have come around to a point where it is a valuable toy—as long as it works. When it works, it is truly amazing.

FIGURE 9.1   Greg Carttar, 3rd St. R & D Production Services, Central Taney County Fire Protection District, Kirbyville, Missouri.

A few weeks before this writing, I had a friend who had just gone to Christchurch, New Zealand, on an extended stay for product training. He is a communications professional with a specialty in voice communications equipment, in other words, radio as you commonly define it.

He is a firefighter, as am I, and we depend on voice communications every time we deploy at a fire scene. We depend on voice for a one-to-many, no keystrokes required, mode of communications. It's impossible to text or use an iPhone with fire gloves on. It's barely possible to use your basic walkie-talkie. Standing in the middle of a raging interior structure fire while texting or pulling Web pages is the most absurd scenario we could possibly conceive of.

I have been in on the confusion that occurs when my young firefighter brothers and sisters resort to texting about department activities or tactics, and then do not understanding why everybody is not on the same page with them. It is because some of us were not on the "send" list.

You could reasonably consider that we had, and justifiably so, a serious case of tunnel vision about our communications.

Strike One: One-to-Many Communications Using SocNet Takes a Lot of Time and Attention

Only a day or so after arriving in New Zealand, my friend found himself in the middle of the New Zealand earthquake. He kept us riveted with Facebook posts of what was occurring, photos of the damage, and welfare updates on himself and the others in his training class.

He described the constant aftershocks, how he was kept awake at all hours by them, and then posted even more photos of damage.

It was incredible. It was immediate. It was ... well, I'll just go back to incredible. I got it. I got how SocNet could be of huge value in quickly gathering short-form data and visual information.

Then, after about 48 hours with no electrical power, the backup batteries at the cell sites in that locality of New Zealand went dead. He was gone. No more bulletins, no more updates. It wasn't until sometime later when his posts resumed that we learned that the loss of communications with him was due to the failure of the *system* that he was working through. "Failure" is a very relative term. Nothing broke, no equipment went bad, nothing went down because it was cheap or second-rate. It went down because it was never intended to provide this kind of service, at this level of endurance, under these conditions.

Strike Two: Control and Maintain of the Infrastructure That Supports SocNet

This infrastructure is controlled and maintained by carriers who may or may not have the same sense of urgency that you do. Put kindly, cell phone service is a "best effort" service with no guarantees.

While watching Facebook for news from New Zealand, another socially engineered Trojan/virus/malware/clickjacking outbreak occurred on Facebook. People should have been suspicious of any posting on Facebook that looked even a little bit scandalous, provocative, or emotionally evocative. I say "should have been" because it was clear that not enough people *were* suspicious, so these attacks went through Facebook like a forest fire and collected the sophisticated and unsophisticated alike.

Unrelated to the social engineering Facebook attacks, one of our firefighters allowed his Facebook account to be hijacked by an unhappy girlfriend. The disgruntled girlfriend posted derogatory statements on his Wall, which caused him much embarrassment.

The point is that it was a false flag and it was untrue. It was calculated misinformation intended to cause controversy, disruption, and mischief, which it certainly did for a day or so.

Project for yourself the effect of deliberate and visceral misinformation into a highly charged environment like the acute phase of a disaster response.

Twitter has had its own set of security issues recently and I don't think they need to be revisited ad nauseum, but Twitter has had its own set of successes as well.

A very recent paper by Mendoza, Poblete, and Castillo entitled Twitter Under Crisis: Can We Trust What We RT? investigates the use of Twitter during the Chilean earthquake of 2010, analyzes traffic patterns, false flags, dependence on infrastructure, and how the Twitter-verse ultimately moves to regulate and resolve false information, but not until it has been an initial disturbance.

If you tried to follow the valiant effort by the Deepwater Horizon Unified Command to maintain the Deepwater Horizon Response Facebook page, you are probably aware that it almost always deteriorated into a political furball with every post, effectively blocking intelligent and informed exchange of information.

Strike Three: SocNet Is Inherently Insecure and Can Suffer from False Flags, Misinformation, and Intentional Disruption

Nor will we get into the three days that my Internet connection was down because a lightning storm took out a pole-mounted remote network switch for the third time in as many months. The phone company just could not believe their equipment had been damaged this many time in such a short time. If I had not had a cell phone, I would not have been able to argue with them about it. If my landline had not been forwarded to my cell phone, my business would have been shut down for three days.

Strike Four: Landline Internet Access Is No More Robust Than Cell Phones When Damage Is Particular to Landline Infrastructure

In the last couple of days while I was thinking this segment through, there have been discussions on some emergency management Websites regarding how to incorporate SocNet into emergency management.

One tongue-in-cheek commenter suggested that EMs recruit the most unapologetically geeky young people to populate a side room of the command post, give them an unlimited supply of Red Bull, and let them go at the text-o-sphere on behalf of the command staff.

Well, that's an interesting idea, and it has a certain real theoretical merit. But, have you read, and I mean *really* read, the posts that seem to dominate the text-oriented world?

Damage report from the field:

"Dude, im all dwn in ths stuff an shizzle is cumin @ me frm evrywhre!"
"Wot?"
"got2go now! L8R!"
"Wot?"

Response from the IC:

272

"What?"

By the way, there is no ICS form hard copy of this report. Does anybody use punctuation any more?

Field: "We already ate Grandma"
IC: "My God! They're eating each other down there!"
Field: "Dude, my bad, We already ate, Grandma."

Strike Five: There Is a Certain Amount of Discipline, Format, Training, and Clarity Required for Important Messaging

As someone remarked, "The people you have trained may not be the ones that show up." So, is this a blanket condemnation of social networking and the public infrastructure? No, it is not.

It is, however, a blanket cautionary tale meant to make the layman aware of just how fragile public infrastructure is, how insecure social networking can be, and how much care has to go into utilizing this technology. It is also cautionary with regard to how essentially unstructured forms of communication can or cannot be integrated into a very structured and ordered emergency management environment.

As long as public infrastructure is intact, SocNet can be extremely valuable if the information can be distilled with accuracy down to 140 characters or whatever the particular SocNet allows. Some information can be effective when it is brief, but sometimes it must be verbose. As long as trolls do not get into the mix, that information can flow with great speed.

The message: "Hi! My name is Natasha, and I invite you to visit my Website for good time!" in the middle of a complex series of messages about damages and health/welfare could be, shall we say, counterproductive.

There is nothing robust enough in these networks to prevent either such spam, hostile code, or to prevent a deliberate false flag attack.

Let's go back to Strike Two (Infrastructure) and look at that in more depth because this is where you can be let down when you need it most. People tend to look at the Internet and Wireless and Cell phone/Smartphone and Radio as different and unrelated technologies, and at the user interface level, they are—different software technologies and/or control surfaces and/or different ways of presenting or transmitting intelligence to the user whether it be Voice, Simple Message Text, Hypertext, whatever. But, if it does not have wires connected to it, it is radio in one of its many implementations.

Your cell phone and your wireless broadband access make it easy to think that you are connecting to some other person or entity directly, but you are not, even if they are standing next to you. You are simply transmitting and receiving to and from a portal not more than a few miles away from you, and, in many cases, not more than a few hundred feet away from you. At that nearby portal, your wireless signal has to get interconnected with a transmission network that is physical.

That physical network is the phone company (Telco), also known as The Cloud. The Cloud is global, regional, and local. Often there is a distinction made between the Public Switched Telephone (PSTN) voice network and The Internet, but in reality and in the global sense they are both simply different types of traffic flowing across the same physical network, as with your DSL connection where voice and data are both flowing on the same wire entering your home or business. But, in any case, once your signal enters The Cloud, you lose control of it and any ability to troubleshoot or resolve problems.

Fortunately, The Cloud is normally very reliable and is supremely engineered to be robust, even if ultimately exhaustible. However, if anything should happen to Telco, or its physical infrastructure, such as copper and fiberoptic cable buried in the ground, all of our modern and convenient means of personal communications would go silent. The Radio component of your cell phone or xG device would still be throwing energy happily into the ether, and, in some cases, the cell site receptor would still be happily gathering that energy; however, the intelligence would have nowhere to go beyond that cell site. The Cloud would become impenetrable fog.

Radio, as defined in this discussion, is voice or data communications independent of any public network infrastructure, is truly peer-to-peer, and truly survivable.

In truth, "Radio transmission and reception" is the core of any "wireless" technology. These terms get recycled every 50 or 100 years or so, and the term *Wireless* was originally coined when the first spark gap Morse code systems were deployed early in the twentieth century. No, that *other* century.

Think: An operator hunched over a Morse code key onboard the Titanic tapping "SOS..SOS..." He was the wireless operator. A magician. He was able to send messages through the ether and get them back.

Wireless is still magic: Energy, with intelligence impressed upon it, flies into the ether and magically finds the proper receptor. But, the fact is that primitive wireless Morse code transmission system from 1912 is much more robust than modern Wireless connectivity. It was global, and did not rely on any intermediate infrastructure except the radio sets at each end.

Radio has never lost the capability of providing local, regional, and global communications, and, in the modern day, can deliver voice, digital data, and, yes, e-mail, anywhere in the world from a box not much larger than a thick hardbound book. All of this, like the Titanic, independent of outside physical infrastructure. No Cloud is required.

If we revisit my friend in Christchurch, New Zealand, during the earthquake, what happened to him is that The Cloud failed from loss of electrical power. The earthquake, for some unknown and miraculous reason, apparently spared the cables in the ground that interconnect the cell site near him to the Mobile Telephone Switching Office (MTSO) in Christchurch, but did not spare the electricity source for the cell site, which reverted to batteries and chugged merrily along until they were exhausted. Until power was restored, or until the Telco got that site running again on a generator, it was dead.

Here we look at another layer of infrastructure that we all take for granted, and another "Cloud" in its own right, Electrical Utility Power. We are more familiar with those failures; who has not experienced a power failure? For the hour or two or 12 or 24 that the power was out, did our cell phones still work? Were we lulled into a false sense of security that our cell phones and, yes, even landlines, were invulnerable because short-term reliability is so robust and those systems were not taxed to exhaustion on that occasion?

Okay, so the power is out, the cell site batteries go dead, but the Telco eventually gets around with a generator to power it back up. Where is the fuel for that generator coming from? There has been an earthquake and, when the local stores of fuel are exhausted, how will more fuel get there across the heavily damaged highway system?

The source, of course, is a pipeline depot and yet another Cloud. Fuel is derived from crude oil at a refinery in some distant locale, potentially hundreds or thousands of miles distant. It is pumped from the refinery by way of underground pipelines to local or regional pipeline depots. From there it is trucked to distributors, or retailers, such as gas stations. The same is true for natural gas, methane is extracted from gas wells or separated from petroleum wells, purified, and pumped great distances through pipelines that branch over and over until finally that little pipe arrives at your home or business. Or, a great big line winds up at the local power plant to fire boilers or run huge engines that generate your electricity.

Wait, wait! ... how did we get from my cell phone and Twitter or Facebook and social networking to pipelines and power plants? Because dissimilar infrastructure Clouds often share the same right-of-ways, those strips of protected land that are granted or sold to entities that transmit or transport products in closed-circuit media, or transport goods like railroads do, and stretch from coast to coast. Much of one of the first transcontinental fiber routes was along the Union Pacific Railroad right-of-way. Power lines, pipelines, and fiber/copper routes often run great distances in close proximity to each other in the same, or in closely parallel, right-of-ways.

Because we are going to talk about the cataclysm, the "Wicked" monster natural disaster that we have not experienced in human history, the one that will attack so many layers of infrastructure that not only will it be difficult to recover from quickly, it will be difficult to understand its magnitude.

The disaster will be inflicted on property and, indeed, people, but the cataclysm will be experienced by people who communicate. If they are of a certain age, they will be isolated in a way that they have never experienced without seeking the solitude of a remote wilderness. The difference between isolation and solitude is perception. You may seek solitude, but you probably won't enjoy being suddenly thrust into total isolation in this constant communications world we now occupy.

Why we have not experienced it in human history is because we have never had such a reliance on a means of communication that is so infrastructure-support intensive on so many layers, to a much greater degree than even the foundation of that means, the PSTN, on which it is built.

No, it's not going to be the comet strike or the super-volcano, since we're not likely, as a global civilization, to survive those. Those last few hundred thousand tweets and status updates would be interesting, though.

It could be, on a lesser scale, the earthquake that causes California to slide into the Pacific, or the tsunami that scours the U.S. West Coast clean that has a localized catastrophic effect. That would pretty effectively wipe out Facebook and Twitter along with the rest of Silicon Valley, so, yes, that could be bad.

The West Coast has a history of earthquake events, and a very high level of awareness, from practical experience, of the effects of these events on critical infrastructure.

No, the one I'm talking about is the New Madrid Seismic Zone (NMSZ). The morning after New Madrid, the sun will shine and the rest of the world will be unaware. If the event is of the magnitude of the 1812 event, eight states along the Mississippi River will take heavy damage and several million people will be impacted (Figure 9.2).

What makes New Madrid so "wicked" is that a large amount of buried infrastructure runs through the fault zone. Liquifaction of the Mississippi River flood plain will cause towers, power plants, and buildings to sink into sandy mud. In 1812, the ground level of land immediately west of the Mississippi flood plain rose by many feet, mud geysers spewed sulfurous sand and mud, and buildings sank. It was said that church bells rang in Boston. The change in terrain caused the Mississippi River to appear to reverse its flow for a time. So much of what actually happened was unknown because most of the area west of the river was still Native American territory and unsettled by the Europeans, and was only revealed by modern forensic geology and aerial photography. There is no recent historical or practical awareness of earthquake hazards and potential damage in this area of the country.

What was not there in 1812 was public and private infrastructure in the ground. That whole area that is projected to take major damage is now crisscrossed with copper and fiber routes, natural

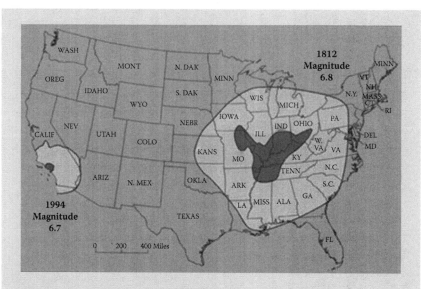

FIGURE 9.2 The 1895 NMSZ quake versus 1994 Northridge, California quake. Source: United States Geological Survey.

gas and petroleum pipelines, chemical pipelines, and primary rail and highway transportation arteries.

A significant amount of the natural gas that goes to the Eastern Seaboard travels through pipelines that traverse the major damage zone (Figure 9.3). If they are not damaged where they lay in the ground, they will likely be damaged where they cross rivers on or under bridges. (More detailed views are available from the U.S. Energy Information Administration www.eia.doe.gov)

It is projected that major damage will occur to hundreds, if not thousands of major and minor highway bridges, which are the means by which copper and fiber routes cross rivers and irregular terrain.

In short, there is a strong likelihood that a very large part of the Mississippi River Valley will go deaf, dumb, cold, and dark for some time. There is a strong likelihood that significant shortages of gas and refined petroleum products will occur between the NMSZ and the East Coast, impeding the ability of industry to act on that damage. It is likely that large areas involving several states that contain

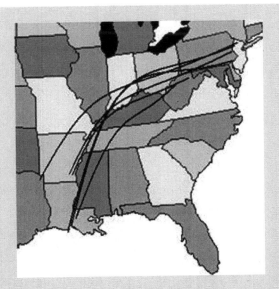

FIGURE 9.3 A simplified view of pipeline routes to the Northeast. (Image courtesy of the Carttar).

large numbers of victims will be blacked out from cell service, texting, and tweeting. The internet (The Cloud), which is a giant and resilient network, will be less impacted with increased distance from the major damage zone, but in the damage zone the nodes (cell sites) that it interconnects will be isolated.

It is likely that many towers that support broadcast media—television, AM and FM radio—will go down or be heavily damaged. Public media will be in short supply.

The real danger to society will be the disintegration of civilization as these victims are cut off from all communications, and are unable to understand what has happened and what they should do. We saw a small example of what happens to civilization in these conditions in Hurricane Katrina, and it happened quickly. Even though the worst of communications loss in Katrina did not last nearly as long as the New Madrid Event may, the effects on civilization were profound.

CONCLUSIONS

There has been an alarming trend in the last couple of years since social media has come into such ubiquitous usage, for emergency managers and other emergency practitioners to believe that the public network and social networking will be available not only as a primary means of communications, but also as a fall-back when all else fails, when, in fact, it is vulnerable on many cascading levels. The belief is that advanced technology will be sufficiently resilient to weather any amount of damage. This abandonment of "old fashioned" but robust, reliable, and simple means of communications, which have independence from infrastructure that they do not control, is of concern.

For reasons I hope I have clearly described, consisting of many cascading layers, public infrastructure and communications media that rely solely on the survival of commercial "best-effort" consumer-grade services is likely to fail practitioners when they most need it.

There is an "optimistic bias" that can lead planners to ignore or deny interrelated failures and how projected damage in one type of infrastructure should be an indicator of projected damage in another. In other words, the infrastructure clouds are not a single layer, they are a hierarchically dependent stack. The most mundane have huge effect on the most complex. The personal devices that provide access to social networking and the services themselves are perched at the very pinnacle of this stack.

Social media is pervasive, and under the right conditions can be a valuable resource, but it is difficult to discipline and very insecure. It can be very time-consuming when message volume is critical and the necessary verbosity in those messages exceeds the transactional capacity of the social medium.

In short, use it when you can in the right circumstance, but don't rely on it for your last line of defense, and definitely not as a sole primary.

When the "Wicked" big one comes as they always do, somewhere, in the dark, running on a battery from a dead car, someone will be tapping...SOS...SOS. And it will work, even if nothing else does.

new information may present itself that has not be identified before, such as the need for social media human intelligence where there are dedicated positions of human resource where information management through the media is needed.

SOME CHALLENGES OF SOCIAL MEDIA

Aggregating Information

Although information can be directed by using hashtags, and keywords, and can be filtered using technology and humans, there remains a need to aggregate the information in one place. This can be accomplished a number of ways. One way to help tightly couple the multiple sites together is to use another application that brings together all of your social identities in one place (Figure 9.4).

This is very important, especially during emergent times, when a stakeholder is in need of information that may be posted not on the site which they are presently on, but on another companion site. For example,

FIGURE 9.4 Social identities listed in one place.

if a user sees an agency's tweet that directs the user to another source for information, the source should be provided as a link to the user in the tweet. On Facebook or on the agency's home page, other icons should be available to directly link the user to corresponding Facebook, Twitter, Websites, or news links. It is important for the user to be able to go from one media to another effortlessly and quickly without having to conduct an Internet search. One such social identity aggregator is DandyID as seen in Figure 9.5.

Another way is by using a site that assists in this endeavor. uStream brings together multiple media in one place and includes a live video stream for real-time data aggregation. Presently, this is used by a number of groups like morning talk shows. For example, as you can see in Figure 9.6 with uStream, the audience can use a Social Stream and can interact using Facebook, Twitter, AIM, or MySpace or they can interact using a chat that is supported by the system. This is great for real-time events to help all of the comments, and information reflects a certain time

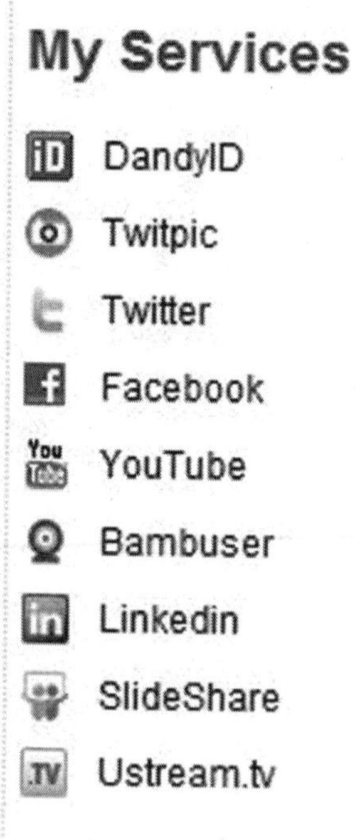

My Services

[iD]	DandyID
[◎]	Twitpic
[t]	Twitter
[f]	Facebook
[You Tube]	YouTube
[Ω]	Bambuser
[in]	Linkedin
[≡]	SlideShare
[TV]	Ustream.tv

FIGURE 9.5   Aggregating social identities in one place.

FIGURE 9.6 Live streaming with social stream.

and point during the live show. This would be an excellent way to cover events where live feed is needed. There are other applications offering the same kind of service. Bambuser, for example, is another free and available system. One added benefit of these systems is that all anyone needs is either a laptop or a smartphone. Most newer laptops and Netbooks have cameras built into the monitor and also have a microphone built into the hardware. All you have to do is point the camera in the right direction and have the sound in close proximity to the laptop. Other hardware is available for better quality and it is all relatively cheap. The laptops and smartphones also support listening using headphones, which may be needed for noisy environments.

Another alternative is to bring components as such together on a Website that can embed other widgets or applications that may be required to fit the needs of the given situation. A Google site along with the many widgets available can be used to bring together information that is needed to help an agency fulfill the objectives of the crisis communications needs as defined.

Marketing Your Social Identities

Getting the word out that an organization has a social media site can be difficult. This can be conducted a number of ways. One is word of mouth within a community. Fliers can be added to utility bills advertising the site and hashtags, and the radio and other more traditional means of media can be used. Self-promoting techniques also can be used where the creators of a medium can reach out to the public or members and request that they join the group.

Stakeholder Acceptance

Stakeholder involvement can be one of the most challenging aspects of all. An article by Gideon For-mukwai addressed approaches in his paper, which can provide the reader more information on this (For-mukwai, 2009). Although stakeholder involvement was very difficult only a couple of years prior to the publication of the book, one would have to have his/her head under a rock not to notice how social media is transforming the way information is exchanged.

New employee positions will need to be created, be they from a volunteer effort from the community or from the in-house public information officer (PIO) group. People need to closely monitor incoming and outgoing information, and they need to be more sensitive to the needs of the public as they move over to this virtual setting and expect emergency management to also do so.

BEST PRACTICES, CONSIDERATIONS, AND OBSERVATIONS

Consider the Tech Savvyness of Population

Cedar Bluff versus Washington, D.C. area and Twitter: There's the old saying: "If a tree falls in the forest and nobody is around to hear it, did it make a sound?" Some areas and the community in the area will be more prone to use social media. This is an obvious component to the success of any social media strategy implemented by an agency. Although social media not only supports the community member, but also those who are friends and relatives who may not live nearby, if the community members are not media users, then the implementation will have an insignificant effect. For example, rural areas that don't have Internet providers will not have the same end result from implementation as a suburb of the Washington, D.C. area.

Some Best Practices

Best practices for using social media are in an article printed every week by someone, and no two are alike. The truth is that these systems are new and we don't really know what best practices exist. Best practices for one community or agency may not be the same as they would be for another. However, one general set worthy of mentioning comes from the NASCIO (National Association of State Chief Information Officers) where they offer several recommendations for best practices on social media usage and management: http://www.records.ncdcr.gov/guides/best_practices_socialmedia_usage_20091217.pdf:

- **Gain comprehensive awareness of existing use and social media tool capabilities.** By reading this book and creating social identities along with the practitioner's experience and expertise, technology can be further utilized for the unique needs of an agency during any phase of emergency management.
- **Develop a documented strategy and goals that establish a policy floor for administering social media.** Policies vary from state to state, district to district, and community to community. It is important to weigh out the needs for information against what outcomes will be a direct consequence of denying information access and availability. The same rules for information that exist for an agency can be transferred on to the online environment. New situations may arise that don't have a precedent, and so a flexible but agile policy may be best to test the waters.
- **Establish a multidisciplinary team that includes business, technology, policy, legal, records, and accessibility stakeholders.** Just as in any emergency planning, all stakeholders that will be involved in the real-world event should be included in the planning and creation for the use of a successful social media design strategy. It is best to identify the objectives and goals of all members before beginning the design to assure that all considerations are made, both public and private, to best fit the overall needs of the community.
- **Confer with your state attorney general to establish mutual understanding of legal issues pertaining to social media.** All social media has a policy that is provided upon the creation of the account. Policies evolve and are being changed all the time. It is very important to stay abreast of any changes that are made and to actively seek out these changes.

- **Know the risk and mediating steps associated with social media use.** Most applications have information provided outlining the positive benefits of use. Using the Google search tools and carefully evaluating the needs of the agency against the tools available will help mitigate any undesired outcomes.
- **Be ready for outages, with the understanding that free services carry no concrete guarantees of reliability.** Although this is true, these systems are huge and supported by some of the best and brightest computer and network specialists. These systems work at being robust and secure. When a system is compromised, it is normally backed up very quickly. However, one major concern that should be considered is that there is normally no support for the social media from these systems. You more than likely will not be able to call Twitter or Facebook. Accounts can be terminated for some unknown reason and can be most difficult to deal with given the lack of a human-driven system support.
- **Continuously monitor terms of service modifications by social media providers, especially where these impact privacy.** Sometimes default settings are put in place that can jeopardize the integrity of the information on a site. Policies and settings can be complex and difficult to find in some cases.
- **Anticipate that provider business models may charge without warning. Are states prepared to pay for what is currently free?** This could happen, but would be cheaper than any proprietary alternative out on the market. Additional services and functionalities are available with a lot of these applications for a nominal fee.
- **Carefully consider branding and representation on multiple social media platforms. Are they consistent and enhancing enterprise marketing strategies?** Multiple social identities should exist. Although there is a limit, there should be multiple alternative ways for communication and information to flow. Use other sites as backup in case one should temporarily go down for some reason.
- **Get started on policy, guidelines, and standards, and expect to update these iteratively as new opportunities arise.** Policies should be considered during the design phase when stakeholders collaborate outlining the objectives and goals desired from social media and the corresponding Web technologies. Applications are updated and modified often. This may eliminate the need for another system being used. New applications and hardware

are constantly being created, offering more functionality faster. Technology ages quickly. It is important to use applications that take full advantage of the information available so that decision makers can have more accurate information in which to implement the best available alternative solution.

- **Use metrics to link analytics and strategic intent. The private sector does this very purposively and with great sophistication; leading states are adopting that strategy**. Factors that influence what is used should be measured against the tools available and their possible consequences and outcomes. Once the system has been active, it should be evaluated and measured against the initial objectives and goals as they were set forth by the stakeholders.
- **Expect surprises**. The nature of social media will present unanticipated challenges and opportunities. It's difficult to really lay out a set of best practices due to the new emergence of Web technologies into the emergency domain. Rigorous scientific studies need to be conducted on the effectiveness of the applications and technology. Real-world experiences also will provide insight through lessons learned. Each area is different with respect to population, demographics, and communications infrastructure and this produces potentially very different outcomes for each case and scenario.

CONCLUSION

Social media has a lot to offer emergency management in many of its facets. Systems should be deliberately designed to meet a set of predetermined objectives and goals laid forth by the stakeholders. There are many social sites that are all different from one another, each providing its own unique set of functions. Communications can be one-way or two-way and relationships are one-to-one, one-to-many, many-to-one, or many-to-many. It is important to determine which set of communication structures are offered to support the many needs of social groups. Although we covered Facebook and Twitter, the goal of this text was not to teach these applications, but to expose emergency managers to the foundations upon which these, and all social networks, are based. By controlling basic features, information can be utilized for its intended purpose between the interested parties and stakeholders.

Social Media has only just begun to surface and a lot remains to be seen and developed. As emergency management officials implement these technologies, opinions and policies are being developed to best fit the needs of an agency in its surroundings. Much testing needs to be conducted on groups using social media to test where it is most effective and under what set of conditions is it best leveraged. What works for one group and area may not work for another group and area given the demographics of the population. It's important not to forget those who do not have social media, but to understand that social networks exist both on and offline and can be used together in order to have a greater reach.

The human element is greatly underutilized. This has been the focus of many chapters and is proved in the larger open source cases that were provided showing how the community is an integral component to any successful system. Like any set of communications, there's a time to know when to use what where and this is no different for social media. It may be great for some situations and may be useless for others. And, as all equipment and plans should be tested, so too must social media once they has been designed and launched. It is important to create an overall system that can be modified for other uses and is flexible enough to adapt to the needs of the public. Social media is in its infancy and has a lot of maturing to undergo. It is by providing a set of guidelines here that we hope to expose you to what is available on the Internet and to better understand the transformative thinking taking place as we enter into this global economy where we all work together collaboratively for a common purpose, to make the world a better and safer place for all.

Book Online Site Extras—SMEMbook.com

Drowning in a Sea of Social Media PPT Voice Over Lecture http://www.authorstream.com/Presentation/conniemwhite-428441-drowning-sea-social-media-emergency-management-basics-education-ppt-powerpoint/

EXERCISE: CREATE A UNIFIED SITE; AGGREGATING INFORMATION

Learning how to use technology is just one component of using it; utilizing it as needed is another. A plan needs to be created before anything is developed and implemented. Careful attention needs to be paid and specific requirements need to be documented. Questions need to be answered, such as: Who are the users, how will the system be used, what are the goals of the Stakeholders? Why is the system being created?

In order for any social media or technology to be successfully implemented, the Stakeholders must accept and support the technology.

Who are your Stakeholders? Who are the user groups of the system?

- For each technology user (Facebook, Twitter, etc.) site created, identify who the target market is = the user group (civilians, first responders, victims, hospital, etc.)
- What types of Groups are needed? Open, Closed, Private.

What Roles need to be supported?

- Creator
- Moderator
- Participants who can add information
- Guest who can only view, but not contribute

User Identifications:

- Pen names
- Anonymous
- Real name—identified personnel (linkedIn, for example, to identify experts needed; resumes, location, referenced)

For every technology used, describe why it was used, including:

- Why the group is open/closed/private.

Describe how the system will be used under the following levels of severity, scope, and magnitude. Include a scenario for each.

- Emergency
- Disaster
- Catastrophe

Describe the information that will be incoming: What kind of information and who (the users) or what is bringing it in: civilians, RSS, official personnel.

Describe the information that will be going out: What kind of information (announcements) and who (the users) or what is bringing it in: civilians, RSS, official personnel.

289

Describe any information that will be accessible and to whom: documents, mapped weather, etc.

Remember other uses, such as the Red Cross texting 90909 to automatically send a $10 donation with the donation added to the cell phone bill; this could be a plan in place for activation after a larger event has occurred.

Different parts of a system should be created and only used under certain circumstances. Private and Secret groups could be used during extreme events. When a system is not used, people forget how to use them. With many of the social media technologies available, there is the added benefit that the user is already using the system in other open or closed groups. So, the user will be able to utilize the system effectively given they will know how to use it.

The creator of a social networking site can modify and update the system's available functions as needed and, if needed, as an emergency unfolds.

REFERENCES

Anderson, C. 2006. The long tail: Why the future of business is selling less of more. New York: Hyperion.

Belblidia, M. S. 2010. Building community resilience through social networking sites: Using online social networks for emergency management. International Journal Information Systems for Crisis Response and Management, Special Issue: A Social Media Tsunami 2 (1), January–March.

Brkan, I. B. 10 ways to build your blog community with Twitter. Posted March 25, 2009. http://blog.shoutem.com/2009/03/25/build-your-blog-community-with-twitter/ (accessed October 10, 2010).

Federal Chief Information Officer Council. 2009. Guidelines for secure use of social media by federal departments and agencies, version 1.0, September, Washington, D.C.

For-Mukwai, G. 2010. The transformative power of social media on emergency and crisis management. International Journal Information Systems for Crisis Response and Management, Special Issue: A Social Media Tsunami 2 (1), January–March.

Friedman, T. L. 2005. The world is flat: A brief history of the twenty-first century. New York: Farrar, Straus, and Giroux.

Harrald, J. 2009. Achieving agility in disaster management. International Journal of Information Systems for Crisis Response and Management, IJISCRAM 1 (1): 1–11.

Harrald, J. 2006. Agility and discipline: Critical success factors for disaster response. Annals, AAPSS, 604, March.

Hiltz, R. and M. Turoff. 1978. The network nation. Cambridge, MA: MIT Press.

Hiltz, S. R. and M. Turoff. 1985. Structuring computer-mediated communication systems to avoid information overload. Communications of the ACM July, 28 (7).

Hughes, A., L. Palen, J. Sutton, S. Liu, and S. Vieweg. 2008. Site-Seeing. In Disaster: An examination of on-line social convergence. Paper presented at ISCRAM08, May 3, Washington, D.C.

Killian, L. 2002. An introduction to methodological problems of field studies in disasters. In Methods of disaster researched, ed. R. Stallings, International Research Committee on Disasters.

Lang, G. and R, Benbunan-Fich. 2010. The use of social media in disaster situations: Framework and cases. International Journal Information Systems for Crisis Response and Management, Special Issue: A Social Media Tsunami 2 (1), January–March.

Leuf, B. and W. Cunningham. 2001. The wiki way: Quick collaboration on the Web. Reading, MA: Addison-Wesley.

291

Linstone, H. and M. Turoff. (forthcoming) Delphi: A brief look backward and forward. *Journal of Technological Forecasting and Social Change.*

Malerba, D. 2010. Tweet me your location, the use of social networks in emergencies. PhD diss., University of Sussex, Brighton, United Kingdom.

Mendoza, M., B. Poblete, and C. Castillo. 2010. Twitter under crisis: Can we trust what we RT? Paper presented at the first Workshop on Social Media Analytics (SOMA '10), Washington, D.C., July 25.

Munoz, C. L. and T. L. Towner. 2009. Opening Facebook: How to use Facebook in the college classroom. Paper presented at the Society for Information Technology and Teacher Education Conference, Charleston, SC.

Okolloh, O. 2009. Ushahidi, or 'testimony': Web 2.0 tools for crowdsourcing crisis information. In *Change at hand: Web 2.0 for development.* eds. H. Ashley, J. Corbett, B. Garside, and G. Rambaldi.

Palen, L., and S. R. Hiltz. 2007. Online forums supporting grassroots participation in emergency preparedness and response. *Communications of the ACM (Emergency response information systems: Emerging trends and technologies)* 50 (3), March.

Palen, L., S. Vieweg, S. Liu, and A. L. Hughes. 2009. Crisis in a networked world: Features of computer-mediated communication in the April 16, 2007 Virginia Tech event. *Social Science Computing Review, Sage*: 467–480.

Plotnick, L. and C. White, eds. 2010. A social media tsunami: The approaching wave. Online Social Networks to Support Community Resilience through Collaborative Web 2.0 Technologies. *International Journal of Information Systems for Crisis Response And Management (IJISCRAM)* II (I), January.

Plotnick, L., C. White, and M. Plummer. 2009. The design of a social networking site for emergency management: One stop shop. Paper presented at the Americas Conference on Information Systems (AMCIS), San Francisco.

Plotnick, L., M. Turoff, and C. White. 2010. Partially distributed emergency teams (PDET): Considerations of decision support for virtual communities of proactive (VCoP). In *Supporting real time decision-making: The role of context in decision support on the move (annals of information systems)*, eds. F. Burstein, P. Brezillion, and A. Zaslavshy. New York: Springer-Verlag.

Prutsalis, M., D. Bitner, P. Bodduluri, F. Boon, C. de Silva, D. König, and G. Treadgold, G. 2010. The sahana software foundation response to the 2010 Haiti earthquake: A new standard for free and open source disaster data management systems. Paper presented at the Information Systems for Crisis Response and Management Conference (ISCRAM), Seattle, WA.

Raman, M., T. Ryan, M. E. Jennex, and L. Olfman. 2010. Wiki technology and emergency response: An action research study. *International Journal Information Systems for Crisis Response and Management, Special Issue: A Social Media Tsunami* 2, (1), January–March.

Sutton, J., L. Palen, and I. Shklovski. 2008. Backchannels on the front lines: Emergent uses of social media in the 2007 Southern California Wildfires. Paper presented at the Proceedings of the 5th International ISCRAM Conference, Washington, D.C., May.

Starbird, K. and L. Palen. 2010. Pass it on? Retweeting in mass emergency. Paper presented at the Information Systems for Crisis Response and Management (ISCRAM) Conference, Seattle, WA.

Starbird, K. and J. Stamberger. 2010. Tweak the tweet: Leveraging microblogging proliferation with a prescriptive syntax to support citizen reporting. Paper presented at the Information Systems for Crisis Response and Management (ISCRAM) Conference, Seattle, WA.

Tapscott, D. and A, D, Williams. 2006. *Wikinomics.* Los Angeles: Portfolio Publishers.

The Red Cross. 2010. Social media in disasters and emergencies. http://www.red-cross.org/www-files/Documents/pdf/other/SocialMediaSlideDeck.pdf (accessed August, 2010).

Turoff, M., M. Chumer, B. Van de Walle, and X. Yao. 2004. The design of an emergency response management information system. *Journal of Information Technology Theory and Applications.* Volume 5, (4): 1–36.

Turoff, M., and S. R. Hiltz. 2008. *Information seeking behavior and viewpoints of emergency preparedness and management professionals concerned with health and medicine.* Report to the National Library of Medicine (NLM), March 6.

Turoff, M., C. White, and L. Plotnick. 2010. Real time decision making. Dynamic emergency response management for large scale decision making in extreme hazardous events. In *Supporting real time decision-making: The role of context in decision support on the move (annals of information systems),* eds. F. Burstein, P. Brezillion, and A. Zaslavshy. New York: Springer-Verlag.

Van de Walle, B., M. Turoff, and S. R. Hiltz, eds. 2010. Information systems for emergency management. In *The advances in management information systems* (monograph series), ed. V. Zwass. Armonk, NY: M.E. Sharpe Inc.

Vieweg, S., L. Palen, So. B. Liu, A. L. Hughes. and J. Sutton, J. 2008. Collective intelligence in disaster: examination of the phenomenon in the aftermath of the 2001 Virginia Tech shooting. Proceedings of the 5th International ISCRAM Conference, Washington, D.C., May.

Virtual Alabama Fact Sheet. http://www.dhs.alabama.gov/virtual_alabama/pdf_files/VirAL_Fact_Sheet.pdf

White, C. and M. Turoff. 2010. Factors that influence crisis managers and their decision making ability during extreme events. *International Journal of Information Systems for Crisis Response and Management* 2, (3): 25–35.

White, C., M. Turoff, and S. R. Hiltz. 2010. A real time online delphi decision system, version 2.0: Crisis management support during extreme events. Paper presented at the Information Systems for Crisis Response and Management (ISCRAM) Conference, Seattle, WA.

White, C. and L. Plotnick. 2010. A framework to identify best practices: Social media and Web 2.0 technologies in the emergency domain. *International Journal of Information Systems for Crisis Response And Management (IJISCRAM)* and *International Journal Information Systems for Crisis Response and Management, Special Issue: A Social Media Tsunami* 2 (1), January–March.

293

White, C., L. Plotnick, J. Kushma, S. R. Hiltz, and M. Turoff. 2009. An online social network for emergency management. *International Journal of Emergency Management* 6 (3/4): 369–382.

White, C. and M. Turoff. The potential for social networks in emergency management. *International Association of Emergency Managers (IAEM) Bulletin*, February special edition. 26, (2): 2010.

White, C., L. Plotnick, R. Aadams-Moring, M. Turoff, and S. R. Hiltz. 2008. Leveraging a wiki to enhance collaboration in the emergency domain. Paper presented at the 41st Hawaii International Conference on System Sciences (HICSS), Waikoloa, Big Island, HI, January 7–10.

White, C. S. R. Hiltz, and M. Turoff. 2008. United we respond: One community, one voice. Paper presented at the Information Systems for Crisis Response and Management (ISCRAM) Conference, Washington, D.C.

White, C., M. Turoff, and B. Van de Walle. May 13–16, 2007. A dynamic delphi process utilizing a modified Thurstone scaling method: Collaborative judgment in emergency response. Proceedings of the 4th Annual Information Systems on Crisis and Response Management (ISCRAM) Conference, Delft, The Netherlands.

White, C., L. Plotnick, M. Turoff, and S. R. Hiltz. 2007. A dynamic voting wiki model. Paper presented at the Americas Conference on Information Systems (AMCIS), Keystone, CO.

White, C., S. R. Hiltz, and M. Turoff. 2007. Finding the voice of a virtual community of practice. Paper presented at the International Conference on Information Systems, Pre-ICIS Sixth Workshop on e-Business (WeB 2007), Quebec City, Canada.

White, C. and M. Turoff. 2010. Factors that influence crisis managers and their decision making ability during extreme events. *International Journal of Information Systems for Crisis Response and Management* 2 (3): 25–35.

294

INDEX

INDEX

Innovative Support to Emergencies,
    Diseases, and Disasters
    (INSTEDD), 34, 226
InSTEDD, 34, 226
International Association of
    Emergency Managers
    (IAEM), 6
International Network of Crisis
    Mappers, 212
Internet
    availability, 218–219
    high traffic conditions, 146–147
    landline disruption, 272
    open source foundation (LAMP),
        262–263
Internet Protocol (IP) level granularity,
    261
iPad, 130
iPhones, 48, 79, 137, 184, 199, 270
Iran, 123–124, 184

J

Jing software, 94, 206

K

Kenya, 168
Keywords, 42–46, 86, 108, 187, 208, See
    also Hashtags

L

LAMP (Linux, Apache, MySQL, PHP),
    262–263
Language translation, 216, 218
Laptop computer features, 94, 199, 283
Law enforcement agency cooperation,
    246–247
    common operating picture, 253–256
Learning environment, 63
Legal issues, 285
LICNOT, 248, 261–265
Lightweight software, 263
"Like" pages, 23, 57

LinkedIn, 7, 56–57
    connections, 56
    groups of experts sharing
        information, 159
    Huddle Groups, 67
Links, 74, 79
    making donations, 76
    real-time preparedness and
        response, 79
    tweeting, 110
Live streaming video, 207, 282–283, See
    also uStream
Long-tail surveillance, 248–252, 261

M

Malerba, Daniele, 215, 216
Management support, 19–20
Many-to-many relationship, 55–57
Many-to-one relationship, 55, 131–133
Mapping, 25, 192, 209
    augmented reality overlays, 35
    border-centric law enforcement,
        253–256
    collaborative tools, 211–213
    Crisis Mappers, 212, 231
    evacuation routes, 79
    Google Earth, 210, 253–256, 261
    Google Maps, 209–210
    Haiti earthquake response, 222–224
    identifying resources, 185
    information mapping, 90
    OpenStreetMaps, 212–213, 222
    preparedness and response, 79
    TxMAP, 253–256, 261–262
    weather observations using tweets,
        114–118
    Wikimapia, 213
Marketing social identities, 283–284,
    285–287
Mechanical Turk, 229, 234
MediaWiki, 241, 253–254
Meeting scheduling, 178–181
Megadisaster, 276–280
"Mention" feature, 99, 103, 108

301